STRATEGIC DETERRENCE in the 1980s

STRATEGIC DETERRENCE in the 1980s

ROGER SPEED

foreword by
EDWARD TELLER

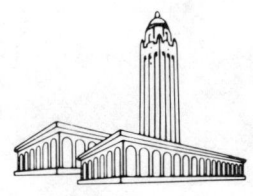

HOOVER INSTITUTION PRESS
Stanford University • Stanford, California

*The Hoover Institution on War, Revolution and Peace, founded at
Stanford University in 1919 by the late President Herbert Hoover,
is an interdisciplinary research center for advanced study on
domestic and international affairs in the twentieth century. The views
expressed in its publications are entirely those of the authors
and do not necessarily reflect the views of the staff, officers,
or Board of Overseers of the Hoover Institution.*

Hoover Institution Publication 214

© 1979 by the Board of Trustees of the
   Leland Stanford Junior University
All rights reserved
International Standard Book Number: 0–8179–7142–4
Library of Congress Catalog Card Number: 78–70887
Printed in the United States of America

For my daughter, Kira

Contents

Illustrations		viii
Tables		ix
Foreword		xi
Acknowledgments		xiii
Introduction		3

I Deterrence and Strategic Forces

I	Deterrence: An Overview	7
II	Assuring Deterrence	17
III	The Survivability of U.S. Strategic Forces	32
IV	Strategic Force Issues	71

II Strategic Policy

V	Extended Deterrence	103
VI	Deterrence by Denial and Defense	113

Appendixes

A	Strategic Forces	131
B	ICBM and Bomber Survivability	137
Notes		147
Index		171

Illustrations

Figure 1 Potential Destruction of Soviet Population and Industry / 25
Figure 2 Estimated ICBM Accuracies / 38
Figure 3 Effect of Accuracy on Minuteman Survivability / 40
Figure 4 Minuteman Survivability / 41
Figure 5 Survivability vs. SLBM Range / 51
Figure 6 Survivability vs. Number of Weapons / 52
Figure 7 Survivability vs. Reaction Time / 53
Figure 8 Minimum Essential Emergency Communications Network (MEECN) for the ICBMs and Bombers / 68
Figure 9 U.S. Counterforce Capability / 77
Map   Counterforce Targets in the United States / 47

Tables

Table 1	U.S. ICBMs and the Soviet Threat / 34
Table 2	History of ICBM Accuracies / 37
Table 3	United States Bombers / 45
Table 4	Modern Soviet SSBNs / 46
Table 5	Important Variables Affecting Bomber Prelaunch Survivability / 48
Table 6	U.S. SSBN Forces / 57
Table 7	Expected SALT II Treaty / 95
Table A-1	Estimated U.S. Strategic Nuclear Forces, 1978, 1985 / 132–133
Table A-2	Estimated Soviet Strategic Nuclear Forces, 1978, 1985 / 134–135
Table A-3	Comparison of Forces: Equivalent Megatons *and* Warheads / 136
Table B-1	U.S. Counterforce Capability: U.S. ICBM Capability and Soviet ICBMs / 142
Table B-2	B-52 Flyout Characteristics / 145

Foreword

It is not easy to discuss the strategic balance in the 1980s. Strategy is always difficult. But the balance, which unfortunately is a balance of terror, is once again threatening to become delicate. The subject, therefore, despite the difficulties, demands careful attention.

Unfortunately, much of the subject matter is shrouded in secrecy. This fact compounds the popular confusion, a confusion that is bound to exist in any case since questions of survival, of peace or war, affect the emotions of every individual. Thus, the popular expression concerning nuclear war is "unthinkable"—with the adjective being applied to a topic where lack of thinking will surely lead to disaster.

On this difficult topic, Roger Speed has written a remarkable book. Using publicly available information, he has created a realistic picture of the strategic problems facing our country, illuminating them from more than one side, which is the proper way to stimulate independent judgment. Moreover, he has discussed strategic matters in their broadest sense, including the difficult problems that would arise in the event of a conflict in Europe. Indeed, American strategy is inseparable from the fate of our allies.

No one who reads this book will fail to be influenced. The reader will find new facts and may change some of his opinions, although I am afraid that of all matter known to man the human brain has the greatest inertia. If anything can help to levitate and mobilize our rational thinking in a forbidding field, this book will do so.

EDWARD TELLER

Acknowledgments

Defense policy formulation in a free society requires the informed participation of the general public. Yet for most people, the intricacies of the debate over strategic policy, strategic weapon system survivability, and arms control agreements remain relatively obscure and inaccessible. It is hoped this book will contribute to a better understanding of these issues, since their resolution is likely to have a critical effect on the preservation of peace in the next decade.

This book was written while I was at the Hoover Institution on War, Revolution, and Peace, and the work was supported by a Peace Fellowship from that institution. I wish to thank all of those at Hoover, particularly Dennis Bark, who made my year there a thoroughly enjoyable experience.

I also wish to thank my colleagues who over the years have contributed to my understanding of the issues discussed in this book, particularly Edward Teller, Albert Latter, Roland Herbst, James Drake, Sam Cohen, David Vaughan, and Richard Greene. To those people who read and commented on all or parts of the manuscript I am grateful: John Barton, Robert Pfaltzgraff, Jr., Richard Staar, Stefan Possony, Darrell Trent, Norris Keller, Frank Chilton, and James Adams. I am especially indebted to Attiat Ott for her unflagging interest in and thoughtful criticism of this book. I, of course, assume sole responsibility for the views expressed.

Introduction

The steady growth of the strategic forces of the Soviet Union has brought the era of American nuclear superiority to a close. This rise in Soviet military power during the last decade has resulted in a new debate over American security policy. While fundamentally American policy remains one of deterring attacks on the United States or its allies, these new circumstances raise many questions about its continued adequacy.

If deterrence is to be assured in the 1980s, serious questions about the vulnerability of U.S. strategic forces, arms control, the defense of Western Europe, and U.S. strategic targeting doctrine must be addressed and resolved. A brief overview of some of the major issues under debate is given below.

STRATEGIC FORCE VULNERABILITY

A policy of deterrence requires the maintenance of strong and survivable strategic nuclear forces. However, improvements in Soviet missile technology suggest that the U.S. land-based intercontinental ballistic missile (ICBM) force may become vulnerable by the early 1980s, if not sooner. In the face of this threat, a number of alternative courses of action have been suggested: deployment of a mobile or multiple-aim-point basing system (with or without a new, larger missile) to increase survivability; deployment of an antiballistic missile system to defend the ICBMs; launching of the U.S. ICBMs on warning before a Soviet attack arrives; or abandonment of the ICBMs altogether.

Another important question in this debate concerns the survivability of both the bomber and submarine forces. Can the bomber force survive a surprise Soviet attack under the present basing arrangement? Can the bombers penetrate the extensive Soviet air defense? And, perhaps most importantly, are the strategic submarines invulnerable as is often proclaimed?

ARMS CONTROL AGREEMENTS

Although attempts to control the size of the strategic forces of the two superpowers are generally viewed favorably by defense strategists, disagreement exists regarding the exact terms of such agreements. Acceptance of any particular arrangement depends to a large extent on one's view of the stability of the strategic balance. Belief in the idea that the United States has a massive overkill capability in its nuclear arsenal and that the Pentagon routinely uses "worst-case" planning to exaggerate the extent of the Soviet threat inevitably leads to the conclusion that deterrence is simple to maintain. From this viewpoint, the political dimensions of arms control agreements (the maintenance of détente) take precedence over security considerations. On the other hand, if the opposite view is held—overkill is a myth and the survivability of U.S. strategic forces is in question—then the terms of arms control agreements are critical because they can either enhance or diminish the survivability of the strategic forces and thus deterrence.

DEFENSE OF WESTERN EUROPE

Since 1954, the United States has had a policy of extending its nuclear umbrella over its Western European NATO allies in order to deter an attack. However, the growth in Soviet strategic forces, it is argued, diminishes the credibility of a threat to launch a nuclear attack against the Soviet Union unless the United States itself is attacked. Because the United States does not possess a disarming first-strike capability, an attack on the Soviet Union could prove suicidal and is thus unlikely.

In addition to the growth of its strategic forces, the Soviet Union has continued to increase its conventional and tactical nuclear weapons forces to the point where they could threaten the security of Western Europe. The Carter administration's response to this threat has been to advocate an increase in the conventional forces in NATO—the same approach taken by every administration since that of President Kennedy.

But is this prescription adequate to cope with the combined arms (conventional and tactical nuclear) military doctrine of the Soviets? Some defense analysts have argued that the use of nuclear weapons would be necessary to halt an invasion by Warsaw Pact forces. However, the use of these weapons is hotly debated. Deployment of the neutron bomb in Western Europe is an example. The neutron bomb is a small nuclear weapon designed to be used on the battlefield that offers the possibility of countering a massive tank invasion of Western Europe while limiting damage to civilians. Its prospective deployment has met with worldwide opposition, including opposition from Western Europe itself. The reluctance to deploy

Introduction 3

this weapon raises questions about the adequacy of NATO's present defense doctrine. Is it possible under this doctrine to provide an effective defense, or must there be some fundamental change both in the doctrine and in the structure of forces in order to preserve deterrence in Western Europe?

STRATEGIC POLICY

The question of how to deal with an attack on Western Europe is part of the larger problem of how the U.S. should respond to a Soviet attack that falls short of an attack on U.S. cities. In an age of strategic nuclear parity, a policy of "assured destruction" that threatens an attack on Soviet cities can hardly be deemed adequate to cope with limited attacks. This problem has led to a search for an alternative doctrine that would allow the U.S. to counter a Soviet attempt to exploit its military strength. Another critical question under debate is what happens if, despite everything, deterrence fails. Can any policy limit civilian casualties? And would such a policy strengthen or weaken deterrence?

This book presents an analysis of these and other important defense issues. An attempt is also made to offer some workable solutions to the threat to the survivability of U.S. strategic forces and to offer a new strategic policy to cope with the growth of Soviet power.

Chapter 1 provides an overview of American and Soviet views of deterrence and of concerns in the West resulting from the growth of Soviet military power during the last decade. In the next three chapters, America's strategic forces and their relationship to deterrence are discussed. Chapter 2 presents the basic principles necessary for assuring deterrence and suggests possible reasons for the recent de-emphasis of these principles. Chapter 3 is a detailed look at the issues surrounding the survivability of the strategic forces. In Chapter 4, actions that can be taken to assure the continuing survivability of the strategic forces are presented. The impact of strategic arms agreements on the problem of assuring deterrence is also discussed in this chapter.

The next two chapters are concerned with the requirements of strategic policy. In Chapter 5, an analysis of America's policy for defending Western Europe is presented. The discussion highlights the fundamental weakness in NATO doctrine that makes it difficult, if not impossible, to develop an effective deterrent against the Warsaw Pact. Chapter 6 suggests that a fundamental change in doctrine is required to deal with a Soviet Union that possesses comparable or greater military power than the United States. As part of this new doctrine, a new approach to defending NATO is suggested. Finally, an attempt to codify prohibition of attacks on civilians is discussed.

I
Deterrence and Strategic Forces

Deterrence: An Overview

In the nuclear era, deterrence of war has become the main theme of American strategic doctrine. This chapter provides an overview of American and Soviet views of deterrence and of concerns in the West resulting from the growth of Soviet military power during the last decade.

DETERRENCE

The concept of deterrence was not born with the nuclear age; it has long been a part of international politics. Countries have always tried to induce fear in an adversary or at least to create strong doubts about the outcome of any possible aggression. But because the consequences of aggression were often difficult to calculate short of actually going to war, deterrence often failed.

The introduction of nuclear weapons potentially changed this situation because it simplified the calculations. The destructive power of these weapons is so great that the outcome of a nuclear exchange is thought to be obvious to everyone, even to those who hold a completely different set of values, as the Russians are often feared to do. If the cost of nuclear retaliation can be seen to exceed any gain obtainable through war, then nuclear weapons, despite their awesome destructive power, offer the hope that a policy of deterrence might work.

In principle, deterrence can be achieved either through the development of a strong defense or through the threat of punishment. In the first case, the aggressor is deterred by the prospect that he will not succeed. In the second case, he is deterred by the threat that the retaliation he will suffer will outweigh any gains he may achieve. Although it is possible to defend against the use of nuclear weapons, a completely effective defense is thought to be impossible. Thus, the United States has generally adopted a policy of deterrence by threats of punishment.

Punishment, however, can take many forms. The United States at present relies primarily on simple retaliation—the threat to destroy Soviet society. This is usually called an assured-destruction policy.[1] The Soviet Union, on the other hand, has adopted a more conventional military approach to deterrence; in the event of a nuclear war the Soviet Union is prepared not only to retaliate but to survive and win the war.

Although current American and Soviet views on deterrence and warfighting appear to be in sharp contrast, this has not always been the case. American policy has always contained elements of war-fighting rather than simply being a policy of deterrence by retaliation alone. For example, during the early 1950s, the United States held an essentially unilateral deterrent since it could threaten massive retaliation against Soviet aggression without fearing extensive damage to the American homeland.[2] The United States had, in effect, a war-fighting and war-winning doctrine.

As the number and variety of Soviet strategic forces increased, there were strong pressures (within the Pentagon and outside of it) to increase the number and capabilities of U.S. forces. The desire was not only to retain an assured-destruction capability but to maintain a damage-limiting capability as well. This meant the targeting of Soviet strategic forces—so-called counterforce targeting—to prevent their use against the United States. The objectives of this strategy were to retain the superiority of U.S. forces and to keep America essentially invulnerable. Without this invulnerability, it was argued, America's commitments to its allies in Europe would appear less than credible. But in order to retain this position of dominance, the United States would have had to maintain a first-strike capability—the capability to destroy enough of the Soviets' long-range nuclear forces to insure that any response they might make following a U.S. attack would be minimal. A vigorous civil defense program was also advocated to add credibility to this posture since even the best first-strike would not be likely to destroy all Soviet nuclear weapons.

However, as the Soviets expanded their strategic missile forces and placed them in submarines and hardened silos, it became clear that it would be very difficult and very expensive to obtain a real damage-limiting capability. Nevertheless, short of obtaining a full first-strike capability, there were still arguments for a counterforce doctrine. If the United States could launch a strike against Soviet land-based missiles, for example, it might then be able to hold Soviet cities hostage and prevent the Soviets from retaliating with their submarine-based missiles. Through such coercive tactics, it was argued, the Soviets could perhaps be compelled to yield in a crisis.[3]

Although the logic of counterforce targeting initially appealed to Secretary of Defense McNamara, for fiscal and philosophical reasons he eventually de-emphasized the damage-limiting aspect of his policy.[4] Around 1967, it was acknowledged that the Soviet Union also had a second-strike assured-destruction capability and that a situation of mutual deterrence existed. Since that time, deterrence in American strategy has gradually become synonymous with retaliation. The primary function of U.S. nuclear weapons now is to assure that retaliation will be effective.[5]

In contrast, the Soviets have always considered deterrence from the more traditional military point of view of possessing a war-fighting capability. The stronger the capability, the stronger the deterrent. This view is particularly important to the Soviets because their assessment is that although nuclear weapons will make wars extremely destructive, their introduction has not overturned all of history, and, as noted by General Secretary Leonid I. Brezhnev, "wars and acute international crises are far from being a matter of the past."[6] Since wars are not inconceivable, the Soviets hold the view that it is the duty of the military to prepare for that possibility. The overriding goal of the Soviet Union, if war occurs, is to survive and emerge victorious.

The core of Soviet doctrine is the development of forces and programs that will limit damage to the Soviet homeland.[7] Thus, counterforce targeting, not assured-destruction retaliation, is the primary role assigned Soviet military forces. According to Marshal Grechko:

> The Strategic Rocket Forces, which constitute the basis of the military might of our armed forces, are designed to annihilate the means of the enemy's nuclear attack, large groupings of his armies, and his military bases; to destroy his military industries; (and) to disorganize the political and military administration of the aggressor as well as his rear and transport.[8]

Similarly, the Soviet navy is assigned the task of blunting the attack from U.S. aircraft carriers and strategic missile-carrying submarines.

Although the Soviets proclaim that they will never start a war, they recognize that a counterforce attack would not in general be effective except in a first-strike. Accordingly, the Soviets are always alert to the possibility that the West will initiate an attack and assert that they will be able to thwart any such "criminal intentions" by launching a preemptive strike of their own.[9]

The Soviets have also long emphasized the importance of air and missile defenses to destroy those weapons surviving a preemptive strike. They have the most extensive air defense system in the world and continue to improve it. They were the first and the only country ever to deploy an antiballistic-missile (ABM) defense system. Although their initial efforts in this area were not considered effective, they are continuing extensive ABM research and development programs.[10]

Soviet counterforce targeting and active defenses are complemented by extensive passive defenses.[11] The Soviet civil defense program appears to be designed not only for general population protection but also for alleviating a number of specific problems that would face a country emerging from a nuclear war.[12] Blast shelters that can protect the political and military leadership are given high priority as are plans for restoring essential services. Through these measures, the leadership hopes to maintain control during the chaotic aftermath of a nuclear war. In addition, blast shelters are being constructed in an attempt to assure the survival of a trained cadre of industrial workers who can aid in rebuilding Soviet industry.

The capability of these preparations to alleviate the difficulties the Soviets would face following a nuclear war is heatedly debated. Although no civil defense program is likely to work perfectly, it is clear that steps can be taken to mitigate the impact of nuclear weapons, either by leaving the target area or by taking shelter.[13] The general assessment of the intelligence community is that "under optimum conditions" the Soviet civil defense program could be largely successful and that it could "reduce casualties among the urban population to a small percentage."[14]

In addition to developing a damage-limiting capability, the Soviets realize that interactions with their neighbors following a nuclear war could well be the factor that determines whether they achieve victory. If a nuclear war leaves the Soviet Union in a weakened condition, it could have serious problems with the People's Republic of China. It is imperative, in the Soviet view, to maintain enough local defense or deterrent forces to keep the Chinese from expanding into Siberia while the Soviet Union recovers. Furthermore, some of the Eastern European countries may attempt to break free from Soviet dominance if the opportunity arises. Since most, if not all, of these countries' industry might not be attacked in a nuclear war, continued Soviet control could be important.

Continued access to world markets, even though the Soviet Union has abundant natural resources, would also be important. Some of the suppliers of these materials, such as Iran, are close to the Soviet Union. However, no country is outside the range of Soviet missiles and thus could be subjected to nuclear blackmail.

Of course, Western Europe could be the most critical element in Soviet recovery and expansion of power. With a combined gross national product about 50 percent greater than that of the Soviet Union, the Western European countries could supply aid that would hasten any recovery. If these countries are fully incorporated into the Soviet bloc, it could eventually make the Soviet Union even stronger than it was before the war.

Finally, it should be noted that the Soviets not only advocate a doctrine of deterrence based on the possession of a war-fighting capability, but they also appear to be taking concrete actions that will give credibility to that doctrine. The continued steady growth of Soviet military power in all areas—strategic and tactical nuclear forces, conventional army, navy, and air forces, and strategic defenses—is designed to be effective in all aspects of war-fighting.[15] These forces are presenting a growing threat to U.S. strategic forces and are placing the Soviet Union in a strong position to dominate its neighbors in the event of war.[16]

SUPERIORITY AND THE LIMITS OF NUCLEAR DETERRENCE

A policy of nuclear deterrence is most credible in the defense of those areas deemed most vital to a country. For America, this policy has meant primarily the defense of the homeland and the industrialized democracies of Western Europe.[17] However, as the Soviet Union increasingly takes on the attributes of a world military power with global interests and expanding global capabilities, there will be danger to the periphery as well as the strategic center. Thus, the Soviets undoubtedly will continue to exploit the strife in Africa, the Middle East, and the rest of the nonindustrialized world during the decade ahead.

It has been argued that this Soviet involvement is facilitated by the growth of their strategic power and that the United States must act to offset what is perceived by many to be an attempt by the Soviets to achieve strategic superiority.[18] Numerical superiority is certainly a possibility. The Soviets, even within the confines of the proposed arms control agreements that call for equal numbers of strategic nuclear delivery vehicles (missiles and bombers), have the potential for more nuclear firepower than the United States because their intercontinental ballistic missiles are much larger in size and much greater in number. Indeed, by the early 1980s the Soviets will have a clear lead in most of the usual indices used to measure the strategic balance, except perhaps in the number of warheads (see appendix A).

Although the growth of Soviet military power has been (and will continue to be) an important factor in world affairs, it is unlikely that the question of numerical superiority will play a significant role in determining the fate of the Third World. The roots of the decay of the Western international system lie not in the shift in the balance of strategic weapons but rather in more fundamental political realities. The rise of Marxist influence and totalitarian governments in the world cannot be attributed to Soviet superiority in ICBMs, and an increase in American ICBMs is not likely to diminish it.

The idea that America's strategic nuclear weapons could deter the spread of communist influence was born in an era of a virtual American monopoly of deliverable nuclear destruction. The threat of using nuclear weapons is thought to have saved Western Europe from potential Soviet aggression and perhaps to have ended the Korean War. At that time, the Western colonial system was still intact, and despite Soviet attempts to cause trouble, communism was thought to be contained.

Although the world has changed greatly since the 1950s, in some quarters the concepts of the deterrent power of nuclear weapons have not. By the mid-1960s the Soviets had a secure second-strike assured-destruction capability. Even though the United States had a large numerical superiority in strategic weapons, this superiority was no longer operative. As Henry Kissinger said in 1965: "This situation reflects the basic paradox of contemporary technology. Power has never been greater; it also has never been less useful."[19]

The achievement of a second-strike capability and the collapse of the colonial system gave the Soviets freedom of action and a multitude of opportunities to expand their influence. Marxism offered an ideal vehicle for aspiring liberators in the underdeveloped world, whose embrace of Marxism often led to military support from the communist states and political support and sanction from Western intellectuals. The Soviets clearly did not need the shield of superiority to support this process, and U.S. numerical superiority could do little to stop it.

The Cuban missiles crisis, however, is often cited as an example of the coercive power of nuclear weapons. The Soviets are thought to have backed down because America had nuclear superiority. There is perhaps some validity to this view because at that time the United States could have launched a damage-limiting first strike against Soviet weapon systems. But however successful a U.S. attack might have been in 1962, it became obvious a few years later that the U.S. no longer had this capability.

Moreover, it is likely that U.S. strategic weapons were not the determining factor in the resolution of the Cuban missile crisis, although they did deter the Soviets from using their own. The United States government did not threaten to attack the Soviet Union (unless America was attacked) but rather threatened the Soviets with a conventional defeat both in Cuba and on the high seas. Because America had overwhelming conventional superiority in the Caribbean, there was little doubt about the outcome of a military confrontation.

Whatever the determining factors in the Cuban crisis were, the incident probably should be viewed as a special case that cannot be extended to the rest of the world. The crisis did not arise simply because of communist intervention in the affairs of an underdeveloped country (even one so close to the United States); it resulted because the Kennedy administration felt that the introduction of intermediate-range ballistic missiles in Cuba threatened to upset the central strategic relationship between the two superpowers. The visible threat of nuclear missles aimed at the United States allowed the president to invoke the "vital security interests" of the nation whereas the presence of Soviet troops and defensive surface-to-air missiles did not cause such a reaction. Similar circumstances are not likely to arise again.

In areas outside of NATO and the Warsaw Pact, the utility of strategic weapons, unless one side has a first-strike capability, would seem to lie primarily in their ability to neutralize the other side's threat of attack. Strategic weapons only permit other factors to come into play, and the resolution of local issues is more likely to depend on questions of national will, determination of vital interests, balances between local conventional forces, and local political factors. If the West wishes to contest the Soviets in the nonindustrial world, it must develop new tactics and strategies that take into account the new strategic reality of (at best) a nuclear standoff.[20]

STRATEGIC BALANCE

Despite difficulties in translating numerical superiority in strategic weaponry into political advantage, there has been a shift in recent years from a simple strategic policy of maintaining an adequate deterrent to a policy of placing more emphasis on the political and psychological aspects of strategic nuclear power. Thus, Secretary of Defense Schlesinger concluded in 1975 that one of the requirements for deterrence was that the United States maintain "essential equivalence" with the Soviet Union not only in forces but in

> throw-weight, accuracy, yield-to-weight ratios, reliability and other such factors that contribute to the effectiveness of strategic weapons and to the perceptions of the non-superpower nations.[21]

Critics of this new approach to deterrence found it difficult to believe that foreign countries would lose confidence in America because of asymmetries in what they considered rather esoteric measures of the strategic balance. Advocates of essential equivalence readily agreed that it was difficult to find relevant measures of the strategic balance by comparing static inventory numbers and argued that a "dynamic" measure of the balance based on what these weapons could do in a conflict was needed. The conflict usually envisioned is a strategic counterforce war in which the Soviets attack U.S. strategic missiles in an attempt to increase their throw-weight advantage (throw-weight being the total weight that a missile can deliver).[22] It was argued that even though the United States would still maintain its assured-destruction capability, a counterforce attack could greatly weaken its overall strategic position and force a resolution of the issue in question on terms favorable to the Soviet Union.[23] The strong residual strategic force of the Soviet Union would deter a U.S. assured-destruction strike, particularly in view of the Soviets' extensive civil defense program that could make them much less vulnerable than the United States to an all-out attack.

However, a Soviet coercive counterforce attack would seem to be unlikely as long as the United States can maintain an assured-destruction capability. The risks of escalation to an all-out nuclear war would appear to be too great for the Soviets to initiate an attack simply to resolve a political conflict favorably, especially since the Soviets could not be sure that the United States would feel compelled to yield in the political issue at stake.[24]

The debate over the possibility of a counterforce war does, however, illustrate an important point: superiority is not only a matter of numbers of weapons but also a question of the capabilities of those weapons. It makes little difference if the United States has the same (or greater) throw-weight as the Soviet Union if its strategic forces are vulnerable to a preemptive strike by the Soviets. By the same token, it matters little if the Soviets have four-to-one ICBM throw-weight advantage if U.S. missiles are survivable.[25]

This view is closer to the traditional military meaning of superiority— the capability of one's weapons and troops to achieve one's objectives. For example, at the beginning of the nuclear age, America had a nuclear monopoly, and throughout most of the 1950s, it had overwhelming nuclear superiority. The operational meaning of superiority in this period was that America, if it chose, could have launched a devastating nuclear attack against the Soviet Union (or China) without fear of similar damage in return.

Today, military superiority has two possible meanings for the Soviets: a damage-limiting, first-strike capability against the United States or an overwhelming military superiority in the European theater coupled with a massive second-strike capability that can neutralize the usefulness of America's strategic forces. Thus, while the political implications of Soviet *numerical* superiority are naturally of interest, the most important aspect of superiority is the capability to achieve military objectives. Concerns about a shift in the strategic balance should therefore not focus on some simple set of indices, but rather on the critical issue of whether the United States can maintain a survivable deterrent and defend Western Europe. All other issues are of secondary importance.

IMPLICATIONS FOR THE UNITED STATES

Much of the recent debate over Soviet military and political philosophy, numerical superiority, and the implications of partial vulnerabilities of U.S. strategic systems has served to obscure rather than illuminate the critical problems facing the West. Whatever the ultimate intentions of the Soviet leadership may be, it is clear that they adhere to a strategic doctrine based upon a war-fighting, damage-limiting capability. From every indication, the Soviets take this doctrine seriously and are diligently trying to translate it into reality. Although there have been protestations of concern about various aspects of this Soviet effort (particularly its political implications), it has not been fully recognized that the world is now entering a period in which the "balance of terror" is once again becoming delicate.

Two decades ago, it was generally assumed that the mere possession of a stockpile of nuclear weapons by the United States and the Soviet Union prevented nuclear war because the consequences of war would be catastrophic. Albert Wohlstetter was one of the first to point out that deterrence was not automatic but depended on the survivability of America's strategic forces.[26] If an American retaliatory strike could be sufficiently limited, war was still possible.

The recognition of this problem resulted in the early 1960s in a new emphasis on survivability. Defense policy was to maintain a survivable second-strike capability at all costs. In contrast, today, even in the face of a threatening Soviet buildup, there is a general air of complacency about the survivability of American strategic forces.

This complacency is unjustified. There is a great deal of uncertainty about the capabilities of the forces that the Soviets will possess in the early 1980s, and within the range of uncertainty, there could be a severe threat to *all* of America's strategic forces—ICBMs, bombers, and strategic submarines.[27] Prudence requires that diligent steps be taken to maintain the survivability of these forces. For deterrence to remain effective, there should be no serious doubts, on either side, about their survivability.

It is not necessary to believe in the aggressive intentions of the Soviet leadership to recognize the danger that can result if the Soviets achieve a first-strike capability; the opportunity for political blackmail and coercion would be great. Moreover, due to U.S. fears of a Soviet first-strike and

Soviet fears of an American preemptive attack, a crisis resulting from Soviet attempts to obtain even limited political objectives could prove destabilizing and result in nuclear war.

However, even if steps are taken to protect America's deterrent forces, their capability to protect anything other than the American homeland (by threats of retaliation) is likely to be greatly circumscribed in the years ahead. Since the Soviets now maintain a large second-strike retaliatory capability of their own, America's capability to extend its nuclear deterrent to other countries has largely lost its credibility. This is particularly important for America's European allies whose defense has ultimately relied on America's threat to launch, if necessary, a full-scale nuclear attack on the Soviet Union. Since it is clear that such an attack would be suicidal, the West must develop a new strategy to cope with the realities of Soviet power.

II
Assuring Deterrence

The general principles for assuring deterrence were expressed by Alain Enthoven, assistant secretary of defense for systems analysis under McNamara:

> If the overriding objective of our strategic nuclear forces is to deter a first strike against us, the United States must have a second-strike capability; that is, strategic forces of such size and character that they can survive a well-planned, large-scale surprise attack with sufficient strength remaining to penetrate the attacker's defenses and still destroy him. This capability to destroy him even after absorbing his surprise attack must be a virtual certainty, and clearly evident to the enemy. This is the foundation of U.S. deterrent strategy. Consequently, as long as deterrence remains the priority objective, the United States must be prepared to offset any Soviet effort to reduce the effectiveness of our assured-destruction capability below the level we consider necessary.[1]

Survivability is thus the key to deterrence. But maintaining the survivability of U.S. strategic forces in the years ahead will be neither automatic nor easy. It will require a policy of prudence that fully recognizes the uncertainties involved, maintains diversified forces, fully accounts for the possibility of a surprise attack, and pursues research and development programs to hedge against technological surprise.

The following sections examine these general principles, which were once widely accepted but are now downplayed or ignored. This attitude of complacency and its possible causes are also explored.

UNCERTAINTIES

Determination of the survivability of each of the strategic forces can be an extremely complicated process marked by great uncertainty. Such assessments depend on many technical details that are often difficult to ascertain. For example, the United States is compelled to undertake extensive test programs to reduce the uncertainties in its knowledge of the accuracy, reliability, and other characteristics of its own weapons. Assessments of Soviet capabilities are much more difficult because they must be based on less direct techniques.

To obtain information on Soviet weapon systems, the United States uses data gathered by satellites and stations around the periphery of the Soviet Union. There are, however, limitations to this approach since the Soviets have some control over the data received. Opportunities to conceal information or to mislead the United States are abundant. If the Soviets take minimal precautions, it is unlikely that even the best surveillance systems will yield enough information to allow a complete understanding of a weapon's capabilities. Thus, information obtained from tests (when available) must be augmented with appraisals of the actual technology available to the Soviets. This, in turn, depends on U.S. understanding of that technology because there is often little direct information on the state of the particular Soviet technology in question. In some instances, this shortcoming will introduce a wide latitude into the evaluation.[2]

Considering the difficulties involved, it is not surprising that different analysts, using the same limited data, frequently arrive at different conclusions.[3] One example of such differences was made public when the so-called B Team of outside experts was commissioned by President Ford to assess Soviet capabilities in several areas. The conclusions of the three panels that constituted the B Team reportedly were quite different from those of the official intelligence community (the "A Team") on the subjects of Soviet missile accuracy, Soviet air defenses, and Soviet strategic intentions.[4] These reported differences are an indication of the wide range of uncertainty that exists concerning Soviet capabilities.[5] More importantly, as former Director of Defense Research and Engineering John S. Foster, Jr., has pointed out, many of these uncertainties are in crucial areas that make it extremely difficult to be confident about assessments of the survivability of U.S. strategic forces.[6]

Despite serious gaps in American knowledge of Soviet weapon systems, the Defense Department has been reluctant to face the full implications of this uncertainty.[7] In this regard, it is worth noting that there is an almost universal presumption that the truth cannot lie at the extremes; if there are two extreme positions, the truth, it is felt, must lie somewhere between them. There is, of course, no foundation for this belief, but it may explain some of the complacent reactions to the large range of uncertainty regarding the survivability of U.S. strategic systems. Although the uncertainty involved in assessing system survivability may not have been critical when the United States had a wide margin of safety, as Soviet capability has increased, the margin of safety has narrowed.

DIVERSE FORCES

The United States has for some time maintained a triad of strategic forces: land-based intercontinental ballistic missiles (ICBMs), submarine-launched ballistic missiles (SLBMs), and long-range strategic bombers. In the early 1980s, it will be possible to add a new element—the long-range cruise missile. The cruise missile is, in effect, a small pilotless aircraft that can be launched from air, sea, or land. Its small size and its capability to fly at low altitudes will help it to penetrate the extensive Soviet air defense. But the cruise missile's chief advantage is that it is cheap and, hence, can be produced in large enough numbers to saturate the defense.

Given the wide range of uncertainties about Soviet and American weapons systems, especially when evaluated within the context of a nuclear war, diversified forces provide a critical hedge against the catastrophic failure of one or more systems and safeguard the U.S. deterrent against Soviet technological breakthroughs. This diversity can also be expected to complicate the execution of an effective counterforce strike because the Soviets must use different tactics and weapons systems to attack the full U.S. force.[8] Diversified forces also complicate the Soviets' defense against a retaliatory strike. For example, ICBMs and SLBMs reenter the atmosphere at different angles, can come from a wide variety of directions, and employ different means of overcoming an antiballistic missile system.[9] And penetrating bombers armed with bombs and Short-Range Attack Missiles (SRAM) present the Soviets with an entirely different set of defense problems.

The diversity represented by the triad is, however, thought by some to be unnecessary. The growing vulnerability of U.S. ICBMs is seen as an opportunity to phase them out and to move to a "diad" of bombers and strategic submarines. In that event, the United States would abandon its target system that consists of 1,000 separate aim-points (the ICBMs) and rely on a 50 aim-point system of bomber bases and a 25 aim-point system of strategic submarines at sea.[10]

Although there is nothing sacred about a trinity of strategic forces, there are a number of reasons for not abandoning a land-based missile system. First, converting to a diad of forces while the Soviets maintained a diversified and flexible triad could have serious political ramifications. Although there is probably a large degree of acceptable variation in the world's perception of the strategic balance of forces, the abandonment by the United

States of its ICBMs while the Soviets maintain a massive ICBM system would be viewed (rightly or wrongly) with the greatest of alarm by America's allies. This dramatic shift in the perceptions of the strategic balance would make a diad politically unwise.

It should be emphasized, however, that the primary objections to a diad are technical and not political. There are already great uncertainties about the survivability of U.S. bombers and submarines. If the United States abandons its ICBMs, the Soviets can then concentrate more of their efforts and resources on finding offensive and defensive countermeasures against these two forces. In addition, a diad instead of a triad would make the Soviets' tactical problem of coordinating an attack and defense much easier.

There is also an important tactical danger in having all U.S. ballistic missiles on submarines. The Soviets could then attack this sea-based force without launching a nuclear attack against U.S. territory. Depending on the nature of the attack, the United States might not even be able to identify the attacking party.[11] In any event, the United States might feel restrained from attacking the Soviet Union for fear of a Soviet counterattack. Because an attack on a sea-based force would not involve the deaths of U.S. civilians, the Soviets might consider this a low-risk option—certainly less risky than attacking a land-based ICBM force with the resulting massive civilian casualties.

In summary, even with a triad of strategic forces, it will become increasingly difficult during the next decade for the United States to maintain a high degree of confidence in its deterrent capability. Under the circumstances, the United States is likely to require more diversity, not less.

SURPRISE ATTACK

The fundamental principle of strategic planning established by Secretary of Defense McNamara was that the United States should be able to survive a surprise (out-of-the-blue) attack and still have sufficient forces remaining to inflict "unacceptable" damage on an aggressor. However, the planning of force requirements on this basis is now viewed by most defense critics as unrealistic and wasteful. In their view, nuclear wars will not occur as deliberate and planned actions. Rather, if a nuclear war occurs at all, it will result from a crisis that escalates beyond all expectation because of miscalculation or accident.

Although the McNamara policy remains official doctrine, the prevalent view of the U.S. government appears to be that the United States would obtain strategic warning of an impending attack.[12] For example, defense officials were recently quoted as saying that "it is impossible for the Russians to launch a massive nuclear attack on the United States without a warning period of at least several days."[13] This statement is based on the relatively low alert status of Soviet strategic forces and on the U.S. capability to detect changes in this status. This viewpoint ignores both the obvious fact that this low alert status is an alterable policy and, more importantly, it ignores the time lag involved in detecting a change in the status of Soviet systems—a time lag that may be long in comparison with the time required to prepare for an attack using modern strategic weapons.[14]

Relying on strategic warning, the United States now maintains only 30 percent of its strategic bombers on alert and depends on a communications network and a command and control system that could be severely degraded by a surprise attack.[15] In Europe, NATO forces are so concentrated that a surprise attack could destroy almost all tactical nuclear warheads and delivery systems as well as much of the conventional forces. This tendency to rely on advance warning of an attack rather than undertaking the steps necessary to assure survivability could prove even more dangerous as the Soviet threat grows.

Although the United States may be confident of its capability to detect an impending attack, the historical record gives little justification for such confidence. Despite modern technologies and intelligence networks, nations have continued to be surprised by their enemies. Several explanations for this phenomenon have been suggested. The predominant viewpoint is that although there are generally clear indications of an approaching crisis, these signals are usually lost in the noise of competing and contradictory signals.[16] Others have argued that deception is the key to surprise.[17] That is, the background noise is not always just irrelevant information but often a deliberate attempt to transmit disinformation to deceive the other party. This was the case not only in Hitler's surprise attack on Russia but also in the Arab attack on Israel in 1973.[18]

Institutional factors are also cited as increasing the chances of being surprised by an attack. Bureaucratic pressures may often lead to the interpretation of incoming information in such a way as to confirm established theories and policy. In discussing the failure of Israeli intelligence in 1973, Avi Shlaim noted: "The monopolistic structure of the intelligence community was largely responsible for the narrow, dogmatic, and monolithic thinking that characterized the estimates presented to the policy makers. It precluded the wider vision, depth, and subtlety which the confrontation of independent evaluations and opposing points of view can produce."[19]

A somewhat different perspective on the causes of surprise is offered by Abraham Ben-Zvi.[20] After examining five outstanding cases of surprise attack (Pearl Harbor, Hitler's attack on Russia, the Chinese intervention in Korea, the Sino-Indian Border War in 1962, and the Arab-Israeli War of

October, 1973), he concluded that tactical indicators of an impending attack did exist and "that the presence of confusing 'noise' did not obfuscate or eliminate the relevant warning signals that were gathered by the observing state on the eve of war."[21] The problem was that these warning signals were in conflict with the leadership's views of the other party's intent, and, thus, the warnings were either rejected or ignored. This tendency to "mirror-image" and to act under the assumption that the other side shares one's own conceptual framework is perhaps the most difficult and elusive barrier to preventing surprise.

Although any resort to nuclear arms would involve grave risks, it is possible that the Soviets will someday face a crisis in which they think they have no alternative other than war. The United States may at that point recognize the seriousness of the crisis and act accordingly. However, in view of the uncertainty involved in obtaining strategic warning, it is extremely dangerous to base strategic policy on the presumption that such advance warning will be available. This is particularly true when the great emphasis in Soviet military writing on the advantages of surprise is taken into consideration. This is not to say that nuclear war could not result from unintentional escalation of an international crisis when both sides had their strategic forces in a high alert status; but to rely on this is to gamble with the nation's security.[22]

RESEARCH AND DEVELOPMENT

The Soviet Union unquestionably has undertaken a massive military development program. For over a decade, new systems and new innovations have continually been introduced. Given the Soviet damage-limiting philosophy, the United States must be alert to the possibility of threatening technological breakthroughs. Technological surprise in such areas as antisubmarine warfare, antiballistic missile systems, and air defenses could pose a severe threat to deterrence. Thus, it is critical for the United States to maintain a vigorous research and development (R&D) program.

The focus of this R&D program should be twofold: to increase understanding of technological innovations that could threaten U.S. strategic forces and to explore new concepts to counter potential threats. U.S. reaction time will thus be reduced should a threat materialize.

Although R&D programs seem to be a matter of simple prudence, some defense critics have suggested that they threaten world peace since they are seen to fuel the arms race.[23] The control of R&D programs is thought to be vital if arms control is to have any real meaning. Agreements between

Assuring Deterrence

the United States and the Soviet Union to limit technological exploration of new weapons systems or of new innovations are thought to be necessary and feasible.

The underlying premises of the argument for R&D limitations—that the United States has been engaged in an ever spiraling arms race, that arms competition is the source of international tensions, and that an arms race inevitably leads to war—are all questionable.[24] Moreover, agreements to limit R&D are more likely to have a destabilizing rather than a stabilizing effect on deterrence. In a closed society like the Soviet Union, any agreement would be impossible to police, and technological advances will continue whether research is called military or civilian. Such agreements could thus severely limit the options available to the United States without decreasing the threat to its forces. Rather than relying on unverifiable treaties, the surest path to peace is for the United States to maintain an effective R&D program to assure that its strategic forces remain survivable.

THE MYTH OF OVERKILL

The basic principles for assuring deterrence are not new. Unfortunately, in some instances they are lessons that in recent years have been downplayed if not completely forgotten. This attitude is fostered perhaps by a psychological aversion to contemplating the possibility of war and, perhaps to a greater extent, by the widely held belief that the American stockpile of strategic nuclear weapons constitutes "overkill" under all circumstances.

It is not uncommon to hear assertions that the United States has the capability to destroy everyone in the Soviet Union ten to one hundred times over. One recent estimate even declared that the United States could destroy the *world's* population twelve times over.[25] This estimate was made by multiplying the casualties per kiloton[26] at Hiroshima by the assumed total number of kilotons in the U.S. arsenal and then dividing this figure by the world's total population.[27] Defined in this manner, overkill is, of course, not unique to nuclear weapons. In World War II, 50 pounds of TNT per person were dropped on Germany, Italy, and Japan. In the Vietnam War, 730 pounds were dropped.[28] This kind of calculation can easily be extended to other lethal weapons, such as guns and bullets.

Contrary to the assumptions underlying these nuclear overkill calculations, the world's population is, of course, not gathered together in the same density and under the same conditions as those that existed at Hiroshima. Much of the world's population is rural and widely dispersed.

And although nuclear weapons are indeed very destructive, the range of this damage is limited. Within the radius of a few miles from the center of a nuclear explosion, the resulting blast, heat, and radiation do an enormous amount of damage, but structures and people twenty or so miles away from the explosion (depending on the size of the weapon) may experience little or no damage.

Thus, Secretary of Defense McNamara set his assured-destruction level at 25 to 30 percent of the Soviet population because he realized that it was difficult to increase casualties beyond this level (see figure 1). Given enough weapons, the United States could destroy most of the Soviet Union's urban population if the people were completely unprepared and unprotected. This would amount to about 47 percent of the total population, located in about 1,000 cities. But even with the equivalent of 5,000 megatons (which is larger than the entire U.S. strategic arsenal), the number of casualties could not be increased much beyond this level because the rural population of the Soviet Union is so widely dispersed.

The estimate of casualties illustrated in figure 1 is, in many respects, an overestimate since it is based on an optimally planned and optimally executed attack designed expressly to kill civilians. In reality, the United States does not target civilians per se but rather the economic, political, and military structure of the U.S.S.R. Furthermore, the United States generally has a second-strike policy in which it is prepared to absorb a Soviet first strike and only then retaliate. Following a Soviet first strike, the number of weapons available for retaliation would be much smaller than the prestrike inventory, and any plans for an optimized attack would be disrupted because the United States could not know beforehand what weapons would survive. Because targeting plans for the retaliatory attack are not likely to be redesigned in the midst of a nuclear war, many important targets with large populations could be missed entirely.[29]

Today, the Minuteman ICBM force has the total equivalent destructive power of about 1,000 megatons (or 1,000 EMT),[30] the submarine-launched ballistic missiles (SLBMs) have around 750 EMT, and U.S. bombers can potentially carry about 1,700 EMT (1,350 EMT in bombs and 350 EMT in SRAMs), a combined total of about 3,500 EMT. The addition of the Trident missile and submarine in the early 1980s will increase this total by about 100 EMT. However, a surprise attack in the early 1980s could greatly lower this inventory number. At a minimum, it could destroy the 70 percent of the bombers and the 50 percent of submarines not on alert. In addition, it is unlikely that more than 15 percent of the Minuteman ICBMs would survive such an attack.[31]

Thus, following a surprise attack in the early 1980s, probably less than 1,000 EMT would be deliverable on the Soviet Union even if it were op-

FIGURE 1
Potential Destruction of Soviet Population and Industry

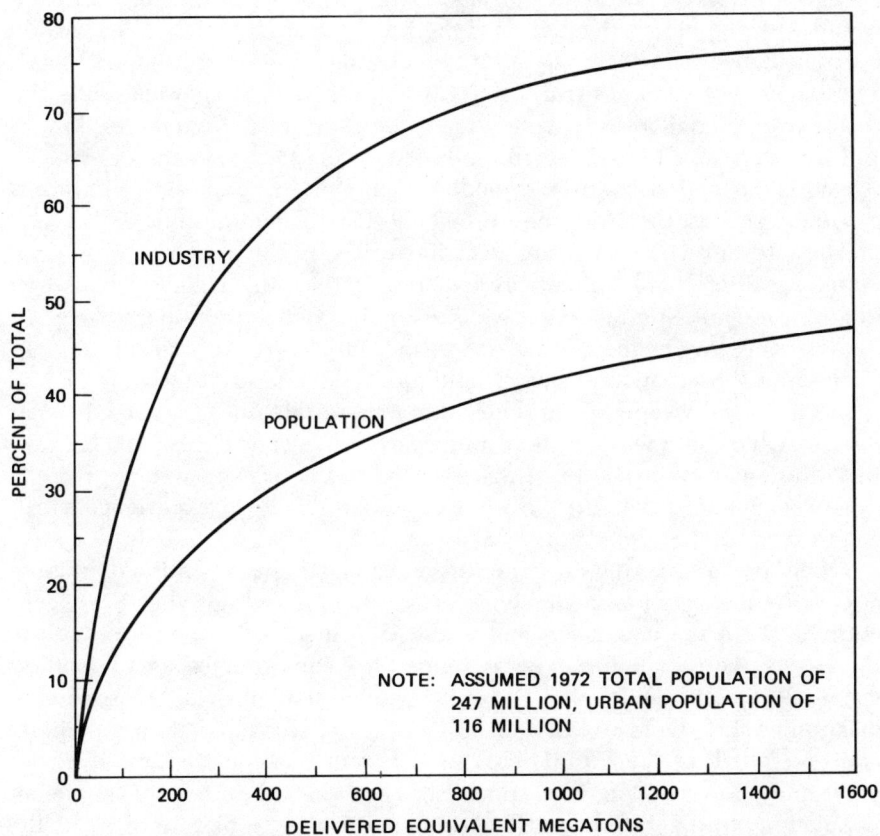

SOURCES: **Population**—Alain C. Enthoven and K. Wayne Smith, *How Much Is Enough? Shaping the Defense Program, 1961–69* (New York: Harper & Row, 1971), p. 207. **Industry**—Derived from data presented in Geoffery Kemp, *Nuclear Forces for Medium Powers: Part 1, Targets and Weapon Systems,* Adelphi Paper no. 106 (London: International Institute for Strategic Studies, 1974), p. 5.

timistically assumed that all U.S. alert bombers survived a Soviet SLBM attack and were able to penetrate the massive Soviet air defense and that the Soviets had no antisubmarine warfare capability nor any antiballistic missile capability.[32] Although it is doubtful that these optimistic assumptions can be relied upon (as will be discussed in chapter 3), the point is that even after making these assumptions, the United States does not have the overwhelming overkill capabilities attributed to it.

There is, however, the added complication of nuclear fallout. If a bomb explodes on or very near the ground, large amounts of dirt and dust are mixed with the radioactive debris of the bomb. This material is then carried high into the atmosphere by the now familiar mushroom-shaped cloud. The larger particles return to earth in the area of the explosion while the rest may be carried away by wind, deposited downrange from the explosion, and threaten anyone exposed to the radiation emitted from the debris. On the other hand, if a bomb is exploded in the air, the radioactive debris is carried high into the stratosphere, and no local fallout results.[33]

The present U.S. targeting doctrine calls for the destruction of economic, political, and military targets rather than the civilian population in general. Thus, in practice, it is disadvantageous to groundburst weapons because this lowers their lethal range in comparison with airbursting. In addition, a conservative planner would more likely desire that there be two chances for the weapon to explode rather than only one. By using a radar fuse to airburst the weapon, he could always use a contact fuse as a backup. But if he relies on groundbursting alone, he has no backup system. Thus, it can be concluded that the Soviet Union is unlikely to experience much fallout from a U.S. retaliatory strike.

Of course, a targeting doctrine can be changed. But even if a deliberate attempt is made to maximize civilian casualties, it will not alter these conclusions about the lack of overkill in the U.S. arsenal.[34] In a recent study, the Boeing Aerospace Company examined the consequences of a hypothetical nuclear exchange in 1985.[35] It was assumed that all U.S. forces were on maximum alert status and that all submarines at sea, most of the bombers, and one-fourth of the ICBMs survived. If there are no shelters in Soviet cities and no evacuation, the report estimated that 36 percent of the Soviet population will be killed by an attack aimed against Soviet industry. If the entire surviving U.S. force is used to attack the population and optimistic conditions (from the U.S. viewpoint) exist, 55 percent of the Soviet population might die from blast and fallout. At the other extreme, with an evacuation and hasty construction of fallout shelters, only about 4 percent of the Soviet population is expected to die.[36]

Pointing out that the United States does not have the capability to annihilate everyone in the U.S.S.R. (or the world) many times over is not meant to downplay the terrible consequences of a nuclear war. A nuclear war would be a disaster whether 5 percent or 55 percent of the population was destroyed.[37] But exaggeration of the number of casualties has had a corrosive effect on rational considerations of actual requirements for deterrence. Defining rationality in this context is admittedly difficult; but the emotionalism generated by the rhetoric of overkill can lead to the discounting of real threats if it is assumed that no matter what happens, the United States will always have too many weapons.

COMPLACENCY

Although the concept of overkill is at best misleading, it has created a psychological atmosphere of complacency not only among defense critics but in the Defense Department as well—a view which is contrary to the public image of a defense and intelligence establishment that continually exaggerates the Soviet threat in order to gain support for greater defense expenditures.[38] This image resulted primarily from the intelligence community's overestimates of the number of intercontinental bombers and ICBMs that the Soviets would choose to deploy in the late 1950s and early 1960s—the famous "bomber gap" and even more famous "missile gap."[39] However, Albert Wohlstetter has shown, through an exhaustive analysis of past National Intelligence Estimates and of statements by the secretaries of defense, that since the time of the "missile gap" projections, the intelligence community has consistently underestimated future Soviet ICBM deployment.[40] Furthermore, others have demonstrated that underestimating ICBM deployments has not been unique.[41] Nevertheless, the image of Pentagon-exaggerated worst-case planning remains substantially intact.[42]

Although Defense Department officials have expressed general concern over the growth in Soviet power, they have in the last few years consistently downplayed threats to specific U.S. strategic systems.[43] This air of complacency is illustrated by then Secretary of Defense James Schlesinger's testimony before Congress in 1975. In discussing counterforce capabilities, he said:

> It is not within the realm of possibility for the United States or the Soviet Union to deny each other the ultimate ability to destroy the urban industrial base of the other's civilization. . . .
> I think it is important for all to understand that nothing for the next several decades—as far ahead as we can see—can remove that ability from either side, and under any circumstances there is no possibility of a high confidence disarming first strike.[44]

Because of Schlesinger's views regarding the assured survivability of the deterrent, a new justification for new strategic systems was deemed necessary.[45] This new policy was based primarily on psychological and political considerations: the United States must maintain essential equivalence with the Soviet Union, and this equivalence must be clearly perceived by the world. Arguments for new weapons systems have thus tended to shift from specific Soviet threats to other grounds.

ICBMs

It has been clear for some time that Soviet development of high accuracy ICBMs would allow them to launch a crippling attack against the U.S. ICBM force by the early 1980s. Nevertheless, until quite recently Air Force arguments for a new, large ICBM (the so-called MX system) concentrated on the capabilities of this missile to redress the growing imbalance in hard-target kill capability (because the MX would have larger and more accurate warheads than the Minuteman) and to offset the perceived large ICBM throw-weight advantage of the Soviets. Although the eventual demise of silo-based ICBMs was acknowledged by the Air Force, the date for this was always set quite far into the future. In fact, until overruled by Congress, the Air Force had planned to begin placing MX missiles in Minuteman silos in about 1985 and then "when the threat developed," to redeploy them in a mobile or multiple-aim-point mode. For example, in 1976, then Secretary of the Air Force Thomas C. Reed, in discussing the basing of MX, suggested that there was no compelling reason to abandon fixed-silo ICBMs because even under worst-case conditions, there was no evidence that any foreseeable Soviet first strike could destroy more than 85 percent of current hardened silos.[46] And in March, 1977, General Alton D. Slay, USAF, deputy chief of staff, Research and Development, testified that although there would eventually be a danger from improvements in the accuracy of Soviet missiles, the recent hardening "program will insure a viable land-based ICBM force into the mid- and late-1980s."[47] He later shifted the ultimate vulnerability of this force to "the late eighties or early nineties."[48]

In the beginning, Air Force arguments against Minuteman vulnerability relied heavily on the issue of fratricide, that is, the inability of the Soviets to target more than one weapon on an ICBM silo because of destructive interference from the explosion of the first weapon. However, after examination, it was shown that with proper timing constraints well within the capability of the Soviets, this problem could be avoided.[49]

After conceding the issue of fratricide, the Air Force continued to argue that Soviet missiles would not be accurate enough to threaten Minuteman for some time. However, public testimony revealed that one would have to make extremely optimistic assumptions (from the U.S. viewpoint) in order to believe that Soviet improvements in accuracy would not be threatening until the late 1980s. Indeed, Secretary of Defense Harold Brown has now admitted that the land-based ICBMs will be threatened in the "early- to mid-1980s."[50]

Despite this newly recognized vulnerability, there has been little overreaction or, indeed, any sense of urgency at all. The proposed system to replace Minuteman—the multiple-aim-point MX system—will not be available until at least 1987, if then. In addition, the Carter administration's initial SALT proposals sought to outlaw this type of "mobile" system completely, an act that would have marked the end of U.S. land-based ICBMs.

Thus, there appears to be no justification for assuming that the Pentagon uses worst-case planning even when there is a clearly identifiable threat. This is even more obvious when the threat is less quantifiable as is the case with both the strategic bombers and strategic submarines.

Bombers

The Air Force's arguments for a new bomber (the B-1) were based more on the fact that the B-52s (which were built in the 1950s and early 1960s) were getting old than on any specific identifiable threat to the B-52. The B-1 would have been faster, less susceptible to nuclear explosions, harder for enemy radars to detect, able to fly at lower altitudes (to avoid detection), and generally a better aircraft than the B-52. Although all these improvements would have aided a bomber in surviving a Soviet surprise attack and then penetrating the massive Soviet air defense system, the reality of the threat that required a new aircraft with these features was not made clear. The effectiveness of the present (and near-term) Soviet air defense system has been continually downplayed. Because the Air Force was reluctant to admit the potential capabilities of the present Soviet air defense system, it tested the bombers against a hypothetical, improved air defense thought to resemble one that the Soviets might deploy in the distant future. This lack of concern for the actual threat was illustrated in a press conference on July 1, 1977, immediately following President Carter's decision to cancel the B-1 in favor of the cruise missile. When asked how long he thought the B-52 would be effective as a penetrating, low-level bomber, Secretary of Defense Brown replied:

> I am convinced that, from what we know, we can be reasonably sure that it will last and survive and be able to penetrate as a low altitude penetrator into the late 1980s, 10 years from now. And I don't say it won't be able to after that. I'm just saying that I can't see further ahead than that.[51]

This can hardly be considered a worst-case view or even a conservative view.

SSBNs

The case of strategic missile-carrying nuclear submarines (SSBNs) is even more extreme. The strategic submarine force is generally viewed as invulnerable both today and for decades to come. The Navy's primary justification for a new submarine (the Trident class) is that in the late 1980s and early 1990s, the present Polaris/Poseidon fleet will be 25 years old and ready for retirement. The longer range C-4 missiles carried by these new submarines will increase their operating area, but this is seen as a bonus because it is deemed highly unlikely that a Soviet threat that would require this additional area will materialize.[52]

Although, as noted above, the root of this attitude of official complacency lies perhaps in the general acceptance of the idea of overkill, there are other strong pressures not to admit publicly that deficiencies exist in U.S. strategic forces. Once the Department of Defense accepted the proposition that worldwide perception of military strength is just as important as the actual survivability of the strategic weapons, it became an exceedingly delicate matter for it to raise questions that might weaken perceptions of U.S. strength. Under these circumstances, what may be perceived as necessities of diplomacy can undermine prudence (particularly when the necessity for prudence is not highly regarded).

This concern for world opinion is illustrated in testimony given by Secretary Brown. When asked why he had expressed annoyance over the debate over the extent of Soviet civil defense preparations, he replied:

> Some of the more alarmist statements made about Soviet strategic civil defense capabilities could have a negative effect, not because we believe them, but because they might undermine deterrence by giving Moscow a false notion that a strategic nuclear attack could be conducted against the United States without U.S. retaliation that would destroy the Soviet Union as a society. Also if our allies or neutrals were to believe that the Soviets could indeed achieve this high degree of protection for their society, that might be translated into a political advantage for the Soviet Union.[53]

The same political argument obviously applies to an even greater degree to discussions of the vulnerability of U.S. strategic weapons.

Interservice rivalry and bureaucratic forces produce other pressures to downplay potential threats. Competition between the Air Force and the Navy over their shares of the strategic forces is always present. Any admission of weakness in one leg of the triad of forces would mobilize the advocates of the other legs to increase their share of the deterrent forces in order to augment or to replace the vulnerable leg. These advocates are not solely, or even primarily, found among the services themselves; rather they are various outside groups with their own views on the proper characteristics of the deterrent. Because many of these groups advocate abandoning one or more legs of the triad, the services are reluctant to substantiate these groups' arguments.

Whatever the underlying reasons, there has been a tendency both in the defense and in the intelligence communities to downplay specific threats to specific weapons systems.[54] Rather than a propensity to exaggerate the threat, there has not even been a full recognition of the underlying uncertainties involved in the determination of the survivability of weapon systems.

III
The Survivability of U.S. Strategic Forces

The United States' strategic deterrent consists of a triad of forces: land-based intercontinental ballistic missiles (ICBMs), ballistic-missile-carrying nuclear submarines (SSBNs), and long-range strategic bombers. Intimately connected with these forces are an early warning system to detect the launching of enemy forces and a command and control network to direct the strategic forces.

Different approaches have been used to insure the survivability of these strategic forces. The ICBMs are housed in hardened underground silos; some of the bombers are maintained on constant alert ready to escape their bases upon warning of an attack; submarines are mobile and hope to use the vast expanses of the oceans to avoid detection. But even under the best of conditions, a large part of the strategic forces would not survive a surprise Soviet attack. For example, only about 30 percent of the bombers and 50 percent of the submarines are on alert, and the nonalert forces are extremely vulnerable to an attack. But far more than the nonalert forces are threatened.

The development of multiple independently targetable reentry vehicles (MIRVs) allows the Soviets to deploy up to ten large-yield warheads on their new, larger ICBMs. If these missiles are sufficiently accurate, they can pose a severe threat to U.S. ICBMs. Furthermore, the Soviets now have a large fleet of ballistic-missile-carrying submarines. If these missiles were flown on short time-of-flight trajectories (depressed trajectories), the survivability of the alert bomber force (with the present basing system) would be in serious doubt. Those bombers that survived would have to penetrate the most extensive air defense system in the world to reach their targets. Finally, there are the strategic submarines, which are considered the most survivable of the strategic forces. However, recent advances in conventional and unconventional antisubmarine-warfare technology could pose a serious threat to the survivability of this critical element of the triad.

It is important to note that even if the strategic forces survive an attack, they are under positive control; that is, the missiles cannot be launched nor can the bombers proceed to target without positive authorization from the president or his designated successor. Thus, the survival of the early warning system and of the command, control, and communications system is critical to the maintenance of a credible deterrent.

Survivability is not only the key to assuring deterrence, but many other issues—arms control, targeting doctrine, and the potential coercive power of strategic weapons—also depend on an understanding of the vulnerabilities of strategic weapons systems. The current debate over national defense policy and defense programs ultimately stems from conflicting views regarding the survivability of these forces (although there are, of course, many other issues involved). In this debate it is often difficult to ascertain the premises underlying the arguments or, for the uninitiated, to understand the importance of these arguments. The following analysis of survivability is presented in order to highlight the critical issues involved and to provide a basis for understanding.

ICBM SURVIVABILITY

The present American ICBM force consists of 1,000 Minuteman missiles and 54 older Titan II missiles. The total number of missiles has remained constant since 1965 although the Minuteman force has been modernized since then. Today there are 450 Minuteman II missiles, each carrying a single reentry vehicle (which contains the warhead), and 550 Minuteman III missiles, each of which carries three smaller reentry vehicles (RVs) that can be directed to three separate targets. The latter are the so-called MIRVs (multiple independently targetable reentry vehicles) and were first deployed in 1970.

The primary threat to ICBM survivability is an attack by one or more nuclear weapons against each underground missile silo. In the past this threat was not considered significant because Soviet missiles were neither very accurate nor numerous. However, the introduction of the fourth generation of Soviet ICBMs (see table 1) has changed this evaluation. The large throw-weight of these MIRVed ICBMs enables the Soviets to install many large-yield weapons on each missile. Because the Soviets are steadily improving the accuracy of this force, the threat to U.S. ICBMs continues to grow.[1] To understand the extent of the threat, consideration of the following factors is important.

TABLE 1

U.S. ICBMs and the Soviet Threat

U.S. ICBMs

Type	Number	Silo Hardness (psi)
Titan II	54	300
Minuteman	1,000	1,000–1,500

Soviet Threat

ICBM Type	No. of Warheads	Yield (MT)	Mid-1978		Mid-1980	
			No.	CEP (nm)	No.	CEP (nm)
SS-18	8–10	1–2	150	0.15–0.2	300	0.1–0.15
SS-19	6	1	250	0.15–0.2	400	0.1–0.15
SS-17	4	1	75	0.15–0.2	100	0.1–0.15

SOURCES: Harold Brown, *Department of Defense Annual Report, Fiscal Year 1979*, p. 49; *Counterforce Issues for the U.S. Strategic Nuclear Forces* (Washington, D.C.: Congressional Budget Office, 1978), pp. 15–16; David Binder, "New CIA Estimate Finds Soviet Seeks Superiority in Arms," *New York Times*, Dec. 26, 1976, p. 1.
NOTES: CEP is missile accuracy measured in nautical miles (nm); see text. Yield is energy released by a warhead expressed in megatons (MT); see text.

Hardness Modern ICBMs are housed in underground concrete silos designed to withstand the severe environment resulting from a nearby explosion of a nuclear weapon. The Minuteman system has recently been upgraded, and each missile is now protected by a suspension system, by foam blocks on the sides of the silo to reduce horizontal shock, by liquid springs on the bottom to reduce vertical shock, by an isolated floor, and by an improved launcher door mechanism that can operate if there is debris on top of the silo. Failure of the missile system can result from damage to the missile itself or from such damage to the silo structure that launch is prevented. In a simplified model, silos can withstand the overpressures of a shock wave (i.e., the resulting pressure that is above the normal atmospheric pressure of fifteen pounds per square inch) up to a certain level and then fail at that point. This is called the silo hardness and is measured in pounds per square inch (psi).

The Survivability of U.S. Strategic Forces

Yield   The energy released by a nuclear explosion is called the yield of the weapon. In a kiloton (kT) explosion, the energy released is the equivalent of one thousand tons of TNT. A megaton (MT) equals one thousand kilotons or one million tons of TNT.

Kill Radius   The distance at which a nuclear weapon can generate an overpressure equal to the silo hardness is called the kill (or lethal) radius of that weapon. For a particular silo hardness, the kill radius increases only as the cube root of yield. That is, to double the kill radius of a weapon, it is necessary to increase the yield by a factor of eight.

Accuracy   The accuracy of a missile is usually measured in terms of its CEP (circular error probable or circle of equal probability) given in nautical miles (nm). CEP is the median miss distance; that is, it is the radius of a circle centered on the target within which half the reentry vehicles would fall if the missile test were repeated many times. By this definition, when the CEP equals the kill radius, the silo has a 50 percent chance of surviving because the RV has a 50 percent chance of landing within the kill radius of the silo.

Probability of Survival   Because the accuracy of a weapon is not some fixed number but can only be predicted in a probabilistic sense, whether a missile silo survives is also a matter of probabilities. In general, the probability that a silo will survive the damage from a single arriving warhead (P_s) is given by the formula:

$$P_s = 0.5^{(r_k/CEP)^2}$$

where r_k is the kill radius of the weapon. The probability of kill (P_k) is

$$P_k = 1 - P_s$$

Reliability   Since not all missiles are completely reliable, some will not arrive on target. For example, if the overall reliability of the Soviet missile force is 85 percent and one Soviet RV is targeted at each of the 1,000 Minuteman missile silos, no matter how accurate the Soviet missiles are, at least 150 Minutemen will survive because they will not actually be attacked.

Multiple RV Attacks   By targeting more than one RV on each silo, the probability of a successful kill is increased (just as the overall chance of tossing "heads" on a coin is increased the more times the coin is tossed although the probability of success for each individual toss remains the same). This also compensates for the unreliability of the attacking missiles and increases the chances that at least one RV will arrive on target.

Fratricide It is thought that in multiple RV attacks if the second (and later) RV follows too closely upon the first, it could be destroyed or deflected from the target by the explosion of the first RV. Unless care is taken to insure the proper timing of an attack, these fratricide effects could diminish the effectiveness of the attack.

Thus, an assessment of ICBM survivability depends on a large number of factors. However, the analysis that follows demonstrates that missile accuracy is the most critical parameter and that for very high accuracies the other parameters are of secondary importance. For example, the expression $Y^{2/3}/CEP^2$ (where Y is the yield and CEP the accuracy) is called lethality or countermilitary potential.[2] It is derived from the definition of ICBM survivability (since the kill radius is proportional to $Y^{1/3}$) and illustrates the dominant effect of accuracy over yield in determining missile survival: a change by a factor of two in CEP is equal to a change by a factor of eight in yield. Similarly, an improvement in CEP by a factor of two can offset an increase by a factor of eight in the silo hardness (see appendix B).

Accuracy

The primary sources of missile error are those associated with the guidance and control system. An inertial guidance system uses gyroscopes, accelerometers, and an on-board computer to calculate the position and velocity of the missile continuously and to send appropriate signals to the control system to insure that the reentry vehicle is being directed toward the target. Other important sources of error are the separation of an RV from its booster (or the postboost vehicle in the case of MIRVs), the dispersion encountered by an RV upon entering the atmosphere, gravimetric and geodetic errors (i.e., errors caused by faulty measurements of the earth's gravitational field and of the exact location of the target), and the method used to fuse the warhead carried by an RV.

From the first crude missiles used as weapons by the Germans in World War II to the present modern ICBMs, the history of missile accuracy has been one of steady improvement. Early ICBMs, introduced less than two decades ago, had accuracies of about one nautical mile (nm). Today, accuracies of an order of magnitude less than this (0.1 nm) are possible. Within a few years, a new American missile (the MX missile) with reported accuracies of 0.05 nm may be available.[3] Indeed, in 1970, D. C. Hoag, director of the Apollo Guidance and Navigation Program, estimated that with present technology, ICBM CEPs of 30 meters (0.02 nm) or less could be developed.[4]

Table 2 and figure 2 give a brief history of the improvement in ICBM accuracies.[5] The hatched portion of the curve for the Soviet Union represents the uncertainty in the assessment of Soviet missile accuracies.

Accuracy assessments are made from data obtained by monitoring Soviet missile tests and from estimates of the quality of the precision equipment (gyroscopes and accelerometers) available to the Soviets for their guidance and control systems. Because the data available are insufficient to make a definitive assessment and because Soviet missile accuracy and the survival of U.S. ICBMs are so critically related, President Ford appointed a panel of missile experts from outside the government (the so-called B Team) to assess Soviet missile accuracy independently of the intelligence agencies.

Significant differences between the intelligence community's official assessment of the accuracies of the new generation of Soviet ICBMs and the

TABLE 2

History of ICBM Accuracies

Era	CEP of U.S. Systems	CEP of U.S.S.R. Systems
1961–63	Atlas E (61) Titan II (63) Minuteman I (63) } 0.75–1 nm	SS-7 (62) 1 nm
1965–66	Minuteman II (66) 0.33 nm	SS-9 (65) 0.5 nm
1970	Minuteman III 0.15 nm	No new Soviet ICBMs
1975	New system considered but not developed (0.1 nm or less)	SS-17, SS-18, SS-19 0.15–0.25 nm
1979–80	Minuteman III 0.1 nm	SS-17, SS-18, SS-19 0.1–0.2 nm
1983–85	MX 0.05 nm	SS-17, SS-18, SS-19 0.1 nm or less New systems 0.1 nm or less

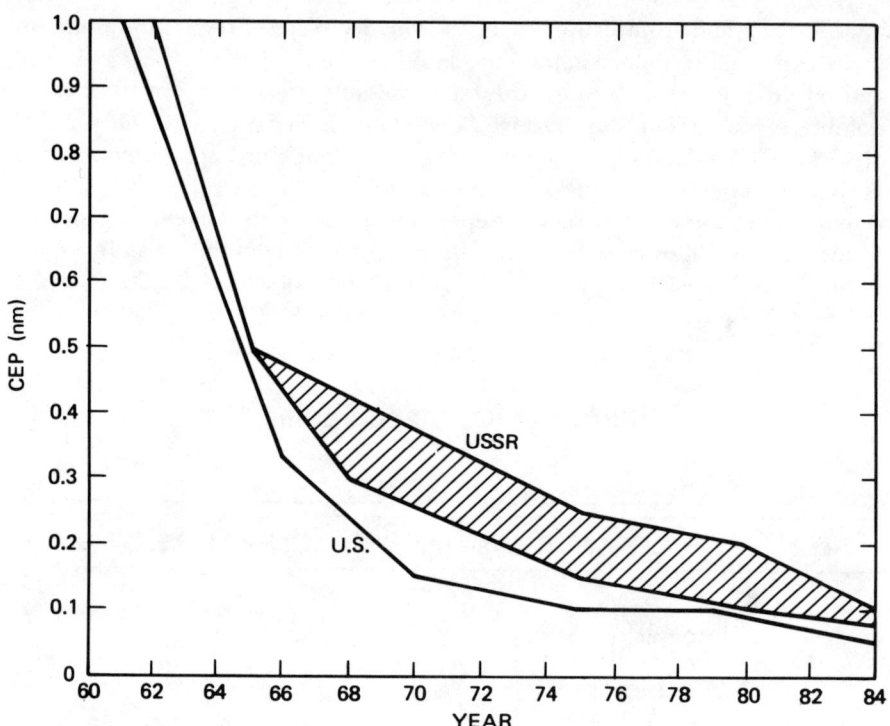

FIGURE 2

Estimated ICBM Accuracies

B Team's assessment were reported in the December 26, 1976 issue of the *New York Times*.[6] According to the *Times*, the National Intelligence Estimate indicated an accuracy of 0.25 nm, whereas the B Team estimated that the missiles were as accurate as U.S. ICBMs—about 0.15 nm.[7] Within a year, the Defense Intelligence Agency (DIA) revised its estimate. General Samuel V. Wilson, director of the DIA, told a congressional committee that the accuracy of Soviet ICBMs was better than previously thought, although they were still thought to be less accurate than the U.S. ICBMs.[8] Although no figures were given, the official estimate of Soviet missile accuracy, as of fall, 1977, probably was closer to 0.2 nm than to 0.25 nm.

Historically, after a missile system has been introduced, improvements in the accuracy of the system have been achieved by testing it and analyzing the sources of error. For example, by changing only the computer software program of the Minuteman III, an impressive improvement in its accuracy was recently introduced, reportedly from 0.15 nm to about 0.1 nm.[9] On the basis of 1976 intelligence estimates and from the general history of accuracy improvements, one can expect that if the B Team estimates are correct, Soviet missiles will have accuracies of about 0.1 nm to 0.12 nm by 1980. If the estimates of the CIA and DIA are correct, accuracies of about 0.15 nm to 0.17 nm (or 0.2 nm at the outside) can be expected.

The Soviets are following the normal pattern of progress, but they appear to have introduced significant improvements much sooner than anticipated by the intelligence community.[10] During the winter of 1977–78, the Soviets conducted a series of tests designed to improve the accuracy of the SS-18 and SS-19. They reportedly have developed a new postboost vehicle (the "bus" used to drop off the RVs at the appropriate time), improved the on-board computer software for the guidance system, made further improvements in their new inertial guidance system, and developed a device to spin the reentry vehicles before deployment from the bus to impart a spin stabilization that will improve accuracy.[11] Some Defense Department officials were quoted as saying that Soviet missile accuracy in this series of tests approached 0.1 nm.[12] This appears to substantiate the B Team's estimates of Soviet missile accuracy.

Minuteman Vulnerability

The controversy over Soviet missile accuracy in the 1980s is more than just academic because, as is illustrated in figure 3, the range of uncertainty happens to be very critical. Under the particular set of assumptions used in making this calculation, about 260 Minuteman missiles would be expected to survive if Soviet missile accuracy were 0.2 nm; only about 30 to 55 would be expected to survive if the accuracy were 0.1 nm or 0.12 nm. (See appendix B for an explanation of these calculations.)[13] The assumptions used in this example (which are generally optimistic from the U.S. point of view) will be discussed below. Variations in those factors affecting Minuteman survivability are illustrated in figure 4. As previously noted, accuracy is the most important factor, particularly at low CEPs.

Silo Hardness

It has been reported that Minuteman silos have been upgraded from a hardness of 300 psi to 1,000 psi.[14] However, a Minuteman hardness of 1,500 psi was used in this analysis because a Soviet planner would probably be conservative and assume that the silo might actually be harder than the designed hardness.

In fact, silo hardness could be considered the greatest source of uncertainty in the Soviets' assessment of the effectiveness of an attack because

FIGURE 3

Effects of Accuracy on Minuteman Survivability

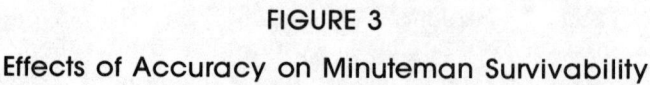

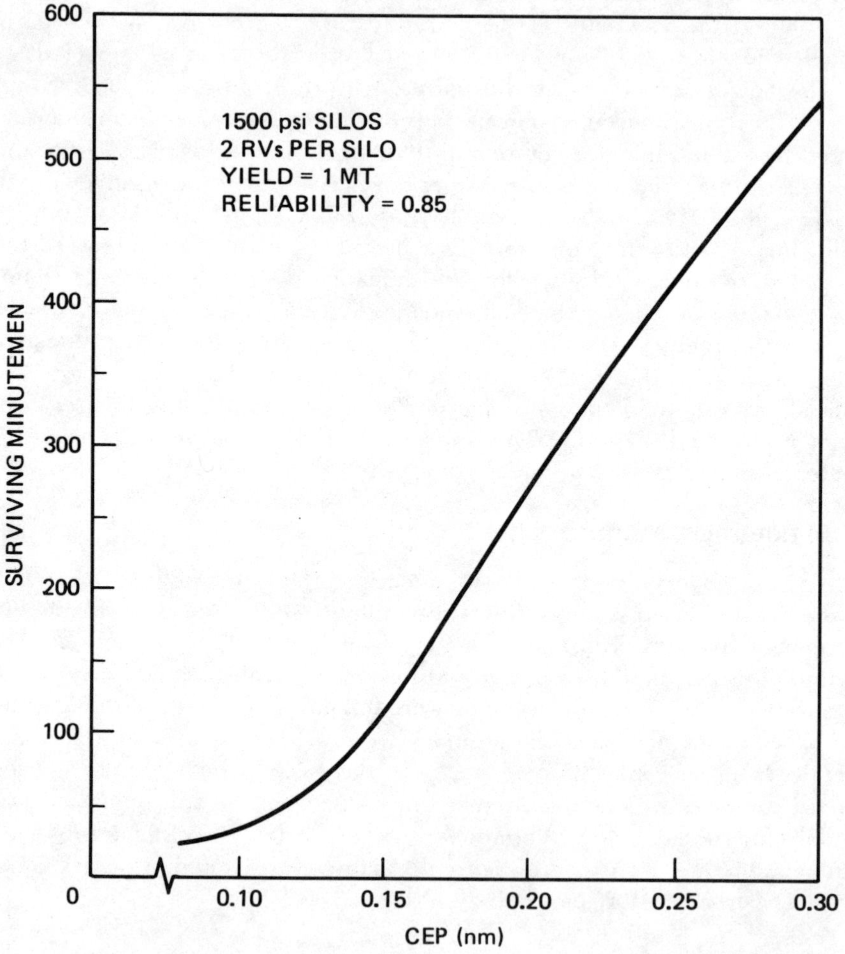

1500 psi SILOS
2 RVs PER SILO
YIELD = 1 MT
RELIABILITY = 0.85

the remaining factors concern their own missiles. However, as noted by Defense Department officials, the Soviets can be fairly confident of the maximum hardness of the silos simply by examining their design.[15] Because the construction and upgrading of the Minuteman silos were put out for bid by private contractors, detailed, unclassified blueprints of the silos were available to the public and presumably to the Soviets. The Soviets also operate an extensive espionage network, and secrets are notoriously difficult to keep in an open society. In any event, as figure 4 illustrates, at

CEPs of 0.1 to 0.12 nm, even a silo hardness of 2,000 psi is not sufficient to solve Minuteman's vulnerability problems.

Yield

The evaluation of Soviet warhead yields has been greatly complicated by the discontinuation of atmospheric testing over a decade ago. It is now more difficult to evaluate Soviet warhead design technology. It is also

FIGURE 4
Minuteman Survivability

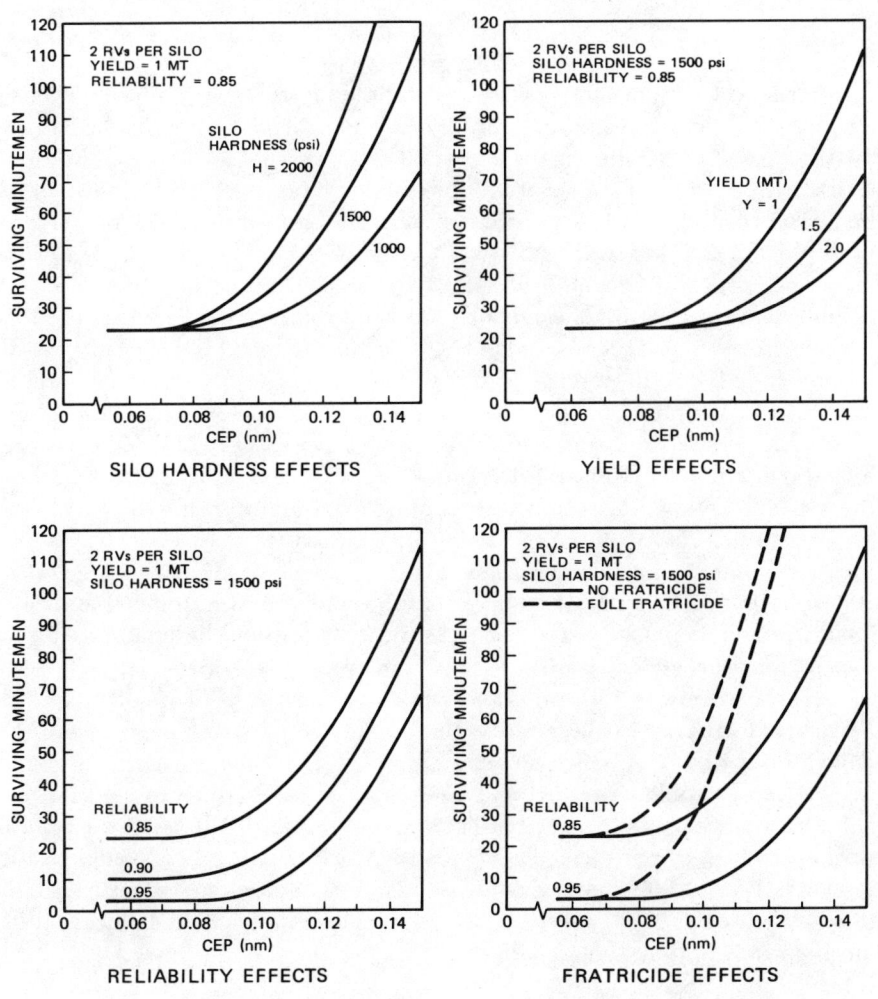

difficult to evaluate the explosive yield of individual underground tests from seismic data alone. Furthermore, there is little way to correlate individual tests with a particular warhead that is actually fielded.

Most public reports of SS-18 warhead yield place the MIRV system warhead (eight to ten per missile) at from 1 to 2 MT.[16] This is probably not an unreasonable range of uncertainty. The lower value of 1 MT, which is optimistic from the U.S. point of view, was used in this analysis.[17] Figure 4 shows the impact of using higher yields. If a more conservative yield (say, 1.5 MT) had been used, the other illustrations in figure 4 would have to be changed somewhat. For example, with a silo hardness of 2,000 psi and a CEP of 0.12 nm, 75 Minutemen would be expected to survive if the yield were 1 MT and 50 if it were 1.5 MT.

Reliability

Mechanical systems are not always completely reliable. Failures in missile systems sometimes occur, and one can expect that some of the Soviet missiles fired at Minuteman silos will fail to reach their targets. At low CEPs where the probability of kill for each arriving warhead becomes very high, the reliability of the attacking system becomes the critical factor. For example, for a 1 MT warhead with a CEP of 0.1 nm exploding against a 1,500 psi silo, the probability of kill is 0.965. Thus if each of the 1,000 Minuteman silos were attacked, only 35 Minutemen would be expected to survive *if* all the warheads arrived. If the Soviet missiles have an overall reliability of 0.85, 15 percent of the warheads will never arrive on target. That is, 150 Minutemen would not even be attacked. However, if there are two waves of attacking warheads,[18] each with a reliability of 0.85, then the first wave will leave 150 Minutemen (15 percent of 1,000) unattacked; but the second wave will result in a total of only 23 Minuteman (15 percent of the remaining 150 Minutemen) being unattacked.

Improvement in reliability at low CEPs is thus quite important, as illustrated by figure 4. With a reliability of 0.95, only 50 Minutemen would be unattacked in a one-RV-per-silo attack; and only 3 would be unattacked in a two-RV-per-silo attack.

Besides extensive test programs and improvements in quality control that may decrease missile failures, the Soviets could also have a system in which they detect missile launch failures in the silos or early in flight (where most problems occur) and then reprogram missiles to replace the failures. By 1980, the Soviets could deploy around 5,000 MIRVed ICBM warheads. Deployment of only 300 SS-18s, each with 10 RVs, would result in 3,000 RVs, 1,000 more than needed for a two-on-one attack. Part of these 1,000 extra RVs could be used to replace early flight failures, thus increasing overall system reliability.

Fratricide

Recently a number of articles have criticized "conventional" approaches to calculating the survivability of Minuteman missiles for failing to consider the operational difficulties that an attacker would face in a real attack. In particular, it is argued that interference effects from the first warhead exploding on a target will destroy the following RVs or at least deflect them enough to severely diminish their effectiveness.[19] This phenomenon is called fratricide.

When a nuclear weapon explodes, there are a number of nuclear-induced effects that can potentially interfere with following RVs:

1. *Neutrons.* A nuclear explosion produces a large number of neutrons, which, if absorbed in sufficient quantity by the nuclear material in the following warhead, can cause that warhead to fail to explode. However, this is a rather short-range effect because most of the neutrons are quickly absorbed by the atmosphere. Hence, proper timing easily avoids the problem.
2. *Blast.* The high temperature resulting from the explosion of the first warhead will create a high-pressure blast wave as well as a fireball of hot gases that will expand and rise into the atmosphere. If the trailing RV followed the first too closely, the blast wave could destroy it. However, if the second RV is at least two seconds behind the first, no severe damage should result.
3. *Ejecta.* If the first explosion is at or near the ground level, large particles of debris (ejecta) will be carried aloft into the stem and the top of the resulting mushroom-shaped cloud. An RV passing through this stem could be destroyed by collisions with the debris. However, if the first warhead is airburst, the fireball will not contain enough dust and water particles to destroy the second RV.

In summary, although there may be difficulties in using several RVs to attack a silo, the operational problems of a two-on-one silo attack can be overcome by a near simultaneous attack. Dust and debris generated by the first explosion can be eliminated as a serious threat for the second RV if the first RV is airburst. The problems caused by the neutrons and the blast wave from the first explosion can be rendered negligible by insuring that the arrival of the second RV is delayed by a few seconds. The trailing RV will under these circumstances encounter at worst the fireball or the stem of the first explosion as it approaches the target (the last few thousand feet of its trajectory). At this time, the RV is so slowed that little erosion would be expected, and, in addition, the erosion would occur too late to seriously affect RV performance. The second RV can also be groundburst to prevent the fireball of the first explosion from interfering with the radar fuse.[20]

It is now generally conceded by the Air Force that a "Soviet ICBM attack could contain two RVs per silo which have been time-resolved to preclude fratricide."[21] However, this point has been disputed by some who contend that it would not be feasible for the Soviets to airburst their warheads.[22] They have argued that barometric-pressure or drag fuses would be too inaccurate and that radar fusing would not be used by the Soviets for fear that the United States would jam the radar. Although the first point may be true, the latter argument would probably not be of concern to the Soviets because it is unlikely that the United States will be able to obtain knowledge of Soviet radar fuses. But even if the United States did and then proceeded to build jammers, the Soviets would in all probability detect this and take appropriate countermeasures.

Although it is quite feasible for the Soviets to overcome the limited technical problems involved in a two-on-one attack, in practice it may make little difference in the outcome of the attack whether they succeed or fail. Their attack could be successful even if there were complete fratricide[23] because at high accuracies (with P_k's approaching 1.0), the main source of surviving Minuteman missiles is that group which is not attacked due to Soviet missile unreliability. Thus, the second wave of RVs is still useful in replacing those RVs in the first wave that fail to arrive. Figure 4 shows, for example, that even with full fratricide, at a CEP of 0.1 nm, only about 55 Minuteman missiles would be expected to survive (assuming 1 MT RVs, 0.85 missile reliability, and 1,500 psi silos).

Therefore, even in this worst-case scenario for the Soviets (and most optimistic for the United States), the second wave is a convenient method of improving the overall reliability and the effectiveness of the attack. Some may consider it somewhat more expensive than reprogramming to replace failures, but the Soviets could still have several thousand RVs left after the second wave (see appendix A).

Conclusion

The present generation of Soviet ICBMs can be deployed in sufficient numbers by 1980 to mount an attack on U.S. ICBMs. Because Soviet progress in the area of missile accuracy is inevitable, it is only a matter of time before the present land-based ICBM system becomes vulnerable. Although a sanguine view of the situation would hold that a serious threat will not develop until 1983 or 1985, based on the analysis of a panel of experts (the B Team) and on recent improvements in the SS-18 and SS-19, there is strong evidence that the threat could develop earlier.

STRATEGIC BOMBER SURVIVABILITY

Although somewhat overshadowed in the space age by ballistic missiles, America's strategic bombers continue to play an important deterrent role. The present force of B-52 Stratofortress bombers can carry a nuclear payload greater than that of the combined ICBM and SLBM forces (see table 3 and appendix A). To deliver this payload, these bombers potentially must be able to survive a missile attack on their bases and then penetrate extensive Soviet air defenses. In the early 1980s as cruise missiles become available, some of these aircraft will be able to launch cruise missiles from outside Soviet borders rather than trying to penetrate themselves; but until that time, all of the bombers must fly over Soviet territory to carry out their missions.

Prelaunch Survival

The primary prelaunch threat to the bomber force is an attack on the bomber bases by Soviet submarine-launched ballistic missiles (SLBMs). In recent years, the Soviets have greatly expanded their strategic submarine force (SSBNs) and now have more than 60 modern nuclear ballistic missile submarines carrying around 900 missiles (see table 4).

TABLE 3

United States Bombers

Bomber*	Number	Nominal Weapon Load
B-52D	75	4 Bombs
B-52G	165	4 Bombs + 6 SRAM†
B-52H	90	4 Bombs + 6 SRAM
Total	330	

SOURCE: *Counterforce Issues for the U.S. Strategic Nuclear Forces* (Washington, D.C.: Congressional Budget Office, January, 1978), p. 18.
*There are also 65 medium range FB-111A bombers which carry 2 bombs and 3 SRAMs
†SRAM—Short-Range Attack Missile

TABLE 4

Soviet Modern SSBNs

SSBN	Number of SLBMs	SLBM Range (nm)	Number of SLBMs	
			Mid-1978	Mid-1980
D-I	12 SS-N-8	4,200–4,800	168	168
D-II	16 SS-N-8	4,200–4,800	144	144
D-III	16 SS-N-18	4,200–4,800	80	176
Y*	16 SS-N-6	1600	544	544
		Total SLBMs	936	1,032

SOURCE: "The Military Balance, 1977/78," *Air Force Magazine*, Dec., 1977, pp. 62, 68.
*At least one of the Yankee class submarines now carries the new SS-N-17 missile.

To counter this threat, the United States maintains 30 percent of its bomber force (around 100 bombers) on a "quick-reaction" alert and deploys them on 16 bases. During a crisis, the number of aircraft on alert can be increased, and the aircraft can be dispersed to a total of 45 Strategic Air Command bases (see map). Upon detection of incoming enemy missiles, these alert bombers will be launched and will attempt to fly a safe distance from their airbases before the SLBM warheads arrive.[24]

An assessment of the prelaunch survivability of the bombers depends on a number of factors (see table 5). Essentially it is a race between the incoming missile (or missiles) and the bomber trying to escape the base. Thus, the most critical variables are SLBM flight time and bomber reaction time following launching of Soviet SLBMs.

Bomber Reaction Time Bomber reaction time depends on two factors: the time required for the SLBM warning system to detect incoming missiles and relay the warning to the bomber bases, and the time required for the bomber crew to get into their aircraft, start the engines, and taxi to the runway. The elapsed time from warning to brake release was estimated by Quanbeck and Wood[25] to be 120 to 150 seconds when the aircraft are on crisis-alert status and 270 to 390 seconds on day-to-day alert status.

The Air Force argues that should a serious threat develop with many Soviet submarines off U.S. coasts, the Strategic Air Command (SAC) can shorten this day-to-day reaction time.[26] It has been estimated that under

Counterforce Targets in the United States

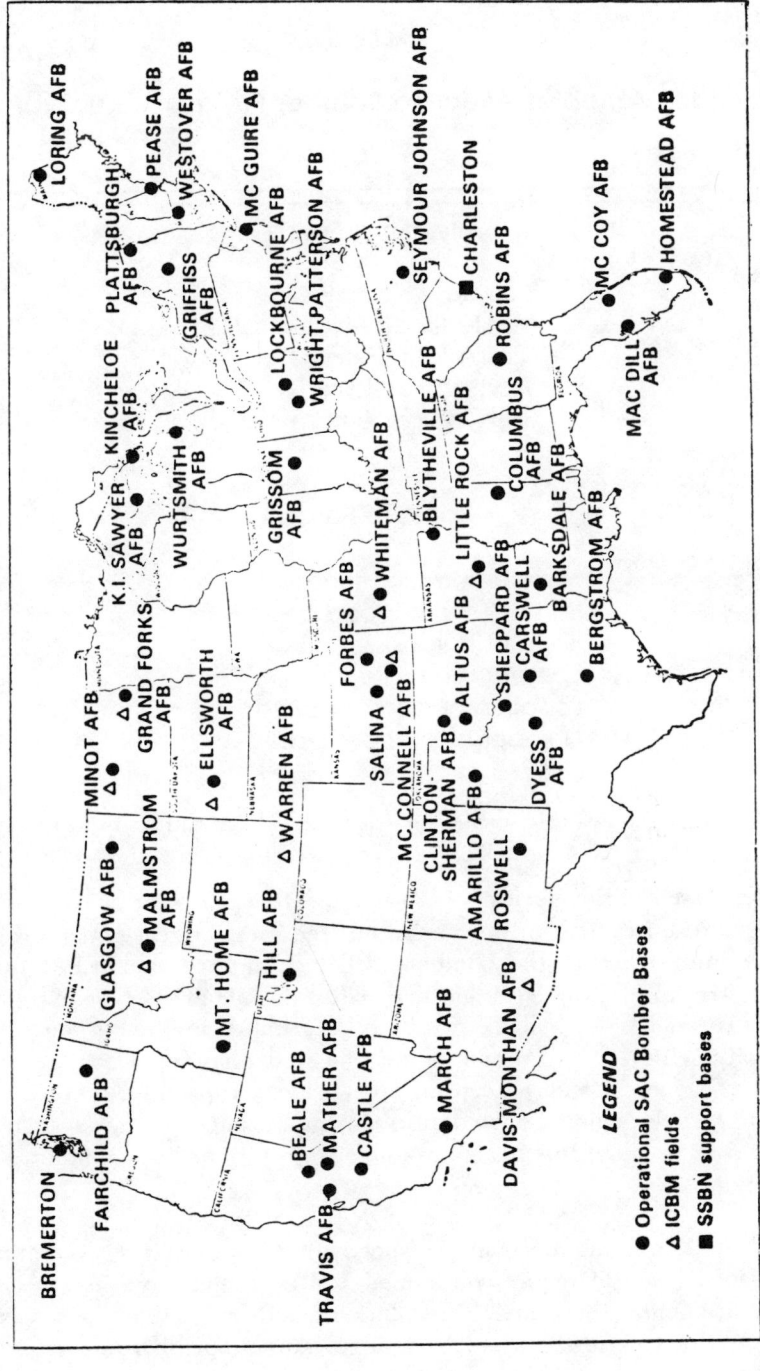

SOURCE: John M. Collins and John S. Chwat, *United States and Soviet Civil Defense: Considerations for Congress* (Washington, D.C.: Government Printing Office, 1976), p. 21.

TABLE 5

Important Variables Affecting Bomber Prelaunch Survivability

Attacking Force

Number of missiles
Missile time-of-flight
Missile launch rate
Warhead yield
SSBN distance from coast

Bomber Force

Bomber reaction time
Bomber flyout speed and pattern
Bomber hardness
Bomber alert rate
Location of bomber bases
Number of bomber bases

these circumstances total day-to-day scramble time can be held to 210 seconds.[27]

Depressed Trajectories Assuming that the Air Force reduces bomber reaction time to the minimum, the most critical remaining factor determining whether the bombers will be caught is the SLBM time-of-flight. This in turn depends on the distance flown and the type of trajectory used. The range of a ballistic missile is determined by the burnout velocity (velocity achieved at the end of the powered phase of flight) and by the angle of launch. Given a fixed burnout velocity capability, there is an optimum launch angle that yields the maximum range for that system. This flight path is called the maximum-range trajectory or the minimum-energy trajectory.

The main Soviet SLBMs, the SS-N-6 and the SS-N-8, have ranges of about 1,600 nm and 4,800 nm, respectively.[28] Because the maximum distance of any point in the continental United States from its seacoasts is about 1,050 nm, these missiles when launched from submarines operating close to the American coasts have a larger range capability than is required to strike any bomber base. This excess capability allows their excess energy to be used to make them arrive at a target sooner by lowering the launch angle. These "depressed trajectories" can shorten the SLBM time-of-flight significantly, and missiles flown in this mode pose the most severe threat to the bombers.

As is shown in the analysis that follows, most of the bomber force as presently based will have little chance of surviving an attack by SLBMs flown in a depressed-trajectory mode even when the bombers are on the highest ground-alert status. The prelaunch survival of the bombers will require the construction of a number of new airfields deep in the interior of the country. As yet the Air Force has made no move to begin construction of new airfields, presumably because they believe that the Soviet Union has not tested SLBMs in a depressed-trajectory mode.

Reducing the flight time by simply depressing the trajectory of an SLBM can severely stress the missile due to greatly increased structural loads and heating. Because of this, Defense Department spokesmen have argued that the Soviets would need two years of testing to verify this capability.[29] This might be true if it were actually necessary to fly the missile through a classical depressed trajectory. However, there is another approach.

An SLBM designed for a conventional minimum-energy trajectory can be flown on a specially shaped depressed trajectory that produces no significant increases in mechanical or thermal loads on its booster and can have a flight time almost as short as that theoretically achievable by maximum depression of the trajectory. During the powered phase of flight, the trajectory flown is essentially the normal one, and only at high altitudes is a turn made to depress the trajectory. To fly this "shaped" trajectory probably would require only minor modifications in the flight control program. In fact, the United States in the late 1960s flew Atlas missiles in this mode to test its experimental ABM system in the Pacific against depressed trajectories.

The Soviets could probably verify their capability to fly SLBMs in shaped trajectories with only a few tests. Because only a few tests would be required, the United States might not detect the tests or might not recognize their significance if they were detected. Soviet SLBM flight tests (using fairly simple instrumentation) could be conducted away from the normal test ranges of the Soviets and away from U.S. sensors. Or, because the shaped trajectory looks essentially like a normal trajectory during the powered phase of flight, it might be possible to mislead the U.S. regarding the actual nature of these flights. The United States might interpret the tests as failures if the Soviets interspersed them with a series of other tests. Because depressed-trajectory flights are threatening to the United States, the

Soviets have a strong incentive for deception. Even if the tests were detected, the United States might have little time to react before this capability was implemented in the Soviet submarine fleet.

Another argument advanced by some analysts for dismissing the SLBM threat is that there are at present only a few Soviet SSBNs on patrol off U.S. coasts (none very close); whereas it is thought an effective attack would require fifteen to twenty SSBNs—a quarter to a third of their fleet. However, Soviet deployment practices can change. Because it would probably take a year or so to construct new auxiliary airfields, it is questionable whether the United States would have the long lead time necessary to react effectively to any increase in Soviet SSBN deployment.

Survivability

The probability of a bomber being destroyed by an SLBM barrage is calculated as follows (see appendix B for details of the model): By subtracting bomber reaction time from missile flight time, one can find the time available to a bomber to escape. Because the flyout characteristics (distance versus time from takeoff) of the B-52 are well known, the radius of a circle within which the first bomber off the ground must be located can be found.[30] If the attacker does not know the bomber flight pattern after takeoff, he must assume that it flies off in random directions and that it can be anywhere within this circle representing maximum bomber range capability by the time the SLBMs arrive.[31] The probability of the bomber being killed is determined by how much of this area can be covered by the lethal nuclear weapons effects. This, in turn, depends on how many weapons are allocated per base. (If all 45 SAC bases are attacked, targeting 5 SLBMs per base still requires only 225 missiles.)

Figure 5 illustrates that even when the bombers are on crisis-alert status with reaction times of 120 to 150 seconds, the probability of survival is essentially zero for all bombers based within several hundred miles of the coasts. With Soviet submarines patrolling 100 nm offshore, only those bombers operating from bases over 600 nm inland have greater than a 50 percent chance of survival. Because few of the 45 potential SAC bases (see map) are located in the deep interior of the country and many are in fact located close to the coasts, the present bomber basing is quite vulnerable to SLBMs flown in a depressed-trajectory mode. The removal of bombers from those bases within a few hundred miles of the coasts does not help because there are so few bases inland.

To maintain bomber prelaunch survivability, bomber bases must be established at a considerable distance inland. There is also some advantage in increasing the number of bases. Doubling the number of bases would put a

FIGURE 5
Survivability vs SLBM Range

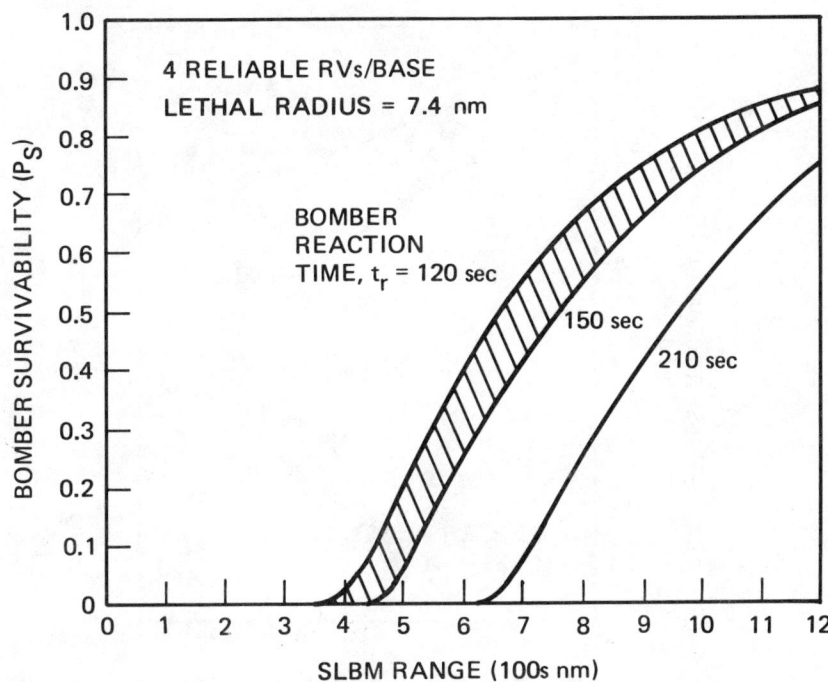

severe strain on the Soviets by doubling the number of SLBMs required to be at attack stations to maintain a four-reliable-warheads-per-base attack. An attack using fewer weapons per base would, of course, be less effective (see figure 6). Distributing the bombers among more bases also insures that more bombers can take off quickly.

Even if bombers are deployed inland and dispersed, the crisis reaction rate of 120 seconds or better must still be maintained to insure prelaunch survivability. And the survivabilty of an effective warning system and quick communications with SAC bases is perhaps the most essential element in bomber survivability. As figure 7 illustrates, even for deep interior bases, a delay of five minutes in takeoff would be catastrophic.

Penetration of Soviet Air Defenses

The Soviet Union has the most extensive strategic air defense system in the world. An area defense is provided by more than 6,000 radars located

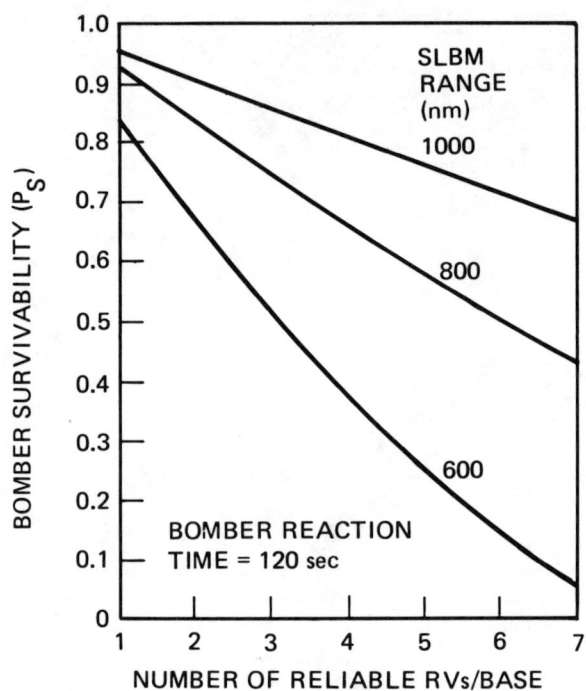

FIGURE 6
Survivability vs Number of Weapons

at early warning and ground control intercept (EW/GCI) radar sites. These radars can be used to vector about 2,600 fighter interceptors to the intruding targets. In addition, there are more than 12,000 strategic surface-to-air missile (SAM) launchers.[32] These SAMs are arranged as barriers across bomber invasion routes and as terminal defenses around prospective targets. The Soviets continue to expand and modernize all these forces.

To overcome this defense system, the United States plans to employ the following tactics:[33]

1. Destruction of defenses by using precursor attacks of ICBMs and SLBMs or by using bomber-launched Short-Range Attack Missiles (SRAMs).
2. Penetration at low altitudes (several hundred feet) to limit radar detection.
3. Degradation of defenses through the use of electronic countermeasures (ECM).

4. Avoidance of defenses. For terminal defenses this means using SRAMs to overfly the SAMs and to attack the target.

Although each of these tactics may be successful, the Soviets appear to have the means to offset these tactics if they operate their systems intelligently. For example, a great deal of American planning appears to be predicated on knowing the exact locations of Soviet defense systems. However, Soviet radars, communications equipment, and launchers are generally on wheeled platforms and are towable.[34] Because they need to be moved only about five miles to avoid destruction by U.S. nuclear weapons, it is possible to move these systems in a shorter amount of time than that required by the U.S. intelligence system to detect and report such a move. (This capability was demonstrated often in North Vietnam.) Thus, the tactic of using precursor missile attacks to open gaps in Soviet defenses cannot be relied on confidently.

FIGURE 7
Survivability vs Reaction Time

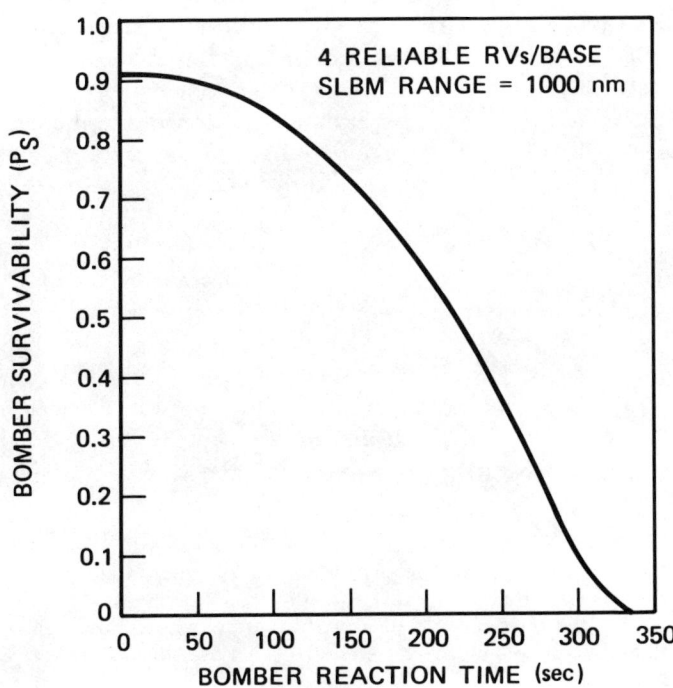

Area Defenses   In the Soviet area defense, the initial alert of incoming aircraft is supplied by early warning radars. This information is routed to a filter center where enemy aircraft are distinguished from friendly aircraft. Reports on hostile aircraft are sent via Morse code to an air defense weapons operation where an air officer directs an air regiment to commit interceptors to engage the aircraft. This engagement is under the direction of a ground-control intercept (GCI) radar. Tracks of the aircraft are relayed to brigade commanders who can commit SAMs either along bomber invasion routes or around terminal targets.[35]

Because radars operate by line of sight, the higher the aircraft, the greater the radars' detection range. American plans call for bombers to penetrate Soviet defenses at low altitudes in order to reduce the detection ranges of the extensive Soviet radar network. However, because there are so many radars and because they can quickly be moved from their prewar positions (thus countering bomber evasion tactics), a large number of radar detections of the bombers is still likely.

Flying close to the ground also makes it difficult for a high flying airborne radar to distinguish a bomber from ground clutter. To be able to detect, track, and shoot down a low-altitude penetrator requires a sophisticated technology generally thought to be unavailable to the Soviets. The Soviets do have a small number of airborne warning and control aircraft equipped with powerful radars and communications systems and designed to perform GCI functions. Although these aircraft are assessed at present to have a limited "look-down" capability over the ocean, they are believed to have virtually none over land. And although the Soviet interceptors SU-15 Flagon and MiG-23 Flogger are given credit for some modest "look-down/shoot-down" capability, no significant threat in this area is expected for some time.* Nevertheless, Soviet interceptors could still pose a significant threat against the B-52.

The actual intercept of a bomber is closely controlled by a GCI operator until the last phase of the operation. An interceptor without a "look-down" capability can be vectored by GCI radar to an intercept point behind the bomber, and visual or IR (infrared) search systems can then acquire the target. The interceptor then pursues the bomber until it is within weapons range. Although this approach dispenses with the necessity for high altitude look-down radar, it does require that the interceptor have a sig-

---

*While this book was in press, the Pentagon announced that the Soviet Union had successfully tested a new "look-down shoot-down" radar and missile system (using a MiG-25 Foxbat fighter) that could seriously threaten low-flying U.S. bombers. It was estimated that the system could be available in the early 1980s. ("Soviet Test of Advanced 'Look-Down' Radar System Reported," Los Angeles Times, Dec. 27, 1978, part 1, p. 18.)

nificant speed advantage over the bomber. The relatively slow B-52 presents no problem in this regard for Soviet defenses.

Because penetrating bombers cannot be confident of avoiding detection by flying low, they are equipped with electronic countermeasures (ECM) that attempt to negate GCI and airborne intercept radars. The Soviets, in turn, employ extensive electronic counter-countermeasures. An actual engagement would be a complicated interaction whose outcome would depend in large part on prewar knowledge of the electronic characteristics and tactics of each side. It is difficult to have a high level of confidence in the outcome, and the heavy reliance by U.S. bombers on ECM has often been questioned. Director of Defense Research and Engineering Dr. William J. Perry in testimony before the Senate in 1977 pointed out that concern over the B-1's ECM capability was one of the reasons why the cruise missile was chosen over the B-1.[36] Since the B-52 has a radar cross section some 25 times larger than that of the B-1, the B-52 is more difficult to "hide" amidst the electronic noise created by jamming and thus can rely even less on ECM.[37] Dr. Perry further pointed out that "in fact, the (B-1's) ECM itself creates a potential vulnerability because the Soviets may use a missile which 'homes' on the jamming signal."[38] Another possible source of vulnerability exists with a jammer. If a bomber uses it, it may alert defense forces to the presence of a low-flying bomber that might otherwise have gone undetected. If interceptors are equipped with radar-warning receivers and direction-finding equipment, they can locate a bomber using a jammer without needing look-down radar.

Finally, the ratio of Soviet interceptors to U.S. bombers is overwhelming—twenty to one (or more, depending on how many bombers survive an SLBM attack). In addition, the Soviets can augment this strategic defense force with over 1,000 other aircraft from their tactical Air Force, the majority of which are the most effective Soviet low-altitude aircraft available. The massing of these aircraft to sweep suspected invasion paths would be a formidable threat even without total GCI vectoring.

SAM Defenses   If the bombers penetrate the aircraft interceptor area defenses of the Soviets, they still must deal with the SAMs, both in barriers along bomber invasion routes and around defended targets. As noted above, destruction of the SAMs cannot be relied on because they can be moved. Nor can the use of SRAMs to bypass air defenses (SAMs are not thought to be effective against the high-speed SRAMs) be relied on. SRAMs have a maximum range of about 70 nm, and the Soviets could move their SAMs more than 70 nm from the targets when they go to a war-mode of operation and could attack a bomber before it releases its SRAMs.

Although Soviet strategic SAMs may be survivable, most (except for the SA-3 system) are generally believed to have only limited capabilities against low-flying aircraft. The Soviets could, however, employ jammers against the bomber's terrain-following radar to force the bomber to a higher altitude where SAMs are more effective.[39] (This tactic could also be used to increase radar coverage for intercept by fighters.) But the Soviets could also augment their strategic SAMs with their highly mobile army SAMs, the SA-4, SA-6, SA-7, SA-8, and SA-9. Some of these weapons were used during the 1973 war in the Middle East and proved to be highly effective against fast, maneuverable tactical aircraft. They should be even more effective against the slower, nonmaneuverable B-52.[40]

An additional method of upgrading their SAMs would be for them to employ nuclear warheads. This could not only correct some low-altitude deficiencies, but also extend the range of the SAMs.

Conclusion

There is little doubt that a surprise attack by Soviet SLBMs flown in a depressed-trajectory mode could destroy most American strategic bombers under the present basing system. Defense Department inaction in this area is apparently based on their confidence that the United States will obtain strategic warning of any threat long before it develops. However, because it is feasible to fly SLBMs on shaped trajectories without causing the strains of classical depressed trajectories, a Soviet threat against the bombers could develop quickly, and the long lead time anticipated by the United States is not likely to occur.

Furthermore, if the Soviets operate their air defense system intelligently, there is great uncertainty regarding the ability of America's strategic bombers to penetrate to their targets. This situation can only worsen as the Soviets continue to expand and improve their defense forces.[41]

SSBN SURVIVABILITY

In view of the possible vulnerability of America's ICBM and bomber forces in the early 1980s, the maintenance of the survivability of the strategic missile-carrying submarines (SSBNs) is crucial.[42] Although the Defense Department has generally discounted any threats to the SSBNs, this view is not shared by the Soviets. The founder of the modern Soviet navy, Admiral Gorshkov, has claimed: "On the basis of the latest advances of science, technology, and production, the mission to repulse and disarm [the U.S. SSBN threat] was accomplished successfully."[43]

The United States presently has 41 SSBNs, and a new Trident-class submarine will enter the fleet around 1980 (see table 6). The 10 older

TABLE 6

U.S. SSBN Forces

Missile Type	Number of RVs	Missile Range (nm)	Number of SSBNs†		
			1978	1981	1985
Polaris-A3	3*	2,500	10	7	5
Poseidon-C3	10	2,500	31	28	20
Poseidon-C4	8	4,000	0	3	10
Trident-C4	6	4,000	0	1	7

SOURCES: U.S., Congress, House, Committee on Appropriations, Subcommittee, *Department of Defense Appropriations for 1979*, 95th Cong., 2nd sess., 1978, part 1, pp. 563, 704–706; Gen. George S. Brown, *United States Military Posture for FY 1979*, pp. 27–31.
*These three warheads cannot be independently targeted.
†Deployment will depend upon outcome of SALT II.

Polaris submarines are all in the Pacific and operate out of Guam. The 31 other boats carry Poseidon missiles and operate out of Holy Loch, Scotland; Rota, Spain; and Charleston, South Carolina. (The United States must leave the Rota base by July 1, 1979.) At any one time, about 55 percent of the boats are at sea.

The Soviet approach to countering SSBNs is likely to be quite different from that of the United States. The U.S. program for strategic surveillance of Soviet SSBNs relies upon passive acoustic techniques,[44] primarily the SOSUS (Sound Surveillance System) network of large hydrophone arrays located along the peripheries of the oceans.[45] The SOSUS network uses sophisticated computer-assisted discrimination techniques and reportedly can detect some submarines halfway across the ocean and distinguish them from surface ships.[46] However, because of geographical constraints, the Soviets cannot readily utilize similar techniques to detect U.S. submarines.

Alternative directions that the Soviet antisubmarine warfare (ASW) program might take are discussed below. A number of potentially serious threats (both acoustic and nonacoustic) to the U.S. SSBN fleet exist, and recent advances in ASW technology could make these threats even more severe. Because much of this new technology is now available to the United States, there is little reason to assume that the Soviets do not have or cannot develop similar capabilities in the near future.

Trail

The primary mode of protecting the SSBNs is to "hide" them in the vast expanse of the ocean. The SSBNs do, however, return to port after two months at sea. The protection of the ocean can thus be negated if the Soviets undertake a trail of SSBNs as they leave port.

Because Soviet attack submarines are faster than U.S. SSBNs, they are an ideal vehicle for tracking. Although it is difficult for the Soviets to maintain a covert trail using passive sonar (because U.S. submarines are quieter than those of the Soviets), a covert trail using nonacoustic techniques (to be discussed below) could be feasible.[47] However, even if the tracking submarine were discovered, the SSBN could find it difficult to break trail if the Soviet submarine used its active sonar system, particularly if the Soviets supported their attack submarines with surface ships.

The argument raised against the possibility of the Soviets undertaking such overt trails has been more political than technical. It has been suggested that such threatening actions would cause the breakdown of détente. Although the Soviets may not be willing at present to damage the chances for détente, a change in world conditions could create a state of tension lasting for several months, and détente may then cease to be a prime consideration in Soviet strategic planning.

Area Searches

If a U.S. SSBN is not trailed as it leaves port, the Soviets face the much more difficult task of finding it in the open ocean. Because the range of the Polaris and the Poseidon missiles is about 2,500 nm and because at any one time, about 55 percent of the SSBNs are at sea, the Soviets must contend with sixteen or seventeen boats in an Atlantic patrol area of around one million square nautical miles. Several acoustic and nonacoustic techniques that could possibly be used by the Soviets for this task are described below.

Towed Arrays   The development of a line array of hydrophones that can be towed through the water represents a potential breakthrough in acoustic ASW technology. According to Larry L. Booda, an editor of *Sea Technology*: "The success of towed hydrophone arrays has been outstanding. They have been designed for towing by surface ships, submarines and helicopters. (They are used as protective detection devices by the ballistic missile submarines.) These arrays offer high gain reception combined with a very narrow beam. Thus two of them deployed one hundred miles or more apart can locate a submarine with sufficient accuracy for the pinpointing detectors of the operating forces to take over to complete the mission."[48]

In the hands of the Soviets, this new technology could pose a serious threat to the SSBNs. If the detection range is, in fact, at least 50 nm, the

The Survivability of U.S. Strategic Forces

SSBN patrol area can be searched in two days or less.[49] The data from the arrays could be processed on board the towing ships or relayed via satellite back to the Soviet Union for processing at a larger computer center. Once a submarine is detected, other forces (aircraft and surface ships) can be assigned to verify the detection and to maintain trail.

Another approach to area surveillance is to augment these towed arrays with small, portable, active acoustic sources, either small, disposable explosive charges or more conventional, very high-powered but portable acoustic generators.[50] A few acoustic sources could be operated by a small number of towed-array ships distributed about the SSBN patrol area. By listening for a signal bouncing off a submarine, it could be possible to obtain a cross-fix and to localize a submarine in a half hour or less. Soviet ICBMs could then be targeted to the suspected targets, or aircraft and ships could be used to verify each detection.[51]

Sonobuoy Surveillance At present, when a submarine is detected, aircraft-dropped sonobuoys are generally used to localize it. The data obtained from these buoys are relayed by radio to the aircraft for analysis. Because the buoys deploy hydrophones with directional capabilities, two or more buoys can give a cross-bearing to localize the target.

Most buoys float on the surface and generally have a short detection range, but this range can be extended considerably by mooring the hydrophones to the ocean bottom. The United States has a program of this type called the Moored Surveillance System.[52] It is an aerially dropped sonobuoy system that is self-mooring and is intended to create a surveillance barrier. The data from these sonobuoys can either be transmitted to aircraft for retransmission to ships and to shore-based processing centers or be sent to shore by satellite relay.

If the Soviets were to deploy a similar system, they could cover a million square nautical miles by using from around 1,000 to 1,500 sonobuoys if the detection radius at the surface were 15 to 20 nm. The sonobuoys could be clandestinely deployed by surface ships and set to start broadcasting at a particular time, sending their data via satellite to the Soviet Union for processing. All designated targets could be attacked using ICBMs within a half hour of the start of broadcasting. Or, on a longer time scale, aircraft and surface ships could be used to investigate suspected targets, bring them under trail, and, if required, deliver weapons against them.

Nonacoustic Threats

Although the United States has devoted most of its ASW effort to acoustic techniques of detection, nonacoustic techniques also exist. Admiral Donald P. Harvey, director of Naval Intelligence, stated in 1978 that "methods of detection could include, but not be limited to, radars, optical systems, and lasers."[53] The United States now has a limited capacity to detect submarines using nonacoustic techniques. A more extensive, operational capability is expected in the 1980s.[54]

Some of the phenomena that the Soviets might exploit to detect submarines are described below.[55]

Surface Effects When a body moves through a stratified medium like the ocean, internal waves are generated that make their way to the surface, and the interaction of these internal waves with the surface changes the reflective properties of the surface. This change reportedly can be detected by radars operating in the millimeter wavelength region[56] and possibly by other systems such as lasers.

Other hydrodynamic phenomena associated with the passing of a submarine can cause a difference in surface temperature. For example: "The sea water used to cool machinery discharged from a submerged submarine is warmer than the surrounding water, and, therefore, represents a heat anomaly in that region of the ocean."[57] According to the Soviets, such temperature differences can be detected by earth satellites.[58]

Another potential threat results from the small rise in the surface level of the water above a passing submarine.[59] Both optical and radar techniques could possibly be used to detect this change.

Finally, there is another phenomenon that reportedly not only affects the ocean surface but also the atmosphere above it and thus may be easier to detect. According to *Air Force Magazine:*

> There's mounting concern that the Soviets may have made significant progress in submarine detection through the energy emissions that surface from the wake of even deeply submerged boats. These irregular emissions, called convective cells, show up as hot spots in the atmosphere and cause moisture. They are detectable by special radar and infrared detection systems on ships or in space.[60]

Internal Wakes A submarine generates a wake of turbulent water that persists for some time after it passes. Several techniques to detect these wakes, such as measuring the temperature and pressure fluctuations associated with the turbulent wake, are available. The use of high-frequency (ultra-sonic), active sonar systems to detect the presence of a wake may also be feasible.

Contaminant Wakes Besides a hydrodynamic wake, a submarine can leave behind other indications of its recent presence. Because some neutrons escape from the nuclear reactor used to power a submarine, it leaves behind a trail of neutrons and radionuclides. It has also been suggested that a submarine leaves a biological track formed by microorganisms killed by its passage.[61] Finally, submarines use electrolysis of water to obtain oxygen for their crews. If precautions are not taken, the residual hydrogen can leave a trail in the water and at the surface that can be detected by such means as lasers.[62]

EM Signals   Electrochemical processes generate varying electrical potentials at different points on a submarine.[63] Because seawater is a conductor of electricity, an electric current (which is modulated at the frequency the propeller shaft is turning) travels between the points of different electrical potential. The resulting low-frequency electromagnetic (EM) field can be detected by a number of devices, such as those using very large magnetic loops or those using superconducting devices based on the Josephson effect.[64]

Direct Detection   Water is opaque to visible light except for a very narrow frequency band. However, lasers operating in the blue-green region of the spectrum can penetrate to some depth underwater and detect submarines. This is of particular concern because U.S. submarines must remain fairly close to the surface for communication purposes.

Conclusion   A serious threat to the SSBNs would exist if nonacoustic techniques could be used by aircraft to make detections. Aircraft with a detection range of around 10 nm could complete a search of the SSBN patrol area in a few hours.[65] Satellites would, of course, be even more effective. The detection of subsurface wakes by surface ships or submarines could also present a threat even though their sweep of the patrol area would be slower. If these subsurface wakes persisted for a long enough time, a covert trail might be established as an SSBN left port since the trailer could remain outside the acoustic range of the SSBN.

Other Threats

In addition to acoustic and nonacoustic threats, there are a number of other methods of detecting submarines that do not fit either of these two categories, although they obviously use one or the other (or both) of these techniques.

Trailing Communications Wire or Buoy   The requirement that the U.S. SSBN fleet remain in constant communication with the U.S. military command poses a serious hazard to the survival of the fleet. Because most radio waves cannot significantly penetrate the ocean, each submarine is required to maintain an antenna at or near the surface. This antenna (which is connected by a buoyant cable to the submarine) takes the form of a long communications wire[66] or a communications buoy.[67]

The Navy has testified before Congress that this arrangement offers many opportunities for detection.[68] Both the wake of the antenna and the antenna itself can be detected by radar, infrared, laser, or visual (photographic and television) techniques.[69]

Other means of communication are possible. Extremely low frequency (ELF) radio can penetrate the ocean to great depths. An ELF communications system (originally called Sanguine but now known as Seafarer) has been proposed for some time by the Navy but has been delayed, primarily because of opposition from environmentalists. Until this or other methods of communicating with the SSBNs are deployed, the trailing antennas will remain a significant threat to the safety of the submarines.

Tags U.S. SSBNs operate from only a few ports and are constantly observed by Russian trawlers as they leave. It is possible that as a submarine leaves port, some device (a "tag") could be attached to its hull by a frogman or a trained animal (sea lion or dolphin). This tag could take many forms and could be designed either to release a device that will rise to the surface at a set time to reveal the submarine's position or to release a series of devices that will reveal the submarine's position over a long period of time. To reveal the position of the submarine at a preset time, a miniature radio broadcaster could be used. To maintain a trail over a longer period of time, a series of devices that remain silent until interrogated by some Soviet surveillance system could be used. A number of such devices are conceivable. For example, recent advances in large-scale integrated circuits make possible the construction of tiny transponders designed to respond only when interrogated by a specially coded pulse from a microwave radar. Thousands of these devices could be placed in a relatively small package and periodically released to form an easily followed trail on the ocean surface.

Sabotage The U.S. SSBN is a formidable nuclear force, but it is also a very concentrated one. Normally, about half the force (around twenty boats) is at sea while the rest are in port and vulnerable to attack. A boat remains at sea for about two months and then returns to port for another month before returning to sea again. If the Soviets ever believed that war was inevitable, they could decide that the sabotage of a submarine while in port would be far easier than attacking it at sea.

There are any number of chemical and biological agents that could incapacitate or kill a submarine crew. They could be brought on board in the ship's supplies (or through other means) and released at a preset time. In this way, the whole at-sea fleet could be attacked at once.[70]

Boost Phase Intercept Soviet antiballistic missile (ABM) systems placed in the vicinity of a U.S. launch area could be more effective than those systems that have to wait until a U.S. RV enters the atmosphere over the Soviet Union. If Soviet ships (and possibly aircraft) with radars and ABM missiles were placed in the U.S. SSBN patrol area, a serious threat would exist to any SLBM that was fired (and also to the submarine because a missile could be backtracked by radar to its point of origin, thus revealing the submarine's position).

Such an ABM system would be designed to attack the booster or the postboost vehicle (the "bus") before the RVs were released. These boosters are easy to track because they make very large targets for ABM radars. Once the booster is above the atmosphere, the computers used for guidance and control aboard the booster and the bus can be incapacitated by a nuclear explosion at a very large distance (perhaps 50 to 100 nm depending on the computer hardness and the yield of the ABM warhead). A successful attack on the computers insures that, at a minimum, the RVs will miss their targets.

Forward-based ABMs are now outlawed by treaty. However, the Soviets have continued a massive ABM research and development program. If the treaty is ever abrogated, they may be able to deploy a forward-based system of this type much more rapidly than they can a land-based system.

Conclusion

The military doctrine of the Soviet Union takes the possibility of war, even nuclear war, seriously, and the Soviets have made a concentrated effort to develop countermeasures to America's strategic forces. By the early 1980s, the Soviets could (if appropriate counteractions are not taken) seriously threaten the ICBM and bomber legs of the triad. It is unlikely that they will fail to try to counter the SSBNs also.

This section has discussed a large number of individual threats, but it should be noted that the Soviets practice "defense in depth." If one technique or system guarantees only partial success, then the Soviets add another to improve their chances. For example, the Soviet air defense system consists of many layers, and the Soviets continue to upgrade, improve, and expand their forces. A similar approach can be expected in ASW, although any one of the techniques mentioned above could be enough to compromise almost the entire SSBN fleet.

Understanding the extent of the Soviet ASW threat is one of the more crucial tasks of the intelligence community, but it is an area in which great uncertainties exist. As Admiral Harvey, director of Naval Intelligence, noted in 1978, the Soviets' "extensive [ASW] R&D effort . . . is the area in which we could be expected to know the least, because it does not have the manifestations in the open seas that their weapons and platforms do."[71] Because these ASW systems often have no easily identifiable characteristics, the Soviets can successfully disguise or hide critical aspects of their program.

It is known, however, that the Soviets have for some time had an extensive ASW program, and there appears to be growing concern recently over the possibility of a breakthrough, particularly in the nonacoustic area.[72] In this field, the Soviets are known to have research programs on lasers, processed optical scanners, advanced radar, and infrared detection systems.[73] It is the evaluation of the U.S. Navy that a "significant advancement in any of these techniques would pose a potential threat to the security of our SSBNs."[74]

Considering the wide range of possible threats (acoustic, nonacoustic, and unconventional) and the intensive Soviet ASW effort, the continued survivability of the SSBNs should not be taken for granted. In fact, unless appropriate countermeasures are taken, the viability of this force in the near future could be in serious doubt.

EARLY WARNING AND STRATEGIC C³

The United States maintains tactical warning systems to detect an incoming attack and a command, control, and communications (C³) network to assure that war orders are implemented. Quick and reliable tactical warning of an attack on U.S. bomber bases is particularly critical because, as noted earlier, a delay of a few minutes could result in almost complete destruction of the strategic bomber force. The maintenance of a communications network between the strategic forces and the National Command Authority (NCA) (the president or his designated successor) is also critical because all strategic forces are under positive control: U.S. missiles cannot be launched nor can U.S. bombers proceed to target without positive authorization from the NCA. The following sections briefly describe these systems and discuss some of their major weaknesses and vulnerabilities.

Strategic Warning

Strategic warning is usually on a time scale of hours, days, or weeks before actual hostilities begin. It might result from an evaluation that a severe international political crisis existed or from positive intelligence that an attack was being planned. Strategic warning is important because it would allow the readiness status (alert rate) of the strategic forces and the C³ network to be raised. At the highest level of alert, the president could be airborne and prepared to direct the retaliatory strike if an attack materialized.

The technical means of obtaining strategic warning (as opposed to normal diplomatic assessment of the political situation) primarily consists of photographic and electronic satellites and numerous electronic surveillance ground stations located around the periphery of the Soviet Union. In addition, some observers believe that the disposition of Soviet missile-carrying nuclear submarines (SSBNs) could offer a means of strategic warning. At present, the Soviets operate only a few SSBNs off U.S. coasts, and none are located very close. Under present bomber basing patterns, alert rates, and reaction times, this small force could pose a threat to much of the bomber force in a surprise attack (at the minimum it could destroy the 70 percent of the force not on alert). However, most defense planners assume that the Soviets will move fifteen or twenty boats closer to U.S. coasts if they are planning an attack.

To follow the movements of Soviet submarines, the United States uses SOSUS, a system of underwater hydrophones.[75] These hydrophone line arrays are generally located along the edge of the continental shelf and feed their data through underwater cables to shore-based stations along the Atlantic and Pacific coasts. Ship-towed hydrophone arrays are being developed to supplement the SOSUS system. Their data will probably be relayed via satellite to a shore-based processing center.

It is likely, but not certain, that the United States would detect a change in Soviet SSBN deployments. Detection depends on the noise level of the submarines, and it is possible that this noise level will be lowered in the future. In addition, there may be gaps in the coverage; apparently, the Gulf of Mexico is not covered, for example. Also, because the SOSUS hydrophones are located in the so-called "deep sound channel" (in order to obtain the low-frequency signals that travel great distances at this depth), a submarine operating close to shore in shallow water could go undetected.

A more important point is that if the Soviets were planning an attack, it seems unlikely that they would suddenly move twenty SSBNs close to the U.S. coasts. If the Soviets were to build up their force over a period of several months, it is doubtful that true strategic warning (in the sense of a conviction that the Soviets were planning a war) would be obtained or acted upon.

In general, strategic warning can be very beneficial, but, as noted in chapter 2, it may fail to materialize at the critical moment. This may not be due to lack of data, but rather to a failure to perceive the significance of the data or to believe data that conflict with preconceived notions of the other party's behavior. In view of the long-held American belief that a deliberate nuclear war is almost inconceivable, the past history of the success of surprise attacks is even more relevant.

Tactical Warning

Tactical warning systems detect an attack after it is underway. ICBM flight times from the Soviet Union to the United States are about 25 to 30 minutes, but submarine-launched ballistic missiles (SLBMs) require only from 5 to 15 minutes, depending on the distance and on the type of trajectory flown. To detect the launch of these missiles, at least two different devices that sense different relevant phenomena survey Soviet ICBM and SLBM launch areas.[76]

Defense Support Program   The United States presently operates at least three Defense Support Program (DSP) satellites that employ infrared sensors which can detect missile firings within 90 seconds after liftoff. The satellites are in synchronous orbit (i.e., they rotate at the same rate as the earth and thus remain fixed at one position above the equator). One is positioned above the Indian Ocean to detect ICBM launches from the Soviet Union or China, and the other two are above the Atlantic Ocean and Central America to detect SLBM launches from the Atlantic and Pacific.[77] Data from the ICBM detection system is sent to overseas ground stations and is then relayed to the North American Defense Command (NORAD) in Colorado.[78] The SLBM detection satellites presumably send their data directly to the United States. In the event of an SLBM launch detection, NORAD immediately notifies the Strategic Air Command, whose commander has the authority to launch the strategic bombers under what is termed "positive control"; that is, although the bombers can leave their bases to escape an SLBM attack, they cannot proceed beyond a certain point (the "hold line") without further, positive authorization from the National Command Authority (NCA).

Radars   A radar system supplements the DSP satellites, but their detections normally are somewhat later than those of the satellites. To some extent, these radars also have the capability to plot missile trajectories and to indicate their targets generally.

To detect ICBMs that have been launched, there are three radar installations in the Ballistic Missile Early Warning System (located in Clear, Alaska; Thule, Greenland; and Flyingdales Moor, England) and the Perimeter Acquisition Radar, which is the sole survivor of the ABM complex at Grand Forks, North Dakota.

To detect SLBMs, there are six 474N radars along the east and west coasts and a phased array radar at Eglin Air Force Base, Florida, to cover the Caribbean (as well as ICBMs coming from the south). There are plans to replace the unreliable 474N radars with two phased array radars, one on each coast.[79]

Strategic C³

In case of nuclear attack, many of the normal means of communication (such as telephone land lines) could easily be disrupted. To maintain command and control over the strategic forces during and after a nuclear attack on the United States, the Minimum Essential Emergency Communications Network was developed. This system is described below.

ICBMs and Bombers   The ICBM and bomber forces that are part of the national war plan, the so-called Single Integrated Operational Plan or SIOP, are under the control of the Strategic Air Command (SAC). Normally, the message to execute the SIOP would come from the NCA through the secretary of defense and the Joint Chiefs of Staff (JCS) to SAC headquarters at Omaha, Nebraska. From there the Emergency Action Message (EAM) would be relayed to missile launch control centers ordering them to fire the ICBMs and to the bombers (which at this point should be airborne) giving them the go-ahead to proceed to their targets (see figure 8).

Although the Omaha headquarters of SAC is underground, it is vulnerable to nuclear attack, and a more survivable alternative is provided by an airborne command post (Looking Glass), which is continually in the air in the Omaha area. In addition, there is an emergency network of aircraft to maintain contact between the NCA and the SIOP forces. Although the airplanes (except for Looking Glass) are normally on ground alert, they can be put in the air in an emergency (if enough warning is given). Foremost among these aircraft is the president's National Emergency Airborne Command Post (NEACP), which is based just outside of Washington. Communications links between NEACP and Looking Glass are provided by ultrahigh frequency (UHF) radio relays through two airborne aircraft, the East Relay and East Auxiliary aircraft. In turn, the West Auxiliary provides a UHF link from Looking Glass to the airborne launch control system (ALCS) aircraft. The three ALCS aircraft cover the ICBM fields and can launch the ICBMs if normal ICBM launch control centers have been destroyed.[80]

Should some of these communications links fail, Looking Glass has another backup system for delivering the go-code (EAM). Some of the Minutemen missiles are equipped with a UHF radio package instead of warheads. This is the Emergency Rocket Communications System (ERCS).[81] ERCS missiles contain a tape recorder into which Looking Glass can transmit the EAM. Upon launch, the ERCS missiles would broadcast the EAM from very high altitudes to the strategic forces.

Bombers   After receiving the warning that an attack is underway, those bombers on alert are launched and proceed towards their targets, but

FIGURE 8

Minimum Essential Emergency Communications Network (MEECN) for the ICBMs and Bombers

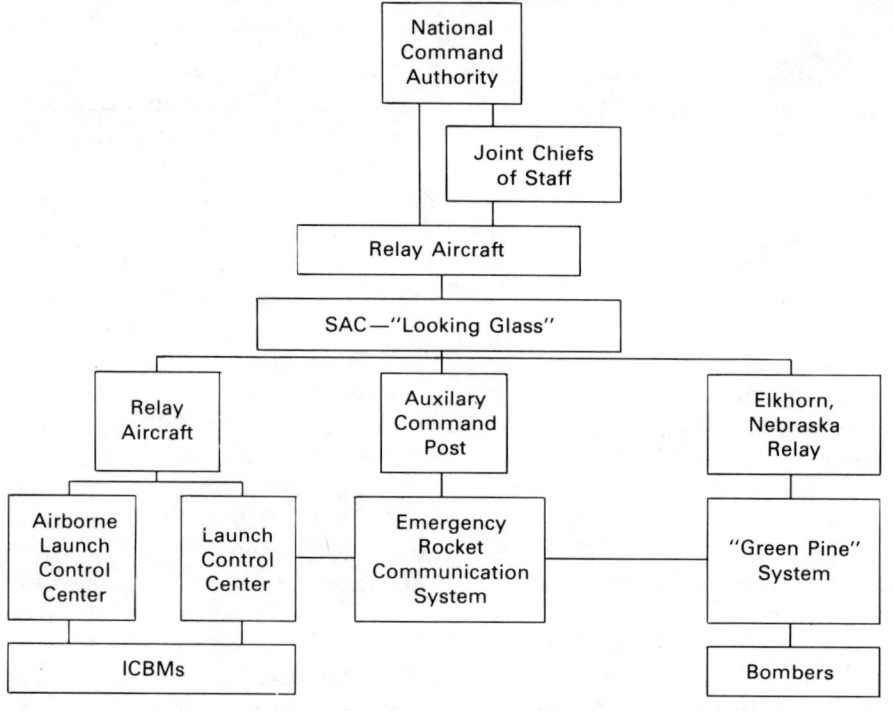

NOTE: Looking Glass and the Auxiliary Command Posts can also launch the ICBMs (and ERCS) but would have to fly to the ICBM fields to do so.

must hold at a certain point until they receive positive authorization to continue. SAC's "alpha net," which uses high frequency (HF) single-sideband radio, is the primary means of delivering the EAM. "To supplement HF radio in the Arctic regions, SAC also has a chain of UHF radio stations located in an arc from the Aleutian Islands to Keflavik, Iceland. This system, called Green Pine, is accessed normally through a UHF station at Elkhorn, Neb."[82]

SSBNs Communications with the strategic submarines are maintained in peacetime by a system of shore-based very low frequency (VLF)

The Survivability of U.S. Strategic Forces 69

radio stations. Because these shore-based stations are vulnerable to attack, there is also an airborne system called TACAMO to maintain VLF communications in an emergency.

Vulnerabilities

There are major concerns about the survivability of the tactical warning and strategic C^3 systems because virtually all sensors, links, and nodes of the current system are vulnerable. Of particular concern is the capability to launch the bombers under positive control and the timely delivery of the EAM to the strategic forces.

Not only are the DSP satellites vulnerable to nuclear attack, but the small number of ground stations could possibly be eliminated by sabotage or paramilitary attacks.[83] Without these systems, the resulting delay in warning the bombers could prove disastrous.

A well-planned surprise attack by the Soviets could reduce the Strategic C^3 system to Looking Glass, ERCS, and TACAMO because the other parts of the communications system are either soft ground stations or aircraft not on airborne alert. Even the survivability of ERCS is questionable because Minuteman is not likely to survive a Soviet attack in the 1980s. (Since the Soviets undoubtedly know which missiles contain the ERCS package, they could target some of their particularly large-yield warheads to these sites.) Also, the TACAMO aircraft must operate in the Atlantic SSBN patrol areas, and the Soviets probably keep close watch on the locations of these aircraft. This area is well within range of Soviet long-range aircraft, and thus the certainty of TACAMO's survival cannot be assumed.

The bombers in the Arctic rely on the Green Pine system to relay the EAM to them by UHF after receiving it from Looking Glass or ERCS. As noted, Looking Glass has access to the stations through a single node at Elkhorn, Nebraska, which could easily be destroyed. Even if ERCS survived to deliver the EAM to the Green Pine network, the network itself could be directly attacked.

Thus, an attack on the strategic C^3 network could delay the receipt of the EAM by U.S. ICBMs, SSBNs, and bombers for hours and could seriously degrade or even prevent effective execution of the SIOP.

SOVIET ANTIBALLISTIC MISSILE (ABM) SYSTEMS

The ABM treaty signed by the United States and the Soviet Union in 1972 restricted both countries to two ABM regions, each with a maximum of 100 ABM launchers, and thus made an overt ABM system virtually inconsequential for country-wide defense. Later agreements further restricted each side to only one site.

Since the signing of the treaty, the Soviets have continued a vigorous ABM research and development program, spending about twice as much on this as the United States.[84] In addition, the Soviets have deployed a number of large, phased array radars around the periphery of the Soviet Union.[85]

It has been suggested that the Soviets are developing the components of an ABM system that could be deployed before the United States could effectively deploy countermeasures.[86] This system would consist of a layered defense with long-range interceptors to attack the U.S. RVs in mid-course high above the atmosphere, and low-level atmospheric defenses against those RVs that escaped the mid-course attack.

The Soviets are developing a new, very large, high acceleration, long-range missile that appears to be designed for mid-course attacks.[87] The new phased array radars could be used to direct these missiles to their targets. For low-level ABM defense, the Soviets could use the short-range, high acceleration missile that they developed several years ago, ostensibly to defend against tactical, battlefield ballistic missiles.[88]

It is also possible that the Soviets already have a "covert" ABM system in place, consisting of the thousands of SA-5 and SA-2 SAMs already deployed. Although this approach has generally been deemed technically inadequate, the evidence for this assessment is still debatable, particularly if nuclear warheads were deployed on the SAMs.[89]

In evaluating the effectiveness of any Soviet ABM system, it should be remembered that by the 1980s the Soviets may have to expect only a limited U.S. response after a surprise attack. Attacks on U.S. C^3 might also cause the U.S. retaliation to be ragged and uncoordinated, making it much easier for an ABM system to handle.

IV
Strategic Force Issues

In the 1980s, the survivability of all U.S. strategic weapons systems may be open to question. Given the wide range of uncertainty in U.S. knowledge of Soviet systems, prudence requires that steps be taken to prevent the materialization of this destabilizing situation. Since the Soviet Union is a closed society, information about Soviet systems will never be complete. Thus, it is imperative that the deployment of U.S. forces be as threat-insensitive as possible. To meet this requirement, the following actions are suggested:

1. The development of a new basing mode for the ICBM force that will be insensitive to Soviet improvements in missile accuracy.
2. The creation, in the shortest time possible, of 50 or more austere bomber bases in the interior of the country to insure bomber pre-launch survivability.
3. The deployment of a large force of cruise missiles to saturate the extensive and growing Soviet air defense system.
4. The enlargement of the operating area of the strategic submarines by deploying new, longer-range missiles or by changing present operating procedures.

This chapter discusses possible means of implementing these suggested changes as well as a number of related actions involving operating procedures, warning systems, and the command, control, and communications network. Counterforce targeting, the need for a strategic reserve, and the impact of possible arms control agreements on maintaining deterrence are also discussed.

ICBMs

Soviet progress in missile guidance technology will undoubtedly continue and will soon undermine U.S. confidence in the survivability of its present ICBM force. In response to the Soviet threat, there are several courses of action that the United States could follow: abandon reliance on the ICBMs, develop some variation of a "launch-on-warning" policy, defend against an attack, or seek a more survivable basing mode for the ICBMs. The arguments against relying on a less diverse strategic deterrent force (a diad instead of a triad) have already been presented.[1] Foremost among these is that there is too much uncertainty regarding the survivability of U.S. bombers and strategic submarines to justify abandoning a land-based ICBM force. It is therefore essential to find and to adopt an alternative to the existing ICBM system.

Launch-on-Warning

One proposed method for insuring the effectiveness of the ICBM force is to launch these missiles before Soviet missiles arrive on target. This method is generally called launch-on-warning (LOW) or launch-on-attack assessment. The latter implies not only the detection of a missile launch but also an assessment of the scope and objective of the attack. The ICBMs could be launched under either of two procedures: (a) after detection of the incoming attack but before the first impact of an enemy warhead or (b) after the first impact but before the full attack arrives. The latter alternative is applicable to Soviet attacks that include SLBM attacks on bomber and submarine bases. If the Soviet ICBMs and SLBMs were launched simultaneously, the SLBMs would begin arriving less than ten minutes after launch, some fifteen to twenty minutes prior to the arrival of the ICBMs. Although in theory a LOW policy could "save" the ICBMs, in practice there are a number of objections to and difficulties with this policy.

The primary reason for maintaining a triad of strategic forces is to guarantee that, at a minimum, the United States can maintain an assured-destruction capability to deter an all-out attack on American cities. If a Soviet attack were directed only at U.S. strategic forces, the launch-on-warning policy would be faced with a dilemma. If the U.S. ICBMs were directed against Soviet cities, this would assure that U.S. cities would also be attacked, which is the opposite of what is desired. If, on the other hand, U.S. ICBMs were directed against Soviet military targets instead of cities, they would no longer be available to deter attacks on U.S. cities. In either case, a LOW policy fails to serve its main purpose—to maintain a U.S. assured-destruction capability.

It should be noted at this point that even if U.S. ICBMs are directed against military targets, they may for the most part be wasted because most Soviet conventional forces, strategic bombers, and submarines can be moved. The United States could attack Soviet ICBM silos; but—apart from the fact that they would be shooting at many empty holes—it is not clear whether the U.S. could severely damage Soviet silos, particularly the new ones (see below). Besides, the Soviets could also launch-on-warning, although they might then be forced to choose cities as targets rather than "riding out" the U.S. attack.

Aside from these considerations, it is not clear whether a launch-on-warning policy would be technically feasible against Soviet efforts to counter it. For example, the president might be killed by an SLBM attack in the first few minutes of the war, and it is not certain that the president's designated successor could make the necessary decisions in the few minutes remaining. Even if the president is not killed, almost all warning sensors, military command centers, and lines of communications are vulnerable to nuclear and in some cases nonnuclear attack. A surprise Soviet attack could thus sever communications links to the ICBMs for some time and prevent an early launch of these forces.

If, in spite of all of these difficulties, a message to launch is issued and received in time, there still remains the additional problem that ICBMS in their launch phase are quite vulnerable to nuclear attack. SLBMs launched to explode high over the ICBM fields could destroy the guidance systems of any ICBM flying through the resulting radiation. This so-called "pin-down attack" could mean that a launch-on-warning policy would destroy the ICBMs rather than preserve deterrence.[2]

Despite the logical and technical flaws in any LOW policy, there are likely to be growing political pressures to adopt this policy as an alternative to the development of a new missile system, particularly if the new system involves the MX missile, which is considered by many to be destabilizing in a crisis because of its counterforce capability. If a LOW policy is adopted, then it will be necessary to give it substance by placing more reliance on automated systems that will try to guarantee launch despite any "disconnection" of the National Command Authority from the ICBMs. To increase the credibility of the threat to launch the missiles before Soviet ICBMs arrive might require either the complete elimination of man from the loop or procedures that would give the president only a few minutes to make a decision. The chances for a mistake and an accidental Armageddon would undoubtedly be increased. In addition, stability during a crisis would be undermined, and the incentive for preemption increased for both sides—the U.S. from fear of losing its ICBMs and the Soviet Union from fear of U.S. preemption.

A U.S. policy that retains the highly vulnerable ICBMs and depends on launching the missiles on warning (or attack assessment) would be the worst possible choice to meet the Soviet threat. Not only would it be inconsistent with the policy of deterring attacks on U.S. cities, but it could also be destabilizing in a crisis, insure escalation, and (if taken seriously) greatly increase the chances of accidental nuclear war.

ABM

The United States has effectively dismantled the one antiballistic missile (ABM) site allowed under the ABM treaty (as amended in 1974) signed with the Soviet Union. Even if the site is reactivated, only 100 defensive missiles are allowed under the treaty. In order to provide an ABM defense for a substantial number of ICBMs, the United States would have to abrogate the treaty. Although this is allowed six months after either side assesses that such action is necessary for its national security, this step may prove politically infeasible. Moreover, strong disagreement over the technological efficacy of this solution is likely. Although progress in defense technology may someday shift the advantage to the defense, at this point, the offense would still seem to have the advantage because it can saturate a defensive system with warheads and decoys and can attack or counter the defense's sensors. Thus, the United States would not likely have confidence in an ABM system to defend Minuteman (or MX) during the next decade.

Nonnuclear defenses of ICBM sites have also been suggested as an interim solution.[3] These proposed defenses should be given some consideration, but they appear to be easily overcome. Their main virtue, it is argued, would be to introduce another element of doubt into Soviet calculations. But deterrence should not rely on assumptions about how the Soviets might view the uncertainties involved in an attack. Instead, it should be based on confidence in the survivability of U.S. forces. No ABM system, either nuclear or nonnuclear, exists that can be relied on confidently to provide that survivability now or in the immediate future.

Survivable Basing

There are several approaches to making land-based ICBMs survivable. The most widely discussed of these calls for the deployment of several hundred new, large ICBMs (designated Missile X or MX) in a mobile or multiple-aim-point mode. The MX missile will be able to carry several times the payload of the Minuteman missile (about 11,000 pounds versus 2,400 pounds) and to achieve accuracies of between 0.05 nm and 0.1 nm compared with Minuteman III's upgraded accuracy of 0.1 nm.

The original method proposed by the Air Force for basing the MX missiles was to place each missile on a transporter that moved along a track in a buried concrete tunnel (or "trench") of ten to twenty miles in length and to fire it by breaking through the roof of the trench and the soil above it. Because the missile could be anywhere in the tunnel, the Soviets would (in theory) be compelled to expend a number of warheads to achieve a high degree of confidence that the missile had been destroyed. The exact number of Soviet weapons required would depend on the length of the tunnel, its hardness to nuclear effects, and the accuracy and yield of Soviet missiles.

Because there was concern that the high pressure shock wave resulting from a single nuclear explosion might propagate down the tunnel and destroy the MX missile, this concept was modified.[4] In the new version, the missile would be moved along an unhardened trench to hardened spurs located off the line of the trench. Once in the spur, a closure mechanism would be activated to seal the missile from the trench. Thus, the Soviets would have to attack each individual spur along the tunnel to be confident of destroying the missile.

Although this approach potentially could provide a survivable ICBM force, a number of objections have been raised against it. Primarily, the estimated cost of $25 to $40 billion is thought to be excessive. With little experience in the construction of this type of system (and certainly not on this scale), it is difficult to have much confidence in the preliminary cost estimates. The final cost could easily exceed present estimates.

There are also great uncertainties regarding the hardness of this unconventional system. Without nuclear testing (which is prohibited by the Nuclear Test Ban Treaty), it will be difficult to be confident that the design-goal hardness of 600 psi can be reached.

Because of the uncertainties regarding hardness and the excessive cost of the tunnel system, two other multiple-aim-point systems are being considered. These schemes are based in part on deception—they envisage a large number of hardened horizontal shelters or vertical silos in which a missile can be hidden. Moreover, the missiles would be transported above ground rather than in tunnels.

A shelter or silo multiple-aim-point system appears to offer a means of obtaining land-based ICBM survivability (as is described below). However, the issue is whether MX or Minuteman should be deployed in this system. Although MX is the Air Force's choice, a number of serious concerns have been expressed about this missile. For example, because MX can carry a large number (8–12) of highly accurate warheads, it inevitably raises the controversial question of whether U.S. strategic weapons should be given a counterforce mission and whether this would enhance or diminish deterrence.

Counterforce Capability The term counterforce usually refers to strategic military targets: the ICBMs, SLBMs, and long-range bombers. Because both sides can destroy "soft targets" (bombers on runways, submarines in port, troop concentrations, most matériel depots, etc.), the primary issue is whether the United States should develop systems with the yield and the accuracy capable of threatening hard targets—primarily, Soviet ICBMs in hardened silos.

Figure 9 illustrates that over the next decade the United States will have only a limited capability against Soviet ICBMs.[5] Not until the introduction of the MX system (which is assumed to occur in 1988) will the United States have the potential for an ICBM counterforce threat.[6] This potential is a source of concern to some and to others the reason to deploy MX.

The essential concern regarding development of an ICBM counterforce capability is the fear that this capability will prove to be destabilizing in a crisis. The threatened side might be tempted to launch its missiles preemptively for fear that if it waited, its missiles might be destroyed in their silos. However, critics of U.S. development of a counterforce capability have, as a group, been rather one-sided in their concern. They seldom view the prospective Soviet development of an effective capability to destroy Minuteman as something that should overly concern the United States. They point to the technical complications inherent in a coordinated attack as perhaps even precluding any real threat to U.S. ICBMs. They also cite the other strategic forces (bombers and submarines) as a means of insuring the maintenance of deterrence. And finally, they suggest that the United States could launch its ICBMs on receiving the warning that an attack is underway. These arguments would seem to apply equally well to the American threat to Soviet ICBMs.

Indeed, the Soviets have long advocated a policy of launching their weapons before a U.S. attack could arrive.[7] They have developed a command, control, and communications (C^3) network that is hardened and redundant to give credibility to this policy. It is doubtful that the United States understands the Soviet C^3 system well enough to prevent a launch by disconnecting Soviet strategic forces from their command structure (by using short time-of-flight SLBMs). Because the Soviets have made a conscious decision to place so much of their strategic force in silos and have continued to replace their older ICBMs with newer, larger ones, it is tempting to conclude that they are unconcerned about losing these weapons. Nevertheless, in a crisis, their confidence in their C^3 system might

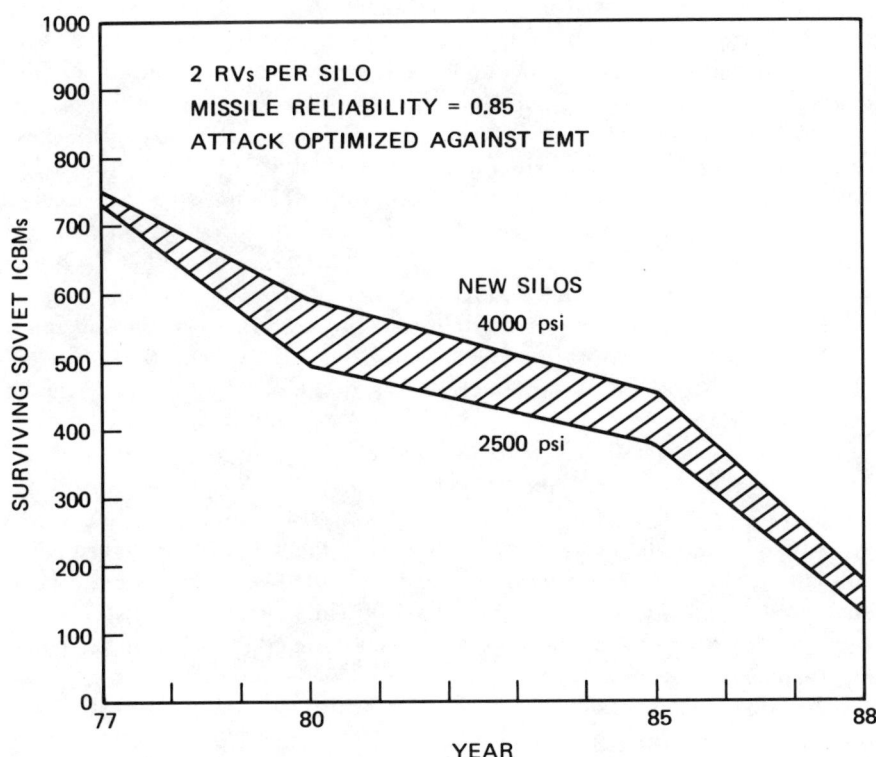

FIGURE 9
U.S. Counterforce Capability

erode, and the temptation to launch preemptively if a U.S. attack is feared cannot entirely be ruled out.

The main arguments for the development of hard-target weapons are: (*a*) to limit damage to the United States if deterrence fails, (*b*) to provide usable nuclear options short of all-out war, and (*c*) to counter the growing threat to U.S. ICBMS. In the 1950s and the early 1960s, "damage limitation" was the primary motivation behind a counterforce strategy. Although Secretary of Defense Harold Brown still lists this as one of the missions of U.S. strategic forces, it is unrealistic to expect that a U.S. retaliatory attack could have more than a minimal impact on limiting the damage that the Soviets could inflict on the United States. Even a U.S. first strike would be ineffective unless forces were also developed to attack Soviet strategic submarines and bombers. Few people still advocate the development of an effective U.S. first-strike capability, and it is even uncertain whether an open society could develop the forces necessary for this capability or could launch a surprise attack if it had this capability.

The suggestion that the president needs a broad range of small-scale usable nuclear options has been offered as an argument for developing counterforce capabilities. In theory, this approach does not envision a full counterforce strike but rather concentrates on improved accuracy and flexibility. Secretary of Defense Schlesinger advocated this Limited Nuclear Options (LNO) doctrine to restore the credibility of a massive U.S. nuclear response to Soviet provocations that fall short of direct attacks on the United States. In particular, with regard to the defense of NATO, he hoped that U.S. willingness to use a small number of strategic nuclear weapons with only limited objectives would restore the credibility of the linkage of U.S. strategic weapons to NATO defense; that is, this policy tried to restore the threat of an all-out nuclear war if the Soviets did not stop an attack on Europe.

Although the possibility of restoring credibility to the doctrine of extended deterrence seems remote (see chapter 5), it is not clear whether a hard-target counterforce capability is necessary to implement this strategy anyway. The targets most often mentioned in the LNO doctrine are either soft military targets or economic objectives such as oil refineries, power stations, and transportation nodes—none of which are hard targets. Nevertheless, it is argued that improved accuracy is needed to minimize collateral damage to nearby people and property. This hopefully would reduce the prospects of escalation.

Improving the accuracy of any U.S. ICBM from 1,000 to 400 feet can have a significant impact on the probability of killing a hard-target, but it has virtually no effect on the collateral damage around a target. A 170 kiloton (Minuteman III) weapon is not a surgical instrument, and neither is the higher yield MX warhead, even if it has zero CEP. Although it is certainly conceivable to build very small yield (a few kilotons or less), highly accurate ICBMs that can limit collateral damage, there has been no move by the Pentagon in this direction. No one seems willing to allocate ICBMs to this limited task, particularly since their more general deterrence role is threatened. Whatever the merits of developing low yield, highly accurate nuclear weapons, they hardly justify the development and deployment of an entirely new and expensive missile system such as MX.

The main arguments for U.S. counterforce capability now revolve around the projected Soviet threat to U.S. ICBMs. As was noted in chapter 1, there is a fear that the Soviets might be able to exploit this perceived weakness politically or perhaps even actually be tempted to attack Minuteman (while holding American cities hostage) to force the resolution of some conflict. It is argued that this tactic might be credible if the Soviets perceived that they could significantly improve their relative strategic position after a nuclear exchange, the usual criterion for judging this being the ratio or absolute difference in the two sides' missile throw-weight. To deter a Soviet attack (the argument goes), it is necessary to have the capability to launch an effective counterattack against the remaining Soviet ICBMs in order to restore the prewar strategic balance.[8] Although this Soviet tactic would seem unlikely and probably be ineffective (short of their achieving a substantial capability against the SSBNs and bombers), it undoubtedly will remain a great concern for many, particularly in a crisis.

Another argument for developing a counterforce capability is that it will compel the Soviets to abandon their present ICBM basing system. Secretary of Defense Rumsfeld suggested in his 1977 posture statement that "the United States should not accept a strategic relationship in which we must bear the heavier costs of alternative basing while the Soviets are allowed the luxury of retaining their fixed ICBMs."[9] It is also argued that if the Soviets (along with the United States) were forced to adopt a mobile system, the strategic situation would be more stable because both sides would now be survivable. These arguments ignore the possibility that the Soviets might still choose to retain their fixed silos and depend on a hair-trigger preemption or launch-on-warning strategy. Furthermore, to argue that this arrangement would increase stability is somewhat self-serving since there are other methods of achieving stability short of developing a counterforce capability.

All these arguments for development of counterforce capabilities miss the main issue—to provide a survivable ICBM force. Developing a second-strike counterthreat to Soviet ICBMs will not save U.S. ICBMs. The solution to the Soviet threat is to negate it by deploying a survivable ICBM system. Of course, the Air Force proposes to make MX survivable by some mobile or multiple-aim-point basing scheme. But once the force becomes survivable, there will be no justification for a U.S. counterforce capability to counter the Soviet capability because the Soviets will no longer have a significant counterforce capability against the ICBMs. Thus, any Soviet temptation to shift the strategic balance by attacking U.S. ICBMs would fail from the beginning, and the United States would not have to depend on counterattacks to redress the balance.[10]

In summary, within the context of present U.S. strategic doctrine, there appears to be no pressing need to develop an ICBM with an effective counterforce capability. Although the arguments against this capability are marginal (except for the cost), the arguments for it are also marginal. The Soviet threat to U.S. ICBMs can be met by adopting a survivable basing mode rather than by developing a counterthreat.

Time Delay Although the high cost of MX and its potential counterforce capability are of serious concern to many, the most serious difficulty with MX is that the system will not be available for almost a decade.[11] For a period of five to seven years or more, the ICBM force could not be relied on as a deterrent, with all the accompanying uncertainties and instabilities this might entail. Although it may be impossible to avoid completely some period in which the ICBMs are endangered, no matter what system is deployed, this period should obviously be reduced to a minimum.

Survivable Basing for Minuteman

The real problem facing the United States is ICBM survivability, not the necessity to match Soviet hard-target kill capability. If a survivable method for basing the present Minuteman force were found, it would offer a satisfactory solution to the impending problem and in many ways would be superior to MX.

One approach is to rebase Minuteman in a multiple-aim-point (MAP) mode. While there are a number of ways of doing this, perhaps the most effective and least costly approach would be to build on the present vertical silo system.[12]

As Soviet missile accuracy increases, the survivability of any single-point target will be in question. The object of a multiple-aim-point system is to create a number of aim-points greater than the number of Soviet reentry vehicles (RVs) available to attack the U.S. ICBM system effectively. For example, an effective attack against the present 1,000-aim-point Minuteman system would probably require at least 2,000 high yield, highly accurate RVs. However, a conservatively designed system would assume that Soviet missile accuracy will continue to improve to the point that the CEP is effectively zero and the probability of kill is equal to 1.0. Thus, each arriving Soviet RV must be assumed to have the capability to "kill" its target, the only restriction being those RVs that do not arrive due to the unreliability of the Soviet missiles. Although assigning two RVs to each target is a simple technique to compensate for unreliable missiles, it would become very expensive as the number of aim-points increased.

In the early 1980s, the Soviets could have around 4,500 reliable, large yield (1 MT) warheads available. To insure that at least half of the Minuteman force would survive, it would be necessary to provide (under conservative assumptions) 9,000 aim-points. To provide these extra aim-points without increasing the number of missiles, it is necessary to depend upon deception. However, the construction of 9,000 silos similar to the present Minuteman silos would be prohibitively expensive. Fortunately it is not necessary to duplicate the present hardened-silo system because the new system would depend primarily on deception rather than on the intrinsic capability of the system to withstand nuclear effects.

The basic concept is to provide a capsule to enclose each Minuteman missile. When placed in a cheaply constructed, vertical, austere silo, the system would be able to withstand shock overpressures from a nuclear explosion of many hundred pounds per square inch. For each Minuteman missile, nine silos (or whatever number deemed necessary to offset the threat) would be constructed. The encapsulated Minuteman would be placed in one of these silos and the other holes would contain dummy cannisters that could not be differentiated from the one actually containing the missile. If it were necessary to do maintenance work on the actual missile (perhaps once every 1.5 years), the cannisters within the nine silos would be shuffled about to maintain the deception.

This system has a number of advantages over the proposed MX tunnel system. It would be considerably cheaper; the technological risks would be far less; there would be less of a problem finding available land; the environmental impact would be less; there would be no destabilizing counterforce threat, which is of concern to many; any arms control agreement limiting the number of missiles would be verifiable; and above all, the system could be available much sooner than MX.

The cost of a 9,000-aim-point system should be considerably less than a similar MX tunnel system. The cost of developing and deploying a new, large, high technology missile could be saved entirely. It is also cheaper to build surface roads to transport a missile than to construct underground subway systems for transportation. The R&D costs to develop a hardened container for the missile should be relatively low, and the successful development of the container is a much lower technological risk than trying to build a hardened underground system. The transporter should not be expensive because its function is to move the cannister, and it is not required as a missile launcher. An estimate of the total cost to develop, procure, and operate the system for ten years is about $12 billion.[13]

Another advantage of this system is that a missile silo requires little land. Many of the present ICBMs are on small fenced-off plots of land leased from farmers.[14] A multiple-aim-point Minuteman system could expand the present missile complexes (there are now six Minuteman missile fields) by utilizing the same facilities. The only restriction is that the new silos must not be located so close to each other that more than one could be destroyed by a single nuclear warhead. On the other hand, the MX tunnel system would require around 10,000 square miles of new land as well as new facilities and new command and control techniques. In addition, the construction of several thousand miles of tunnels would raise many environmental and ecological concerns.[15]

Any arms control agreement could be verified by on-site inspection, a procedure the United States has often insisted on in other contexts. For example, the missile system could be arranged in a thousand complexes of nine silos each, with one real missile and eight dummies in each complex. The Soviets would be free to select at random a number of such complexes for inspection and to verify that only one missile was present in the set of nine.[16] Other, even more stringent schemes involving the inspection of missile production facilities or missile/cannister assembly areas could obviously be considered.

The Soviets in the past have rejected on-site inspection. But as a general principle, any arms control agreement should contain a provision that if one side deploys a mobile or multiple-aim-point system, it must provide for adequate verification that the number of missiles is within the agreed limit. The Soviets can avoid on-site inspection simply by not deploying a mobile or MAP system.

The advantages of austere silos over a tunnel system would also apply if MX were deployed rather than Minuteman.* However, the date that the MX missile is to become operational has been postponed several times and may not be until after 1987. A long period of vulnerability before a new system is available is clearly undesirable. By retaining the Minuteman missile and by proceeding with a fairly simple, technologically straightforward approach, a multiple-aim-point system could be available several years earlier than MX, perhaps by 1982.

Of course, no solution to the Soviet threat is problem-free. Any system that depends upon deception is subject to compromise. The concern is that through external sensors, the location of the real missile might be discovered. However, it should not be too difficult to have the dummy cannisters duplicate any external characteristics (weight, appearance, monitoring signals, etc.) of the real missile. It should also be possible to devise a system in which only one person knows the location of the missile within the complex of nine aim-points. Since each complex could have a different person in charge of selection, there would be a thousand different people, each knowing the location of only one missile.[17] This should make it quite difficult for the Soviet intelligence apparatus to subvert the system.

Another major concern is that the Soviets might increase the number of RVs on each missile, thus increasing the threat. The question then be-

---

*By January 1979, the Air Force appeared to be favoring the MAP system for MX basing.

comes how expensive it is to proliferate aim-points in order to offset the increase in warheads. If, for example, a 20,000 RV threat developed, it might require an additional $11 billion to insure that at least half the Minuteman force survived.[18] This new 20,000 RV force would cost the Soviets around $10 billion to deploy (assuming that no new missiles are required and that the cost of each new warhead [with a "bus" and R&D but excluding operating costs] is about $0.5 million). In general, it is probably cheaper for the United States to proliferate austere silos than for the Soviets to proliferate warheads. In this case, the defense may have the advantage over the offense.

Conclusion

Even though there are a number of difficulties with the MX system, it could be justified if it were the only alternative available to replace the present (and eventually vulnerable) system. However, the multiple-aim-point system for Minuteman described above is a viable alternative and can solve the problem of ICBM survivability at a lower cost and in a shorter time than MX.

STRATEGIC BOMBERS / CRUISE MISSILES

The strategic bomber force remains an important component of the American deterrent since it makes a Soviet surprise attack more difficult and complicates the Soviet defense against a U.S. retaliation. It is also the most flexible of the strategic systems. Although the launching of missiles on warning of an incoming attack is an inherently dangerous posture, this is not a problem with the bombers because they can be recalled if a mistake is made. In fact, under the positive control launch procedures, they are automatically recalled unless presidential authorization is given to proceed to target. Furthermore, those bombers that complete their missions are potentially reusable if a war becomes protracted. Bombers might even be useful for battlefield support of a defense of Europe. In addition, the strategic bomber force can potentially carry almost as much nuclear explosive power as the combined ICBM and submarine-based ballistic missile forces. This is often cited as an important factor offsetting the large throw-weight advantage of the Soviet missile force.[19]

The current bomber force would face serious difficulties in a nuclear war. As presently based, it could suffer severe losses if it were attacked by Soviet submarine-launched ballistic missiles (SLBMs) using depressed (or "shaped") trajectories and launched near the U.S. coastline. Furthermore, even if the bombers survive an initial attack, the current Soviet air defense system (if operated with intelligence and skill) should be able to protect most, if not all, valuable targets. And the Soviets continue to improve this already formidable air defense system.

Prelaunch Survival

The aging B-52 bomber force is not the ideal system to counter the potentially serious threat posed by modern Soviet forces. One of the seldom mentioned advantages of the cancelled B-1 bomber was its prelaunch survivability. The B-1 was faster and somewhat more resistant to the effects of nuclear weapons than the B-52, greatly increasing its chances of escaping an SLBM barrage. The B-52 is a marginal system, but with serious effort and great care, this force could be made more effective.

Against SLBMs flown on short time-of-flight depressed trajectories, the present basing mode of the strategic bombers would result in a complete disaster. Even the evacuation of those air bases close to the coasts would not help appreciably because there are so few bases inland. To increase their survivability, preparations should begin to rebase the alert bomber forces at a large number (50 or more) of separate bases at least 500 nm from the coasts. These would be satellite, austere bases with training and maintenance performed at the existing main operating bases. The cost of each new base should be from $10 to $20 million.[20]

Although the necessity of rebasing inland to counter short time-of-flight SLBMs is generally recognized, the Defense Department has been reluctant to undertake this program until they have confirmed that the Soviets have flown their missiles in this mode. As noted in chapter 3, the amount of time between the testing of missiles in this mode until they were fully operational could be quite short, and the United States may not even be able to detect such tests. In either case, the United States could be confronted with a severe threat before it had time to react. Thus, the time to begin construction of the required bases is today.

Tactical warning is crucial to bomber survivability. Delays in reaction times of five minutes or less could result in complete loss of the force even with optimal basing. One potentially serious problem results from the present system of channeling data from the early warning satellites through a few ground entry points that could be subject to sabotage. An alternative to this system would be to provide direct readouts of the satellite data to the Airborne Command Post (Looking Glass) and to provide secure communications links from Looking Glass to the Strategic Air Command bomber bases. In addition, the entire procedure for launching bombers in the event of an attack could be made more automated to overcome any commander's natural reluctance to launch his bombers without further confirmation of the attack. Automated systems are an advantage with bombers (as opposed to missiles) because bombers automatically return to their base if it is a false alarm.

The reaction time from sounding of a warning to take-off must be reduced to an absolute minimum. Bomber crews should be located next to their aircraft, and procedures for simplifying and shortening engine start should be developed. Today's extremely lax procedures, with many crews not even confined to the "ready building" close to the runways, should be altered.[21]

Finally, the number of aircraft on alert should be increased to about 60 percent of the force. With 200 bombers on alert, it would increase the chances that a substantial force would escape and be able to participate in the next phase of the operation—the penetration of Soviet air defenses.

Penetration

In order to reach their targets, U.S. bombers must penetrate a formidable Soviet area defense system. The Soviets have a sizable advantage over the United States in terms of the number of air defense weapons compared with the number of bombers. Furthermore, even if a bomber eludes Soviet area defenses, each bomber must visit ten to twelve targets to deliver all of its weapons, overflying four to deliver its bombs and approaching within about 30 nm (the average operational range of the SRAM missile) of the others to fire its missiles. With each encounter with Soviet defenses, the probability of survival decreases. The likelihood of a bomber completing its entire mission may approach zero unless the bomber avoids defended targets or is able to suppress or otherwise neutralize the defenses. Soviet tactics of movement, activation of reserves, and the use of field army air defense capabilities could negate such U.S. tactics.

Perhaps the only way to overcome the uncertainties regarding bomber penetration is to saturate the defense. Thus, the United States should deploy long-range stand-off cruise missiles as quickly as possible, ideally as many as the carrying capacity of the B-52 allows—twenty per bomber.[22] This option has the virtues of (*a*) diluting the defenses by increasing the number of penetrators by a factor of ten or more and (*b*) increasing the total payload and the number of warheads carried by surviving bombers. If, for some reason, bombers really need to penetrate, they could do so more successfully when masked by ten to twenty times the number of threatening penetrators.

Cruise Missile Carriers

The deployment of cruise missiles on other carriers as well as on bombers could be an effective means of assuring deterrence. By placing these weapons aboard attack submarines, various naval surface ships, other aircraft, and perhaps even ground-based mobile systems, a Soviet disarming attack would be greatly complicated if not completely negated. However, currently proposed arms control agreements (discussed later in this chapter) would effectively prevent this approach. The proposal to limit the total number of MIRVed systems could even severely limit the effectiveness of bomber-delivered cruise missiles. By counting each bomber carrying cruise missiles as a MIRVed system, the number of such carriers allowed under a treaty could be limited to far below 100 unless the deployment of other MIRVed systems (the Poseidon or Trident submarines or Minuteman III missiles) is reduced in order to allow more bombers. This would not provide enough surviving weapons to saturate the Soviet air defense system confidently.

If the proposed arms restrictions are adopted, it may become necessary to deploy large aircraft such as the Boeing 747 as cruise missile carriers. Each of these aircraft could carry 50 to 75 cruise missiles. Under other circumstances, this approach should be avoided because it greatly concentrates the missile force in a relatively small number of lucrative targets. Secretary Brown has also stated that aircraft of this type could not be available until 1988 or 1990.[23] Deployment of this force may become advisable, but the long time delay predicted by Secretary Brown should be avoided so that the United States can maintain a triad during the 1980s.

STRATEGIC SUBMARINES (SSBNs)

Given the obvious weaknesses in the other two legs of the triad, the United States must rely more heavily on its strategic submarine force to maintain deterrence in the immediate future, particularly if the MX system is chosen to replace Minuteman (because MX is unlikely to be available before the late 1980s) and if the deployment of a substantial cruise missile force is delayed. Furthermore, since saturation is the most effective response to a quick deployment of a (covertly developed) Soviet antiballistic missile system, the submarines with their large number of warheads provide an important hedge against a breakthrough in this area. On the other hand, the warheads carried by SSBNs are relatively small (40 kT), and the total submarine force at sea in the Atlantic carries only about 300 EMT, part of which (about 15 percent) is assigned to NATO for military targets.[24] Most analysts would consider this amount to be the minimum required for deterrence, making even a partial loss of the fleet at sea unacceptably dangerous.

Although the general opinion of the Defense Department (and its critics) is that the submarines are "invulnerable," there is a significant number of

Strategic Force Issues

potential threats that could drastically reduce or eliminate the fleet (see chapter 3). America's lack of knowledge of both the technical aspects of some of these threats and the details of Soviet antisubmarine warfare programs makes it impossible to have confidence in the continued invulnerability of strategic submarines. Despite the uncertainties, there are measures available that could make it more difficult for the Soviets to attack the fleet.

The Trident I Missile

One of the most worrisome aspects of the Soviet antisubmarine warfare (ASW) threat is that the short range (2,500 nm) of the present Poseidon C-3 missile confines the SSBNs to a relatively small area because they must be "on station" (within missile range of their targets) while on patrol. This weakness could be mitigated, if not eliminated, by accelerating plans to replace the C-3 missiles in Poseidon submarines with Trident I (C-4) missiles. Because the Trident I missile has a range of around 4,000 nm, the total operational area of the Poseidon submarines will be increased to about ten million square nautical miles. However, the Defense Department should also consider replacing the C-3 in all 31 Poseidon submarines rather than just the 12 now planned.[25]

Out of Area Deployment

Before the long-range C-4 missile becomes available, it would be possible to increase the submarines' patrol area by deploying the SSBNs "out of area"; that is, at locations where their missiles could not reach their targets. This would require changes in the present war plan, which demands that the submarines always be on station, but this is unlikely to be an insoluble problem since few, if any, targets are "time urgent" requiring immediate attack.[26]

This deployment procedure would increase the chances for survival during the initial phase of a conflict, but it is not an ideal solution. Because the submarines would have to return to positions closer to the Soviet Union, their survival is problematic. Although the Soviets might not be able to intercept the SSBNs as they approached their launch positions, the most prudent plan is still to proceed as quickly as possible with C-4 deployments.

Arctic Deployment

Another means of countering possible Soviet ASW breakthroughs is to give the SSBNs the capability to operate under the Arctic ice cap or in the so-called marginal ice zones surrounding the permanent ice cap. The ice cover of the Arctic Ocean and its adjacent seas occupies an area of approximately five million square miles at its greatest extent, and decreases about 30 percent during the summer season. There are many openings and leads throughout the cap, and the submarines would probably, on the average, never be more than 10 nm from a section of ice less than four feet thick.

In this new environment, many of the open-ocean threats enumerated in chapter 3 would no longer be applicable. In addition to the nonacoustic threats, the potential for active acoustic trails could be lessened. While the Soviets might be able to trail a submarine to the marginal ice zones around the ice cap, once it is under the ice, it becomes almost impossible to follow. Active sonar is no longer effective because reverberations from the ice surface prevent the identification of a target. In the marginal ice zones, the use of passive sonar is of no avail because the constant interaction of the ice, the open sea, and the wind in these regions produces enough noise to mask a submarine's signals easily. Deep under the ice cap, the background noise is quite low. But if a SSBN should be followed that far, the release of a noisemaker would allow it to escape and then to sit quietly under the ice. Since the sound channel is just below the surface, the SSBN would be in an ideal position to listen for an approaching submarine. An SSBN could also use an excursion under the ice as a means of breaking trail. If the United States were confident that the Soviets did not have an effective open-ocean acquisition system, the SSBN could then simply return to the sea.

Although there are some operational difficulties with this plan, the capability of operating in the Arctic would provide a significant hedge against Soviet ASW breakthroughs in many areas.

New Communications System

If there are surface phenomena that can be used by the Soviets to detect the SSBNs, this problem can perhaps be mitigated, if not eliminated, by patrolling at greater depths than at present. This would require the development and deployment of a new communications system because the present "trailing wire" system requires submarines to remain relatively close to the surface. The Navy and the Defense Department have been trying for some time to reduce this problem by developing an ELF (extremely low frequency) system that eliminates the surface antenna and allows communications with submarines at great depths. The ELF system requires a very long transmitting antenna because its radio wavelength is about 2,500 miles long. The Navy proposes to install in Upper Michigan about 50 underground antennas (in a grid pattern), each being 30–80 miles long, with spacing of perhaps 3–5 miles between parallel lines.

Because this is such a large system, it has been met over the years with continued opposition from people concerned with safety and the impact on the ecosystem in the vicinity of a buried electrically energized cable. The Navy contends that there is no cause for concern because the electromagnetic fields associated with the grid are very weak, but the opposition continues.

An alternative would be a much smaller ELF system (similar to the Navy's test facility in Wisconsin) that would function as a negative "bell-ringer" system. As long as the ELF system was on, a submarine would know that all was well; if it stopped transmitting, the submarine would send an antenna close to or on to the ocean surface to receive further instructions. Since the ELF system would be small and vulnerable, it could not be relied on to survive a nuclear attack and to relay the president's instructions (the "go-code") to the submarines. But it is unlikely that either a larger system or the present ground-based VLF (very low frequency) communications system would be more survivable. The go-code could be relayed directly to the submarines by UHF (ultrahigh frequency) satellites or specially launched rockets as well as by present aircraft systems. During peacetime, daily messages would be delivered to each submarine via UHF satellite relay. Using modern communications techniques, an entire message can be so compressed in time that a submarine would need to expose a very small antenna for only a few seconds once a day, thus assuring its security.

Improved Security

Unorthodox approaches such as the "tags" or sabotage noted in chapter 3 are possible and particularly worrisome since the SSBN force is concentrated in so few places. There is no simple way to describe the steps necessary to relieve concern in this area, but the problems should be taken seriously.

The Trident Submarine

The Navy has proposed replacing some of the older submarines with the new, gigantic Trident submarines. This boat will carry 24 rather than 16 missiles, and its launch tubes are large enough for the eventual replacement of the Trident I C-4 missile with the Trident II missile, which has a range of 6,000 nm. Although the Trident I and Trident II missiles would greatly increase the operational range of the SSBNs, the submarines are so expensive (well over one billion dollars each) that they are not likely to be deployed in great numbers, perhaps not even the ten or twelve now planned.

Besides its cost, the Trident boat has a number of other drawbacks. First, it greatly concentrates the force in an even smaller number of targets. Moreover, it is likely to exacerbate any potential ASW problems. It is much larger than the present submarines, making it much easier to detect using any active acoustic technique. Its larger size also makes any hydrodynamic phenomena (either in the ocean or on the ocean surface) that much more pronounced and that much more detectable. The development and deployment of a smaller, cheaper boat in great numbers would have been a more prudent alternative. Little can be done about this in the near future, and procurement of most of the planned Tridents should proceed. But an alternative should be found for the future.

STRATEGIC RESERVE

One image of a nuclear war is that of a spasm war in which both sides fire all their weapons in a crescendo of slaughter and destruction, but it need not happen that way. The Soviet view of nuclear war is that although the first stage may be decisive, they should be prepared to fight a long, protracted war to ultimate victory. In the past, it was a truism that no country would intentionally become involved in a war without reserve forces. This policy may be even more critical in a nuclear war. If there is a war of attrition, reserve forces may play an important role in intrawar deterrence of attacks on cities, in deciding the terms of a peace agreement, and in assuring that a reestablished, postwar deterrence is maintained. Thus, it is important for the United States to maintain some strategic forces that are completely separate from those forces designated as part of the war plan and that can remain survivable for an extended period of time.

One approach to providing a strategic reserve is to designate some part of each element of the triad for this role. However, confidence in the survival of these forces is not so high that many weapons could be taken from their primary deterrent role without generating some concern. Furthermore, except perhaps for submarines deployed outside their normal patrol areas, there can be little confidence in the long-term survival of these forces.

There are several approaches to providing a reserve force (separate from the usual triad forces) and a means of controlling this force. A few of these are briefly discussed below.

ICBMs

There are probably a number of ways to make a moderate force (100–200 missiles) of ICBMs survivable if they are not required to be immediately available for launch. For example, there may be techniques to make silos "superhard" if they need not be operational. Missiles could also be placed in deep underground centers (under mountains or plateaus) that could withstand massive attacks. However, if the outside openings were sealed off by nuclear explosions, the missiles would have to be retrieved by digging them out, either from the outside or from the inside.[27]

Cruise Missiles

A strategic reserve could also include cruise missiles. If there are no arms agreements restricting their deployment, these small weapons can, for example, be stored aboard the many operational naval vessels at sea, particularly attack submarines. However, future arms control treaties are likely to include prohibitions against this, and other techniques will probably have to be sought. To be effective, the cruise missile force must have survivable means of delivery, survivable missiles, and survivable warheads. Although all three factors may be colocated (as they will be on the alert B-52 cruise missile force), if they are in the reserve force, they could be separated in peacetime and brought together after an attack.

Delivery Vehicles   Since it is unlikely that many B-52s will survive a nuclear war, particularly if it is a protracted war, it may be necessary to utilize cargo and commercial aircraft to deliver the missiles within the required range of the Soviet Union. At least one-third of America's large commercial aircraft are in the air at any one time and thus would survive a nuclear attack.[28] A sizable number of large military cargo planes also would perhaps survive. It might be neither too difficult nor too expensive to develop modular packages that allow these aircraft to be converted to cruise missile carriers once they land. (Surface ships might also be used, but they would probably be more vulnerable to attack while moving within range.)

Missiles   Although the cruise missiles could be placed under mountains, it might be more convenient and cheaper to seek survivability through mobility. Missiles could be placed on trains or trucks and constantly moved about the country, but the nuclear warheads would have to be separated from the missiles because the carriers would be traveling along public roads.

Warheads   Nuclear warheads could be stored in a number of ways, but perhaps the most survivable would be aboard underwater platforms, such as nuclear attack submarines or new, special purpose systems. These submersibles could be deployed in the Pacific or Atlantic far from the usual strategic submarine patrol areas, greatly complicating Soviet attempts to find them. If war came, a rendezvous with a seaplane that would pick up the warheads might be arranged, or the submersibles could return directly to the United States. If arms control agreements do not foreclose the possibility, these submersibles could act as storage facilities for both missiles and warheads.

Postattack Command, Control, and Communications

To assure the deterrence value of a strategic reserve (and, for that matter, of war-plan forces), a survivable command center to direct the use of these forces must be maintained. This command post must be able to receive information as well as to communicate with the forces. At present, the United States relies on airborne command posts to perform this function. However, only one of these aircraft (Looking Glass) is in the air in peacetime. Even if it can survive attacks while airborne (which is by no means certain), it must eventually land to refuel and to allow the crew to rest.

A command post that can survive for a longer period of time should be considered. One approach considered in the past was a deep, underground center. Although this is still a possibility, there are a number of difficulties with it (but perhaps not insurmountable ones), particularly in maintaining communications following an attack.[29]

An alternate approach is a submersible command post—either a modified SSBN (perhaps one of the older boats being replaced by Trident) or a specially designed system. This command post might operate off the coasts or in the Great Lakes and could deploy various antennas to receive information and to send commands through a system of buoys, balloons, or cruise missiles in order to maintain the secrecy of its location.

An additional (and perhaps the most important) function of this system could be to act as a hedge to insure that the Emergency Action Message (the go-code) is delivered to the strategic forces. As noted in chapter 3, there is some concern that this message may not be delivered in a timely fashion to all the forces. The submerged command post could launch on warning a communications rocket into a high orbit to assure that the message is relayed to these forces. Additional communication and reconnaissance satellites could be launched by the command post to help in the postattack period.[30]

ARMS CONTROL

During the last decade, negotiations with the Soviet Union to limit or to reduce strategic armaments have become an important element of American foreign policy. These negotiations are viewed as an integral part of a strategy of détente—an attempt to reduce tensions between the Soviet Union and the United States. Arms control advocates view the arms competition as one of the chief sources of "tension" between the two superpowers and feel that if arms control agreements are not reached, the ever accelerating "arms race" will get even further out of control and greatly increase the chances of war.

The notion of an action-reaction arms race has been strongly criticized for being simplistic.[31] But even if it were correct, neither logic nor history would suggest that an arms competition inevitably leads to war[32] (although if only one side competes, it obviously can lead to increased opportunities for war if that party has aggressive intentions). The concept of an arms-race-induced war is a mechanistic explanation that confuses cause and effect. Hostility between nations is the source of arms competition and not the other way around.[33] Unless underlying political realities change, arms competition is not likely to stop, although it can be modified by agreements. And while arms control agreements may serve some useful purpose, a headlong pursuit of an agreement for political rather than for security reasons can have an effect opposite of that intended by increasing rather than lessening tensions.

Arms limitation agreements should have as their goal the establishment of international stability and mutual security.[34] They can do this by limiting the threat to each side's strategic forces. However, since arms control also has the potential for being destabilizing, care must be taken with the details of any agreement. This is particularly important since the Soviets still adhere to a damage-limiting strategy[35] and are thus not necessarily in concert with the U.S. view of stability and security. Under this strategy, the Soviets have a great interest in limiting the alternatives that the United States can pursue in protecting its strategic forces. That is, the Soviets would undoubtedly like to have assurances that if they counter one U.S. system, they will not have to worry about the production of another system or a new mode of basing for which they have developed no counter.

In this context, it is important to consider recent arms negotiations which have sought restrictions on U.S. systems that can be counterproductive to the maintenance of deterrence. Of special concern are attempts to severely restrict cruise missiles, the mode of ICBM deployment, and, to a lesser degree, MIRVs.[36]

Cruise Missiles

Although not a panacea, the cruise missile could be a positive, stabilizing influence. Because of its small size and relatively low cost, large numbers of these weapons can be produced and deployed on various platforms. While this in itself does not automatically preclude a disarming counterforce attack (as some of its advocates have suggested), it can, if proper care is taken, increase the chances for the survival of a substantial force. This force does not threaten the Soviet Union (cruise missiles are slow and cannot be used effectively for a first strike), but it is required to compensate for the massive, Soviet air defense system.

From the point of view of arms control, it is impossible to keep track of these weapons because they are small and easily concealed. As an alternative, it has been suggested that the number of delivery vehicles (aircraft, ships, and submarines) be limited. Demands to limit the range of these missiles have also been made. However, adherence to these limitations cannot be monitored through such "national means of verification" as photographic satellites. Thus, any limitation on cruise missiles would in effect be a unilateral restriction on the United States. Because cruise missiles are important in the maintenance of U.S. capabilities to overcome Soviet air defenses, the suggested restrictions would diminish rather than enhance strategic stability.[37]

Mode of ICBM Deployment

In the face of growing Soviet counterforce capabilities, any restrictions on the mode of basing U.S. ICBMs should be viewed as destabilizing. Multiple-aim-point basing does not increase the threat of war; it is a purely defensive measure. The United States can certainly devise methods to assure the Soviets that American systems are limited by offering on-site inspections. Furthermore, it is difficult to give much weight to arguments which suggest that it is important to ban mobile ICBM systems and thus prevent the Soviets from deploying the mobile version of the SS-16—a system that is neither a threat to U.S. ICBMs nor particularly critical to the Soviets. Since a survivable ICBM force remains critical to national security, any agreement banning multiple-aim-point systems should be rejected.[38]

MIRV Limits

In a second-strike strategy, MIRVs are valuable in assuring that a significant number of warheads will survive even if many missiles are destroyed. They are also an important hedge against Soviet breakthroughs in ABM technology and the quick deployment of an ABM system. However, with sufficient accuracy and yield, they are also a potent offensive weapon and allow one ICBM to be used to attack several targets. Thus, any limitations on MIRVs must be considered as a trade-off between the threat to one's ICBMs and the requirements of assuring a second-strike capability. However, the suggested restrictions on MIRVs are at such high levels that any Soviet first strike would not be inhibited. Limits on MIRVs, with present systems and modes of deployment, act only to inhibit U.S. response to a Soviet threat, and thus, they lower strategic stability. However,

Strategic Force Issues 95

in order to preserve a multiple-aim-point system, there may be some point to MIRV limits—even the fairly high limits usually suggested—because the number of RVs required to attack a multiple-aim-point system is much higher than that required to attack the present Minuteman system.

SALT

By January 1979, the Strategic Arms Limitations (SALT) negotiators for the U.S. and U.S.S.R. had not agreed upon all terms of a treaty, although they were reported to be in 90 percent agreement. The treaty is reported to consist of three elements: a formal treaty to run through 1985, a protocol (to run for three years) that puts temporary restrictions on systems that are subject to further negotiations, and a statement of principles that will serve as guidelines for negotiations over the next phase of SALT. The essential provisions of the SALT II Treaty are given in table 7.

Some provisions of this treaty have met with strong opposition. The emphasis on the number of launchers instead of their throw-weight is seen as perpetuating Soviet superiority in this area with ill effects on strategic sta-

TABLE 7

Expected SALT II Treaty

Category	Limit
Total Number of Launchers*:	
Initially	2,400
By 1980–82[†]	2,250
Aggregate of MIRVed missiles and bombers	
with cruise missiles	1,320
MIRVed Missiles	1,200
MIRVed Land-based ICBMs	820
Modern Large Ballistic Missiles (MLBMs)[††]	308

*ICBMs, SLBMs, and "heavy" bombers. The Soviet Backfire bomber is excluded from the count. The U.S.S.R. is providing a variety of assurances in a unilateral statement designed to put a ceiling on the production rate of the bomber and to assure that it is not configured in an intercontinental role.
†Still under negotiation. Earlier date is U.S. proposal; later date is Soviet proposal.
††These are the Soviet SS-18s (or comparable size replacements). The United States is not allowed to deploy missiles of this size.

bility and perhaps on the political sphere. The terms of the agreement are also unequal in other ways. According to Congressman Jack F. Kemp:

> The Soviet Union will be permitted within the terms of the agreement to deploy and operate systems which are denied to the United States. For example, the U.S. is prohibited from deploying "heavy" ICBMs, while the Soviets are permitted to deploy 326 SS-18s, each with the ability to deliver five times the payload of our most modern ICBM, the Minuteman 3. Similarly, the Soviet bomber known as the Backfire, with the unquestioned intercontinental capability by inflight refueling and landing at Cuban bases, will not be counted against their ceiling on strategic delivery vehicles, while U.S. intercontinental heavy bombers will be counted against the U.S. ceiling.[39]

These matters are important not primarily because they create the impression of inequality, but because they allow a larger threat to U.S. forces than would be the case under a more equitable treaty. For example, the large Soviet throw-weight advantage makes it much more difficult for the U.S. to protect its ICBMs. In addition, if the Soviets are not required to include the Backfire, the number of missile systems allowed them is correspondingly increased, again increasing the threat.

Also of great concern are the provisions affecting U.S. ICBMs and cruise missiles. Although it is unclear at this point whether there will be restrictions on multiple-aim-point systems, there are severe limitations on cruise missiles. Unless the Carter administration is prepared to curtail procurement of the Trident submarine or dismantle some Poseidon submarines or Minuteman III missiles, the number of cruise missile carriers will be restricted to around 100 or less. Plans now call for converting the B-52 Gs to cruise missile carriers. If all 150 of these aircraft were converted and if double the present number were kept on alert, only 100 of them would be available to counter a surprise attack. The number surviving a surprise attack would, of course, likely be smaller, and the effectiveness of the system would be reduced even further.

This restriction on the number of cruise missiles contravenes the principle of an equitable, stabilizing arms agreement. The cruise missile, as noted above, is not a first-strike weapon and is required only to overcome (mainly by saturation) the massive Soviet air defense system. To be equitable, any limitation on the number of cruise missiles would have to be matched by a corresponding reduction in the Soviet air defense system.

In addition, the Soviets have sought to limit the range of the cruise missile to 2,500 kilometers. This would make Soviet forward defenses against the bombers (before the cruise missiles are launched) more feasible since the bombers must then approach quite close to Soviet territory in order to reach many important targets. There appears to be no legitimate reason for establishing this short range, and it is clearly contrary to the principles of stability since it makes a survivable deterrent more uncertain.

Despite the weaknesses in the proposed SALT II Treaty, advocates suggest that it is imperative to sign it since the Soviets have the capability to build even more forces than allowed by the treaty.[40] Conceding that the treaty allows for numerical inequities, they argue that if there were no treaty, in 1985 the Soviets could have an even larger lead in the various static quantities (indices) used to measure the strategic balance. This viewpoint ignores the fact that the strategic balance is not primarily a "numbers" game, but a matter of maintaining survivable strategic forces.

In general, the proposed treaty would not significantly lessen the threat to U.S. strategic forces, and would in fact restrict important actions that could be taken to reduce the Soviet threat. Thus, under the terms of the treaty:

1. U.S. ICBMs can still be threatened in the early 1980s by only a small part of the Soviet ICBM force, and the throw-weight advantage allowed to the Soviets will make it more difficult to develop a more survivable U.S. system in the future.
2. No restrictions are made on Soviet submarine deployment to reduce the prelaunch threat to the bombers.
3. Restrictions on cruise missiles reduce U.S. chances of penetrating Soviet air defenses.
4. No restrictions are placed on the Soviet ASW threat to the U.S. strategic submarine fleet.

Furthermore, it is not even clear that the proposed SALT II Treaty would result in substantial savings in the defense budget. With or without SALT II, the United States will have to spend money to increase the survivability of its strategic forces. For example, steps must be taken to counter the growing vulnerability of U.S. ICBMs. Because the treaty imposes restrictions, both on cruise missiles and on other systems, there would be increasing pressure to replace Minuteman with MX. This system is not only more expensive than the multiple-aim-point Minuteman system, but (because MX will not be available until the late 1980s) it will leave the entire ICBM force in jeopardy for many years. In the interim, the United States could be tempted to rely on a dangerous and destabilizing launch-on-warning doctrine.

Because so few cruise missile carriers are allowed under SALT II, the Carter administration has already begun studies on the development of a new cruise missile carrier by modifying large transport aircraft, either commercial or military. The Defense Department is studying the option of deploying 100 of these aircraft with a total of 6,000 cruise missiles.[41] Although this represents a reasonable course of action under the terms of SALT II, it would be costly (about $8 billion for the aircraft), would dangerously concentrate the force, and would considerably delay the deployment of a substantial cruise missile force.[42]

Without a SALT agreement, it could be more costly for the United States to make its ICBM force survivable because the Soviets could continue to build large MIRVed ICBMs beyond the SALT II's limit of 820. However, the Soviets might not do this because with a multiple-aim-point Minuteman system, the United States could probably increase the number of aim-points (austere, cheap silos) as cheaply as the Soviets could produce warheads, if not more cheaply. Under these circumstances, the Soviets could not gain an advantage by increasing the number of missiles and thus might be dissuaded from the attempt.[43]

Stabilizing Agreements

There is little doubt that if all forces were survivable, both superpowers would have more than enough for deterrence. Thus, reductions from present levels are justifiable if survivability can be maintained.[44] Moreover, because it is easier and cheaper to make a small number of ICBMs survivable (through mobility and deception), restrictions on the number of U.S. ICBMs need not be disadvantageous, particularly if similar restrictions are placed on Soviet ICBMs. Some aspects of the Carter administration's original proposal to the Soviets (in March, 1977) were along this line but did not go far enough.[45] This proposal would have restricted the number of MIRVed ICBMs to 550 and reduced the number of Soviet modern large ballistic missiles from 308 to 150. Placing stronger restrictions on the ICBM payload advantage of the Soviets would have been useful although, in view of the Soviet rejection, difficult to negotiate. Reductions in the U.S. bomber force from 330 to 250 could be offered as compensation for Soviet throw-weight reductions.

To increase the survivability of the bomber force, an agreement to restrict the operating areas of strategic missile-carrying submarines (SSBNs) would be required. The increase in SLBM flight time resulting from keeping one side's SSBNs at least 600 miles from the other side's shores would significantly improve the chances of the bombers escaping their bases. Because this agreement could easily be abrogated, it would be necessary to maintain and improve present ocean surveillance systems to monitor the restricted area. The development of a capability to place the bombers on a very quick reaction, high alert status would also be necessary.

Devising agreements to reduce potential threats to SSBNs would be difficult because much of potential ASW technology would be unmonitorable. However, some restrictions might be possible. Outlawing of active acoustic trail could be considered. Even further, enemy submarines or ASW surface ships could be forbidden to approach within, say, 200 miles of the other side's coasts. Although these restrictions, like those regarding SSBN operating areas, could be easily abrogated, the breaking of an international treaty would at least give clear warning of a developing threat.

Conclusion

Although many agree that there is little to be gained from the proposed SALT II Treaty, they argue that it is more important to sign an agreement (even a bad one) than to risk a breakdown in détente.[46] This view assumes that the arms competition is the source of tensions between the U.S. and the U.S.S.R. A more fundamental point is that the advocates of the proposed treaty are willing to make numerous concessions in the belief that strategic stability is almost automatic in a world of massive overkill and exaggerated worst-case analyses. From their viewpoint, it is not unreasonable that foreign policy aspects of arms control take precedence over any particular military details of an agreement.

However, the basic issue confronting the United States in the coming decade is the survivability of its strategic weapons systems. Because there is no great margin of safety, the task of achieving survivability can be made extremely difficult, if not impossible, by unwise, politically motivated arms control agreements with the Soviets. Agreements must be made with a full understanding of the risks involved and not under assumptions of automatic stability. Treaties concluded for the sake of détente rather than for security are likely in the long run to threaten not only true détente but international peace as well.

II
Strategic Policy

V
Extended Deterrence

The NATO military doctrine adopted by the Eisenhower administration in the 1950s was generally one of deterrence based on massive nuclear retaliation in the event of an attack by the Soviet Union on Western Europe. Conventional forces were de-emphasized, and reliance was placed on strategic forces and, to a lesser degree, on tactical nuclear forces. The credibility of a policy of "massive retaliation" to a Soviet conventional or nuclear attack on Western Europe depended upon the willingness of the United States to initiate an attack against the Soviet Union. During the early 1950s, America held an essentially unilateral deterrent and could have attacked Soviet targets without fear of major retaliation. Under these circumstances, the credibility of an extension of the American nuclear umbrella over its allies was quite high.

As the number of Soviet long-range forces (first bombers, then ICBMs) increased during the late 1950s and early 1960s, the damage that the Soviets could inflict upon the United States in a retaliatory attack also increased. Although during this period the United States tried to develop various damage-limiting capabilities, by the mid-1960s it was clear that the Soviet Union possessed a second-strike assured-destruction capability of its own. America no longer had a unilateral deterrent, and a situation of "mutual assured destruction" prevailed.[1]

With the growth of Soviet nuclear power, the threat of initiating a nuclear attack against the Soviet Union—a policy developed in a different era and under different circumstances—no longer seemed credible to many. Such a strike would now likely result in the destruction of America as well. As French military strategist Pierre Gallois stated:

> If resort to force no longer merely implies the loss of an expeditionary army but hazards the very substance of national life, it is clear that such a risk can be taken for oneself—and not for others including even close allies.[2]

A new policy for defending America's allies was clearly needed. In 1962, Secretary of Defense McNamara introduced the policy of flexible response to replace the doctrine of massive retaliation. It was asserted that forces should be able to respond appropriately to all levels of threats. This meant, in effect, a renewed emphasis on conventional forces to handle any military threat from Warsaw Pact forces.

The ensuing effort to improve NATO's conventional defense capability was widely perceived in Western Europe as an attempt to decouple the use of U.S. strategic weapons from the defense of Europe. De Gaulle in particular came to mistrust the American pledge to defend Europe, and he withdrew French forces from the integrated NATO system in the summer of 1966. Nevertheless, in 1967, NATO formally adopted the doctrine of flexible response, and it remains the official policy today.

In the decade following the introduction of this new NATO doctrine, not only have the Soviets built up their intercontinental strategic forces, but they have also made similar advances in their theater forces: conventional army, air, and naval forces; battlefield tactical nuclear weapons; and intermediate-range nuclear-weapon-carrying bombers and missiles.[3] The Carter administration has expressed serious concern over this buildup and in particular over "an increasingly precarious conventional balance between NATO and the Warsaw Pact in Europe." According to Secretary of Defense Brown:

> We have also seen the expansion and modernization of the Soviet ground forces oriented toward Western Europe, with increased numbers of improved tanks, armored fighting vehicles, assault helicopters, and self-propelled artillery, and with greatly enhanced support from modern, interdiction-type aircraft. If these forces are purely defensive, we must ask why they have such strong offensive capabilities and why the Soviets in their military doctrine place so much emphasis on deception, tactical surprise, speed, and shock in their operations.[4]

The Carter administration's approach to stabilizing this "precarious balance" has been to reiterate America's commitment to the policy of "flexible response" and, as every administration since that of President Kennedy has done, to advocate strengthening NATO's conventional forces. This is in line with the American preference to deter Warsaw Pact aggression through a strong conventional defense. Because of fears of escalation to a general nuclear war, the United States demands that a high threshold or barrier be maintained against the use of any nuclear weapons.

Suggested improvements in the conventional capabilities of the NATO alliance call for increasing the readiness and capabilities of forward defense forces (to cope with the possibility of surprise attack by Pact forces stationed in Eastern Europe if they act without waiting for reinforcements); improving the rapid reinforcement capability of the United States; and integrating the alliances' forces in a more rational manner.

How effective these changes would be in countering a conventional attack by Warsaw Pact forces is uncertain. European members of NATO have never been enthusiastic about America's "conventional emphasis" approach to meeting a Warsaw Pact invasion, and the imbalance in conventional forces in Europe has always been great. Today, it is estimated in various war scenarios that the superiority of the Warsaw Pact in conventional forces ranges somewhere between two-to-one and three-to-one.[5] As presently envisioned, any attack by Warsaw Pact forces will be met far forward by an armored "covering force" to slow the enemy advance (trading space for time) until U.S. and other forces are in place to halt the invasion. A counterattack will then be launched to restore the prewar boundaries. However, even with NATO initiatives to improve the readiness and effectiveness of this covering force, there will remain a strong reliance on air units to stop the rapid advance of Warsaw Pact armor that could result from a surprise attack. Control of the air space over the battlefield thus would be critical.

At present, the Warsaw Pact has at least a two-to-one advantage over NATO in air power with 3,000 tactical combat aircraft in forward areas and another 1,000 stationed in the western U.S.S.R. within striking distance of Western Europe. In addition, the Soviets have about 500 medium-range bombers available and are deploying the new Backfire bomber. In the past, NATO has relied on qualitative superiority to offset the Pact's quantitative superiority, but this situation is changing. From a basically short-range defensive air force, the Pact air arm has been transformed into "a powerful offensive force for both close air support along the entire breadth of the battle area and deep interdiction throughout NATO Europe."[6] Because NATO air forces are vulnerable to these aircraft, there is some question whether "Soviet tactical aviation has deprived NATO's own air power of its traditional role as the great 'equalizer' of Pact preponderance on the ground."[7]

In addition to improving its air power, the Warsaw Pact has substantially increased its surface-to-air missiles (SAMs) and antiaircraft systems. Reportedly, each of the five Soviet ground armies in East Germany has about 1,000 SAMs and 1,000 antiaircraft gun systems,[8] giving them a significant low-level air defense capability to counter NATO's "equalizer" capability.

Although there are many factors that could affect the course of a war, few observers would disagree with the statement that a few days after the beginning of an attack (when second echelon Warsaw Pact forces arrived from Poland and the Soviet Union), NATO would have to relinquish substantial territory even if the war were confined to the use of conventional weapons. Some observers, such as Belgian Major General Robert Close, suggest that a concerted conventional attack could bring the Warsaw Pact armies to the Rhine within 48 hours, well before the ponderous NATO decision-making apparatus could reach a decision on the use of nuclear weapons.[9] In a review of NATO defense policy, a more generous assessment was made by the Carter administration (Presidential Review Memorandum-10), which suggested that with a substantial conventional buildup, NATO forces might be able to stabilize a front along the Weser and Lech rivers.[10] Even this optimistic analysis conceded the loss of over one-third of West Germany, making some of its most populated areas the center of the battlefield. To the Germans, this would be the "suicide war" that they have rejected. They have insisted on a forward defense that will hold losses to a few kilometers at most.

Considerations such as these have led Manfred Worner, chairman of the Defense Committee of the West German Bundestag, to conclude:

> It is impossible, therefore, under present circumstances to come up with a realistic scenario of *conventional* conflict in Central Europe that holds any prospect of a successful outcome for NATO—that is, the restoration of the territorial *status quo ante*. Achievement of this potential through a genuine conventional balance in Europe is effectively foreclosed. No NATO country is today prepared, or in a position, to pay the financial—and, in the final analysis, political—costs that are entailed.[11]

THEATER NUCLEAR WAR

To the discomfort of its allies, the United States appears intent on replaying the Second World War in its war plans. But the Soviets hold an entirely different view on how a war in Europe would be fought. Although there has been some Soviet discussion of the possibility of a conventional phase in a war with NATO, "Warsaw Pact forces are, in fact, postured and trained for theater-wide nuclear strikes against NATO nuclear and conventional military forces and for follow-up attacks by their armored and conventional forces to exploit the nuclear attack and rapidly seize NATO territory."[12]

To support their combined arms (conventional and nuclear) war-fighting doctrine, the Soviets continue to develop and deploy a modern arsenal of theater nuclear forces. These forces include sea- and land-based medium- and intermediate-range ballistic missiles,[13] tactical and intermediate-range aircraft (carrying bombs and cruise missiles), tactical rockets, surface-to-surface missiles, and sea-based cruise missiles. Most formidable of these new systems are the Backfire bomber and the 3,000-mile-range, mobile SS-20 IRBM with its three MIRVed warheads.

NATO has some 7,000 tactical nuclear weapons (under U.S. control) in the European theater to back up its conventional forces and to act as a deterrent against Soviet use of nuclear weapons. In contrast to the Warsaw Pact, most of these systems are short-range and can only be used on local battlefields. To support a theater-wide strike, NATO relies upon a small number of strip-alert aircraft, carrier-based aircraft, Pershing missiles, and 400 warheads (about 40 SLBMs) from the strategic submarine force.

If the theater nuclear forces are to act as a military deterrent, they must be able, in combination with conventional forces, to provide an effective war-fighting capability—that is, to slow an attack, stop it, and perhaps expel the aggressor. Unfortunately, NATO has no plan to use these weapons in a militarily effective fashion on the battlefield. Its conventional forces are neither trained nor equipped to fight in a nuclear environment. Furthermore, theater nuclear forces and their support systems are almost completely vulnerable to a preemptive attack by Soviet long-range theater missiles. All nuclear weapons in Western Europe are stored at about 100 easily identifiable sites that are vulnerable to both nuclear and conventional weapons.[14] There is perhaps a similar number of NATO airbases, aircraft carriers, fixed Pershing missile sites, and critical command, control, and communications centers. Similar concentrations of conventional forces exist. For example, the U.S. Army, Europe, stores over half its theater ammunitions reserves at a single location.[15] Thus, the destruction of a few hundred targets by a Soviet preemptive attack could dramatically affect the outcome of a European war.[16] Under these circumstances, the ability of NATO's theater nuclear forces to provide an effective military counter to a massive Warsaw Pact attack is extremely low.

But, in fact, these weapons are no longer intended to be militarily effective. Secretary Brown, in reaffirming what by now is the traditional view, stated that it is not at "all clear that anything approximating a traditional military campaign could be fought with nuclear weapons. Nonetheless, . . . the U.S. theater nuclear forces have a symbolic importance that transcends their direct military value. They are the visible linkage between our deployed posture and the strategic nuclear forces."[17] Thus, the United States prefers a strong conventional defense, but if this fails, its only recourse under the flexible response doctrine is a political policy of deliberate nuclear escalation up to and including the threat to use American strategic forces in a massive strike against the Soviet homeland.

INCALCULABLE RESPONSE

The United States has attempted to give credibility to its apparently incredible policy (of threatening a general nuclear war) through what nuclear strategist T. C. Schelling calls a strategy of risk manipulation.[18] Because the United States can no longer credibly threaten immediate nuclear retaliation, it can only attempt to raise uncertainties concerning its future actions. As described by Professor Richard Rosecrance:

> They [the Soviets] could not be sure that a conflict would not escalate. In Schelling's terms that "object of the threat that leaves something to chance" is to put oneself in a "slippery slope" which leads down to Armageddon. It is possible to maintain a footing, but the risks of falling are greatly increased. The enemy knows that even with the best will it may not be possible to hold on; hopefully, therefore, he is deterred from pushing further.[19]

NATO's response to the dilemma arising from the increase in Soviet power was described by General Alexander Haig, Supreme Allied Commander Europe:

> At the same time, NATO long ago recognized that trends in the strategic balance would tend over time to erode our ability to make credible, in all circumstances, a threat of escalation. Certainly strategic parity has complicated an already difficult nuclear decision. Notwithstanding, we dare not permit our adversaries to conclude that we are incapable of reaching—or, for that matter, carrying out—such decisions. To do so would only encourage them to test our determination, and thereby bring on the very situation we seek to avoid.
>
> To deprive a potential aggressor of such confidence, we have adopted a strategy which requires him to face uncertainties—uncertainties regarding how we would respond, where we would respond, and to what level of conflict his aggression might ultimately propel him. To be effective, such a strategy requires a full range of military capabilities—strategic nuclear, theatre nuclear and conventional. And it is essential to recognize that the deterrent value of those forces lies not in their independent war-fighting capabilities, but in their interdependent contribution to the uncertainty of our potential response.[20]

This de-emphasis on the military effectiveness of nuclear weapons is expressed more explicitly in a West German White Paper on defense:

> The initial use of nuclear weapons is not intended so much to bring about a military decision as to achieve political effect. The intent is to persuade the attacker to reconsider his intention, to desist his aggression, and to withdraw. At the same time, it will be impressed upon him that he risks still further escalation if he continues to attack. Such further escalation would mean that strategic nuclear weapons would be used against the attacker's own territory.[21]

The Germans expect any decision to use nuclear weapons to be made before NATO's forward defense lines are breached because they have no desire to see Germany used as a nuclear battlefield. But because the Germans have no strategic nuclear forces of their own, they must rely on the "linkage" between NATO's tactical nuclear weapons and the U.S. strategic response. The expectation is that once tactical nuclear weapons are used, the Soviet leadership will fear that a general nuclear war will "automatically" follow if they continue the war.

The basic premise of NATO defense policy appears to be unrealistic in that it seems to assume that the Soviets will not pursue an attack to the point (or at least beyond the point) where NATO is compelled to use nuclear weapons. The entire NATO policy in effect precludes the possibility of a deliberate, intentional war undertaken by the Soviets with the object of pursuing it to victory.

If the Soviets were to ignore America's implausible threats and start a "serious" war, then NATO policy would collapse into meaninglessness. Without an adequate defense to cope with a full, combined arms (nuclear and conventional) assault, defeat would likely be assured.[22]

CREDIBILITY

There is a sharp dichotomy between America's view of how to deter attacks on itself and its view of how to deter attacks on its allies. The basis of America's deterrence policy is that there must never be the slightest doubt in the minds of the Soviet leadership about the consequences of an attack on the United States—the United States will retaliate. However, with regard to attacks on America's allies, the opposite view is held—the Soviets must be completely uncertain as to the U.S. response.

Although the leadership of the Soviet Union would be faced with a great number of uncertainties if it decides to attack Western Europe, it might consider America's ultimate threat to use strategic weapons to be a bluff. From the Soviet point of view, it is difficult to imagine that a U.S. nuclear attack on the Soviet Union in defense of NATO has much credibility. For example, the United States is not in the same position as its European allies; it does not face the possibility of Soviet conquest. Although the Europeans may choose suicide over defeat, this is not the choice facing the United States. But as long as the United States cannot disarm the Soviet Union, an escalation to general nuclear war would be an act of deliberate suicide.

It can be argued, perhaps, that a U.S. threat to attack the Soviet Union is credible because the loss of Western Europe might ultimately endanger

America's security. While such a loss, whether through military conquest or the internal political process, would be a severe blow to America, it is hardly reasonable to argue that a suicidal nuclear attack on the Soviet Union would be an appropriate response.[23] The loss of Europe could have serious psychological and geopolitical ramifications, but it would not necessarily pose a serious military threat to the United States. In the nuclear age, the industrial capacity of Western Europe, even when combined with that of the Soviet Union, has no clear relevance to modern nuclear warfare. What is relevant is strategic nuclear power. The Soviet Union has enough nuclear weapons to destroy the United States today if it is willing to pay the price of its own destruction. The addition of Western Europe would have at best only a marginal impact on the capability of the Soviet Union to acquire a disarming first-strike capability.[24]

More importantly, an attack on the Soviet Union would not likely save Western Europe anyway. NATO lacks an effective defense, and Warsaw Pact military forces would probably still conquer Europe, and thus little would be accomplished other than the destruction of over 100 million Americans and perhaps between 5 and 100 million Soviet citizens.

As Soviet strategic power has grown to equal, and in some regards to surpass, American power, it has become increasingly obvious that the strategic weapons of the United States are in fact now decoupled from the defense of Europe (at least in the sense of providing deterrence by threatening a massive attack against the Soviet Union). Thus in 1975, Secretary of Defense Schlesinger noted in his annual report to Congress:

> Today such a massive retaliation against cities, in response to anything less than an all-out attack on the US and its cities appears less and less credible.[25]

In his 1976 report, he also stated:

> To threaten to blow up all of an opponent's cities, short of an attack on our cities, is hardly an acceptable strategy, and in most circumstances the credibility of the threat would be close to zero, especially against a nation which could retaliate against our cities in kind. Granting the need for such a withheld force in order to deter coercive attacks against our cities, we must surely go on to something else if our deterrent is to be credible over a wide range of contingencies.[26]

LIMITED NUCLEAR OPTIONS

It is, indeed, imperative that the United States go on to something else if an effective defense for Western Europe is to be achieved. However, most efforts to date have not really sought something else but have attempted to restore credibility to the present inherently incredible flexible response policy. Secretary Schlesinger's advocacy of "limited nuclear options" is an example of an attempt to recouple U.S. strategic weapons to the NATO deterrence policy.

One possible approach to making the U.S. threat to launch a nuclear attack credible is to arrange the threat and associated actions in such a way that should the United States attack, no massive response would be called for. By limiting the possibility of catastrophic consequences, the initiation of nuclear war will appear more "reasonable" and consequently more credible.

When introduced by Secretary Schlesinger, the idea of achieving the flexibility to make limited nuclear strikes (rather than massive ones only) was presented primarily as an attempt to develop a deterrent against the launching of limited nuclear attacks by the Soviet Union against the United States. This policy generated heated debate because it was feared that it would lower the nuclear threshold and thus increase the chances for an all-out nuclear war.[27] However, if the main thrust of the policy had been only to develop the capability to respond to limited attacks against the United States, there would undoubtedly have been little controversy.

The most significant aspect of the Schlesinger doctrine was that the United States would have had the capability to initiate limited nuclear options (LNOs). Because an attack would have been limited and deemed an appropriate response to Soviet actions (say, a conventional attack on Europe), it was felt that a limited attack would not automatically have led to a full-scale war between the two superpowers. This attack would, however, have demonstrated that the United States was willing to risk escalation if the Soviets did not desist. Thus, the real objective of the LNO policy was to restore the credibility of America's nuclear umbrella by "recoupling" America's strategic nuclear weapons to the defense of Europe.

Although it represented an interesting attempt to solve the dilemma facing the policy of extended deterrence, the Schlesinger LNO doctrine seems unlikely to prove any more credible than previous policies for several reasons. A limited nuclear attack policy requires a high level of communication: the Soviets must understand what the United States is doing and what it intends to do. Also, since the attack is limited, the Soviets might be able to defend against it, and it thus might constitute no deterrent at all. But foremost, the United States is as vulnerable (if not more so) to limited responses as the Soviet Union, and, in addition, the United States may not possess the political institutions capable of pursuing a series of nuclear exchanges. Once nuclear weapons explode on the United States in response to a limited strike on the Soviet Union, there may be overwhelming public pressure to discontinue those attacks. Soviet leaders are not likely to be subject to similar pressures.

CONCLUSION

The political, economic, and cultural ties between America and Europe have a long history. The survival of these states as free and independent nations remains a vital and important goal of American foreign and defense policies. However, there appears to be no way to restore credibility to the present policy of extended deterrence. Furthermore, it is dangerous to rely on an unbelievable threat to deter aggression while at the same time failing to provide an adequate defense. In a future crisis, this combination may prove too tempting to the Soviet Union. As British military historian Liddell Hart pointed out:

> Clumsy efforts to forestall a feared aggression have too often provoked it—particularly where politically inspired moves have jumped beyond strategic possibilities. There have been too many recent examples. Chamberlain's "Guarantee" to Poland, in 1939, a sudden reversal of his policy of appeasement, had the obvious effect of combining provocation with temptation. No dictator, especially one like Hitler, could be expected to submit to such a slap in the face. At the same time the palpable impossibility of Britain giving any effective help to a country so remote as Poland tempted him to show the futility of the guarantee. Yet the captured German archives show that Hitler had not intended to deal with Poland in 1939, and that he only made up his mind to attack her *after* Chamberlain had made his unfulfillable offer of support. It acted like throwing down a gauntlet, or waving the proverbial red rag in the face of a bull. So the guarantee merely guaranteed that war would start at the time and in the circumstances most disadvantageous for the Western Powers.[28]

While, of course, the Allies eventually prevailed over Germany, the long-term prospect of this occurring was not sufficient to deter Hitler. The immediate gain was too obvious, and the long-term threat from Britain and France, too unbelievable. Today, guarantees by the United States for European security may seem even less credible.

VI

Deterrence by Denial and Defense

The overriding objective of U.S. strategic policy is to deter an attack on the United States or its allies. To this end, it is necessary to maintain a survivable second-strike capability. However, a strategy of assured destruction to meet all contingencies is clearly inadequate in an era when the Soviet Union has an assured-destruction capability of its own. If deterrence fails at some level lower than an all-out city attack, the United States will have to acquiesce in Soviet actions or push on to Armageddon. America's flexible response doctrine and, more recently, the policy of limited nuclear options were attempts to cope with these new circumstances. However, since threats of escalation are mutually deterring, it is important for the United States to devise a new strategy to meet the realities of Soviet power.

To maintain a continuum of deterrence, a cohesive doctrine of denial and defense that integrates conventional, theater nuclear, and strategic forces is needed. With a policy of flexibility and restraint, the United States would be prepared to meet the Soviet challenge at whatever level the Soviets choose, either at the theater level or at the strategic level. Instead of threatening nuclear escalation, which the Soviets might well conclude was a bluff, the United States would confront the Soviets with the prospect of defeat. If the Soviets perceived that they would be denied the gains of a war (even one for which they were willing to take great risks), the chances of a deliberate attack would be diminished, and deterrence would be strengthened.

This concluding chapter discusses the application of this doctrine to the theater level (Western Europe) and to a nuclear exchange between the U.S. and U.S.S.R. Because the possibility always exists that deterrence could fail, a policy that might inhibit attacks on civilian populations is also suggested.

DEFENSE OF WESTERN EUROPE

The emphasis on conventional forces in NATO's flexible response doctrine consistently ignores the Soviets' widely proclaimed doctrine of preemptive use of nuclear weapons.[1] Although the possibility of war may be small, Soviet aggression against the West would have strong implications not only for the fate of Western Europe but for that of the Soviet Union as well. Soviet ideological and nationalistic doctrines have always demanded that the greatest of caution be exercised—neither the revolution nor the state must be risked on adventuristic policies. Any Soviet attack on the West would undoubtedly be backed by overwhelming military superiority and be aimed at a quick victory. If war comes, the primary concern of the Soviets is not likely to be the particular instruments of war but rather victory. The primary "firebreak" will not be the use of nuclear weapons but the decision to go to war. In the words of military historian and strategist Bernard Brodie:

> Can anyone believe, with confidence, that the Soviet Union would challenge us to so deadly a duel and yet leave the choice of weapons entirely to us? Can anyone seriously think that if the Russians launched such an attack, they would not be determined to win it as quickly as possible by offensive action, with whatever weapons were necessary to accomplish that victory? Surely we do not need to be told—although their public discussion of strategic affairs does, in fact, tell us—that they would indeed be so determined.[2]

If NATO defense policy is to have a deterrent effect, it must be able to cope with a serious Soviet attack. To be effective, a defense must rely (at least as a backup) on the battlefield use of nuclear weapons, not just as a symbolic gesture but as a means of stopping and destroying the invaders. This would require a drastic revision of defense plans and perhaps a change in the underlying premises of NATO's flexible response doctrine.

Prerequisite for Change: A No-First-Offensive-Use Policy

The use of nuclear weapons is so intimately connected with a policy of deliberate escalation that fears that any use of nuclear weapons will automatically lead to a complete holocaust are strong. Although this policy is designed to inhibit the Soviet Union, it is self-paralyzing for the West.

This problem is illustrated by the controversy over the so-called neutron bomb or enhanced radiation weapon, which the news media represented as being "designed to kill people and not buildings." This representation created an outcry over the sinister distortion of values involved in this particular weapon—a weapon designed as it were to kill off populations while leaving real estate intact.

In fact, the purpose of the neutron bomb is not to kill the general population but rather to save it. This weapon is designed for battlefield use against armored Warsaw Pact invasion forces. Because it is to be used primarily as a defensive weapon on Western European territory, one of its main functions is to reduce any unintentional civilian damage ("collateral effects") caused by a nuclear explosion. To achieve this, the explosive power of the weapon is reduced some five to ten times below that of other tactical nuclear weapons. The design relies primarily on the fusion process (the hydrogen bomb) rather than on the fission process used by most tactical weapons.[3] The fusion process creates an abundance of high-energy neutrons that can penetrate the armor of a tank and kill its crew. Because it is primarily a fusion weapon, there are few radioactive by-products that lead to fallout that could kill civilians. And because it has a low yield, the blast and heat from the weapon are relatively short-range, which also protects civilians in the neighborhood of a battlefield.[4]

Although the emotional issues have served as a focus for protest, the real objection to the neutron bomb is that it may be effective at what it is designed for—to fight wars. Because it is a small weapon, it can be used on a battlefield to halt enemy advances without, at the same time, posing a threat to the civilian population. Because older tactical nuclear systems are more dangerous to the civilian population, the new system would be much more credible as a defensive weapon. Its critics fear that if the neutron bomb is actually useful, there will be stronger pressure to use it.

American opponents of the bomb consider this dangerous because it lowers the nuclear threshold, a threshold which once crossed could lead (under flexible response) to all-out nuclear war between the U.S. and U.S.S.R. Europeans oppose the neutron bomb for the opposite reason: if the weapon is truly effective, the United States may move towards a policy based on defense rather than on threats of escalation, which would even more visibly decouple America's strategic weapons from NATO.

Thus, within the framework of the present policy, any effort to generate an effective alternative defense policy is met by strong pressures and fears from both sides of the Atlantic, although often for different reasons. The only way to escape this paralyzing impasse is to change the framework.

The flexible response system has not only prevented the search for alternative policies, it also raises many moral questions that may in the future undercut the whole defense of Europe. Even the morality of America's second-strike policy is often questioned because it threatens to destroy millions of civilians. There are indeed serious moral questions inherent in that policy, although some hold that the circumstances in which the policy would be implemented (that is, only after American society itself had been attacked) mitigate, if not justify, the policy. However, there would seem to be no mitigating circumstances in the case of an attack initiated by the United States.

Perhaps the most serious drawback to present NATO policy is that an attack on the Soviet Union might lead to the destruction of over 100 million Americans by a Soviet retaliatory strike. There is no way to justify such a policy on either pragmatic or moral grounds. Defense of an ally, no matter how valuable, cannot justify the destruction of one's own society.

Because of these problems, the present flexible response policy should be fundamentally changed. As a prelude to this change, the United States should adopt a policy of "no first *offensive* use" of nuclear weapons.[5] That is, it will not initiate nuclear strikes against the Soviet Union. More generally, NATO should renounce the use of nuclear weapons on Warsaw Pact territory as long as Warsaw Pact forces do not use nuclear weapons on NATO territory.

The renunciation of a first strike does not mean that NATO should renounce the first use of nuclear weapons. If a country is attacked, it should, of course, be free to choose what weapons it will use to defend itself.[6] If militarily effective nuclear weapons are necessary for a defense, they should be used as long as they are confined to NATO territory. Of course, if the Warsaw Pact attacked NATO with nuclear weapons, NATO's nuclear strikes could naturally be extended into Pact countries. But they should be confined to military targets. Strikes against civilians could invite attacks on Western European and American cities and would only make it more difficult to end the fighting.[7]

Breaking the link between a defense of Europe and the threat of an American initiated attack on the Soviet Union would stimulate debates on more rational alternatives.[8] Neither the exploration nor the implementation of alternatives can be accomplished as long as discussions of policies are confined within the old framework.

Requirements for Defense

To be effective as a deterrent, any defense of Europe must be able to cope with the full range of Soviet military capabilities, both conventional and nuclear. In principle, being defensively rather than offensively oriented makes NATO's task easier than that of the Warsaw Pact. NATO need not create a massive war machine that can push all the way to Moscow; NATO need not seek victory, only Soviet defeat. Or more precisely, NATO need only raise the prospect of that defeat to a level that is unacceptably high for the Soviets.

Deterrence by Denial and Defense 117

To be credible as a deterrent, a NATO defense policy must be one that NATO is willing to implement if put to the test. Thus, the policy must be nonsuicidal; that is, its implementation must not entail the destruction of Western Europe. In practice, this would mean conducting and containing the primary battle as far forward (along the West German–East German/Czechoslovakian border) as possible. The defense must be able to stop a surprise attack and to provide sufficient time for NATO to make a decision on the use of nuclear weapons if they are required. This time would be necessary only to evaluate the scope of the attack on the slight possibility that it was an unauthorized, accidental, or inadvertent small-scale incursion. If it were a full-scale attack, the use of nuclear weapons in a defensive mode to stop the assault would almost automatically be authorized. Of course, if the initial invasion involved Warsaw Pact use of nuclear weapons, the deliberation time required would be minimal. Finally, because the defense must be able to cope with a surprise attack, the necessary forces would have to be far more survivable than at present.

All of these considerations suggest that a significant reorientation of strategy, forces, and doctrine is necessary in order to provide a credible war-fighting deterrent for NATO. Although a number of useful approaches may evolve once the doctrine of flexible response is dropped, the following approach is suggested as one that has a reasonable chance of meeting the requirements outlined above.[9]

A New Defense Concept: The Nuclear-Conventional Barrier

One possible approach to a forward defense of NATO's Central Region would contain the following elements:[10]

1. A hardened, fortified barrier along the eastern border of West Germany to blunt a surprise Warsaw Pact armored blitzkrieg. This barrier would delay the Pact advance and give NATO time to evaluate the scope of the attack and to decide whether the defensive use of nuclear weapons would be necessary. The barrier would also compel the Pact to concentrate its forces in an attempt to penetrate the defense and would thus provide lucrative targets for nuclear and chemical weapons. The primary goals would be to contain the battle along the less densely populated barrier zone and to destroy the invading army. The barrier would be manned by conventionally armed troops and supported by rearward-based mobile forces (perhaps including U.S. strategic systems) armed with conventional and nuclear firepower.

2. A highly mobile counterstrike force with strong firepower capability to cope with any penetrations of the barrier.
3. Highly dispersed conventional and nuclear forces to ensure greater survivability. These forces (particularly the nuclear systems) could be quickly reinforced by U.S. based systems.

The barrier system is envisioned as lying within ten miles of the West German border. It would consist of a layer of antitank and antipersonnel barriers reinforced by three rows of hardened, manned fortifications. Additional fire support would be supplied by widely dispersed forces to the rear of the barrier. The obstacle barrier would use all the advantages of the natural terrain and would be about 100 meters deep and consist of antitank and antipersonnel minefields, armored-vehicle barriers, and antitank ditches with wire entanglements. An extensive array of preemplaced sensors to facilitate the targeting of the invaders would be placed throughout the barrier and in the area between the barrier and the border. The obstacle field would be covered by direct-fire weapons placed in the fortifications and by indirect artillery fire and helicopter-delivered munitions. The manned fortifications would consist of hardened underground bunkers (able to resist around 100 psi from a nuclear explosion) that would contain a variety of defensive weapons such as wire-guided antitank missiles and (as a backup) antitank rocket systems. These bunkers would be about 500 meters apart along a line with three separate rows, each row also being about 500 meters apart. The bunkers would be mutually supportive and all would be connected by hardened tunnels. In addition, for each bunker there would be perhaps six austere satellite "foxhole" bunkers for short-range anti-tank engagements. Finally, the whole barrier belt would be supported by hardened air defense weapons within the belt and mobile air defense units behind the belt.

The number of belts (obstacles plus fortifications) in any particular area of Germany would depend upon the nature of the terrain and its value to the Warsaw Pact as an avenue of attack. In some areas, such as the North German Plain and the Fulda Gap (about 50 miles northeast of Frankfurt), up to three belts, each perhaps two miles apart, might be required to prevent a rapid breakthrough and penetration.

To overcome this barrier, the Soviets would probably have to attack with nuclear weapons. Because the fortifications would be hardened, this would require a large number of nuclear weapons in order to break through over a significantly large area. But even this might not ensure a rapid penetration. If the barrier were built to take advantage of the terrain, nuclear explosions could create their own obstacles. Rock slides and knocked over trees can be particularly bothersome to advancing tank armies.

In areas where terrain features could not be exploited, the obstacle barrier could be seeded with sodium carbonate (soda ash), which becomes very radioactive when exposed to the neutrons from a nuclear explosion. In this way, a Soviet nuclear attack on the barrier could create a radioactive barrier that could make the area unsafe for obstacle removal for many hours and possibly delay the "blitzkrieg" for several days.

If the Soviets managed to blast a hole in the barrier, any attempt to move through it in force could be countered by NATO's own conventional and nuclear counterattack against the by then very concentrated Pact army.[11] Nuclear fire support could be provided by mobile units with nuclear artillery, short-range ballistic and cruise missiles, helicopters, and tactical aircraft.[12] Artillery and small missiles (with or without their truck-launchers) might initially be housed in the extensive tunnel network of the barrier to insure their survivability. These forces could be supplemented, if necessary, by a number of missile-carrying aircraft on continuous airborne alert, possibly operating from the European-based aircraft carriers. Also, U.S. strategic missiles (most likely, submarine-based missiles) could be used to deliver nuclear land mines to reclose the gap, or, because progress through the devastated barrier region could be relatively slow, the missiles might be directed against the advancing Pact army itself. These forces could be expected to hold at least for the few hours necessary for U.S.-based bombers and cargo planes to arrive with new battlefield nuclear weapons.[13]

To meet any penetrations, either through the barrier or over it with airborne units, a highly mobile armored counterstrike force capable of bringing massive firepower to bear on the enemy would be available.[14] In peacetime, this force could be widely dispersed to insure greater survivability.

The cost of a 1,860 km belt system (including bunkers, tunnels, armored vehicle barriers, mine fields, weapons, equipment, and land) is estimated at around $5 billion.[15] This compares with an annual NATO budget of around $60 billion (1975). Because this concept is in sharp contrast to the conventional emphasis of the present doctrine in which a long battle along the lines of World War II is envisioned (on the hope that the Soviets do not win in the first days), a restructuring of NATO's military forces would be necessary. De-emphasizing many of the more vulnerable elements of NATO forces, such as highly sophisticated and very expensive aircraft, and emphasizing nuclear firepower could result in considerable savings. A Brookings Institution study suggested that a nuclear-emphasis force could save around $5 billion annually compared with a conventional-emphasis program.[16] Although the concept proposed here differs from that advocated in the Brookings study, the cost savings are at least indicative of what could be accomplished by a change in doctrine. However, the primary purpose in advocating a change is to develop a viable defense of Western Europe rather than merely to save money.

Although the barrier concept may not be the only solution to the problem, it does illustrate that a defense against a Warsaw Pact nuclear-supported, armored blitzkrieg is likely to be feasible, especially if the defense is designed around the early use of nuclear weapons.[17] As a French analyst of military affairs, Colonel Marc Geneste, has written concerning a similar concept:

> Surface movement (i.e., offense)—hampered by engineering obstacles, traps, mine fields, etc., faced with the latest antitank devices (forcing attackers' concentrations heavier than ever) and the area destructiveness of tactical nuclear weapons (the power of which could nullify the effects of dispersion)—seems almost infeasible. Today movement is eclipsed by its arch foe, firepower, as in World War I, and the advantage of offense versus defense is cancelled out, provided the defender can survive an initial "carpet bombing" of nuclear weapons. For the time being, and for the foreseeable future, offense has lost to defense. . . . Today is the time of the panzer's twilight, and we should witness the end of the "Blitzkrieg War" in the history of modern warfare, until such time as movement catches up with firepower, which is presently not in sight.[18]

Objections to a nuclear defense are often raised because of the fear that it will necessarily result in widespread civilian destruction. Soviet tactics call for a quick breakthrough of NATO's "screening" forces to allow Soviet forces to mix with the local population. Thus, previous analyses have envisioned a nuclear war fought throughout Germany. The barrier, however, allows the nuclear engagement to occur along the less densely populated German border.

Some observers also fear that an initial Soviet nuclear counterforce strike in Europe would be rather indiscriminate and cause mass destruction. However, Soviet publications in recent years have indicated the desirability of discriminate strikes that avoid unnecessary civilian damage.[19] Under Soviet doctrine, all military operations are subordinate to the political objectives of a war. If the Soviets initiate a war, their aim is unlikely to be the physical destruction of Western Europe—their most logical objective would be to capture it as intact as possible.[20]

NATO also has some control over damage to civilians. By moving its military forces away from heavily populated areas, NATO could greatly reduce the "collateral" damage to civilians from a Soviet preemptive nuclear strike. NATO could also modernize its tactical nuclear weapon stockpile, replacing some of the larger yield weapons with small-yield "enhanced radiation" weapons that greatly reduce the area of destruction while at the same time being militarily effective.

These qualifications are not meant to imply that a war in Europe could be fought without major damage. Any war, whether nuclear or conventional, would undoubtedly result in hundreds of thousands, if not millions, of casualties.[21] Of this there is little doubt. However, the important concern is not how to fight a low-cost war, but how to deter any war. And to deter a war, one must be willing to fight. The relevant question is which is more likely to deter the Soviets: a defense that envisions a willingness to employ nuclear weapons on the battlefield along with a credible, nonsuicidal plan for doing so or a conventional-emphasis defense that would undoubtedly collapse under a Soviet nuclear assault. It is clear that a strategy that presents the Soviets with a significant risk of defeat on the battlefield is the more prudent of the two.

A European Deterrent

Although a defense of Europe may be technically feasible, Washington's fear of nuclear escalation may preclude a move toward adoption of such a policy. But the continuation of the present policy poses a threat to both American and European interests. If no effective defense policy can be achieved under present institutional arrangements, it may be advantageous to both the United States and its European allies for the Europeans to assume primary responsibility for their own defense.

The development of a European defense may, of course, be more difficult to accomplish than a shift in NATO defense policy. To most observers, this solution presupposes some political confederation of European states, with a joint Western European Commander. This proposal has always led to an impasse because of the problem of nuclear sharing. All parties recognize the particularly sensitive problems that prevent West Germany from obtaining direct control over nuclear weapons, even within a confederation. Germany, moreover, does not desire nuclear weapons of its own. At the same time, Germany must have some concern about leaving its fate entirely in the hands of Britain and France, which do have nuclear weapons. The concept of deterring Soviet attacks by a nuclear barrier defense (manned by European forces) may provide the key to overcoming these heretofore insurmountable political problems.

A European policy based primarily on defense rather than retaliation would place the security of West Germany and Europe in the hands of the entire confederation instead of simply in the hands of the two Western

European nuclear powers.[22] Having a voice in the formulation and execution of its own defense could give Germany the confidence to join a European union. A purely defensive posture, as would be indicated by the construction of a fortified barrier, would set the appropriate tone and lay the foundation for the development of a united Europe. All members of the confederation would take an active part in the defense—at first as separate nations and later as a "European" force. The short-range, low-yield nuclear weapons necessary for the defense of the barrier could be stationed in Germany under European control, or perhaps with a two-key system with joint European and German control.[23] Longer range weapons capable of striking the Soviet Union (although they would most likely be used to support the barrier) could remain in French and British hands to allay whatever fears that would arise from German possession of these weapons.

The development of a defense of this type is certainly within the resources of Western Europe, particularly with the aid of the United States. What has been lacking is the political will on the part of the Europeans to take the responsibility for their own defense. The development of the requisite political institutions has not materialized, and the dream of a united Europe remains unrealized. To many observers, there is a close connection between these two situations. A fundamental characteristic of a sovereign power is the control over its own defense. Having abdicated this control to some degree, the Europeans have felt compelled to put relations with the United States ahead of all other considerations. In the words of French political analyst Michel Tatu: "In the last analysis, the main obstacle to European unity is Europe's military dependence on the United States and, among other things, the presence of American troops on the Continent."[24]

Although America's presence in Europe may be a strong impediment to European unity, it is obviously not the only one. The forces of nationalism remain strong in spite of a common European culture and heritage. However, as long as Europeans cling to the illusion that America's nuclear umbrella is all that is required to protect them from Soviet expansionism, they are not likely to submerge their national differences and to develop a common defense. An announcement of an American plan to leave the defense of Europe primarily to the Europeans could have a sobering effect on Europe, creating the atmosphere required for unification.

The disengagement of America from the European defense structure would require delicate diplomatic maneuvering, and there would be many pressures against such a move. Europeans have grown accustomed to thinking of themselves as small powers and are reluctant to surrender the feeling of security that comes from America's long presence there. America, for its part, would probably find it difficult to give up the power and influence that it holds in NATO councils. Moreover, many Americans would not look magnanimously on the creation of a strong Europe that could compete diplomatically and economically with the United States.

These views are shortsighted, however. The best hope for maintaining Western European independence (short of relying upon the benevolence of the Soviet Union) may lie in the creation of a strong European defense. Furthermore, the creation of an independent power on the European continent may in the long run be America's best hope to counter the spread of Soviet power.

American disengagement would not mean a break in the NATO alliance but a recognition of the need to deal with Europe as an independent and equal partner. The change should not be precipitous, and some transition period would be required to allow for the necessary adjustments in defenses as well as political institutions. Although there might be support for this move in Europe, it is something that Europeans are not likely to initiate; the leadership for this change would have to come from America.

Unless some change is made in the flexible response doctrine, it may, because of its weakness, eventually become a political liability for the United States. This could cause a precipitous withdrawal from Europe that could greatly lessen the chances for the creation of a united Europe. As long as America is committed to the defense of Western Europe, it should insist on the development of either a credible (nuclear) NATO policy or, if this is politically untenable, an independent European deterrent. In the long run, it would appear in the best interests of both America and Europe if America supported both—a credible defense and an American disengagement to encourage European union.

WAR-FIGHTING

The previous section dealt with situations in which war is confined primarily to the European theater. As long as the United States prudently provides for the survival of its strategic forces, there would seem to be little incentive for the Soviets to combine an attack on Europe with an attack on the United States because of the dangers of escalation. Whether the Soviets would risk such an attack would probably depend on their views on the effectiveness of their counterforce attack, their fears of a U.S. preemptive attack, and their estimate of the capability of U.S. strategic weapons to deny them their objectives. If a Soviet counterforce attack on the United States should occur, the primary objectives of the U.S. strategic response should be the defeat of Warsaw Pact military forces. Any force above that necessary to maintain a counterthreat to Soviet cities should be used for war-fighting to the extent that is possible.

War-fighting usually has the connotation of massive counterforce strikes against strategic, tactical nuclear, and conventional military forces throughout the Soviet Union. But this approach to war-fighting may not be helpful. In the first place, despite claims of overkill, the number of discretionary strategic weapons available (above the withheld counter-city force) may not be great, particularly if the Soviets launch a surprise counterforce attack. Under these circumstances, the United States would have to be selective in its targeting. As a war advances, relative nuclear strengths may play an important role in assuring that intrawar deterrence of city attacks is maintained. In addition, the maintenance of a reserve force is necessary to insure that any bargaining to end the war will not occur under completely unfavorable conditions. Secondly, the launching of a U.S. strategic attack against conventional and theater nuclear forces throughout the Soviet Union may be a futile gesture. Much of their military is mobile and undoubtedly would move if war were imminent. Although there are a number of valuable fixed targets, most of U.S. strategic weapons might be wasted on empty barracks.[25]

An attack on strategic forces, unless it is possible to disarm the Soviets (and thus remove the threat to American cities), may not be an effective use of U.S. strategic weapons.[26] In a war of attrition, the United States could conceivably begin to destroy a significant number of the Soviet strategic forces. However, it is unlikely that either side would wait to be disarmed of their long-range weapons. To do so would deprive them of the bargaining chips needed to maintain intrawar deterrence against city attacks. If a U.S. counterforce campaign looked as if it were succeeding, the Soviets would have an incentive to begin coercive bargaining by escalation to (limited) city attacks. Thus, U.S. strategy might prove counterproductive unless it could disarm the Soviets in one quick attack, which would be most unlikely.

If war between the United States and the Soviet Union should come, the main focus of the struggle will probably be the battle for Europe. If the Soviet military machine is to be defeated, it will most likely be defeated where it can be engaged—on the battlefield. The possibility of a successful U.S. attack is much greater close to NATO's own lines rather than in the vast expanse of the Soviet Union. These local targets are also more important because they have a direct bearing on whether the Soviets achieve their objectives.

In the European land battle, strategic forces could play an important role, but only if integrated into an effective theater defense (e.g., they could be used to support a barrier defense as previously suggested). Without a comprehensive NATO war-fighting plan, the strategic forces would be of little military value in themselves and thus of limited deterrence value.

Ultimately, deterrence of war between the United States and the Soviet Union may depend as much, if not more, on the theater forces as the strategic ones.

Objections to War-Fighting

Critics of war-fighting strategies fear that such doctrines create the illusion that low casualty, surgically fought wars are possible and that to the extent that this illusion is believed, it lowers inhibitions against use of nuclear weapons. They feel that this increases the possibility of the all-out war that the United States is trying to deter.

Many of these concerns are understandable since much of the discussion in recent years of countermilitary and countereconomic strategies that fall short of an all-out war has focused not on deterring attacks on the United States but rather on restoring credibility to America's tattered nuclear umbrella. That is, under certain circumstances, the United States, to protect its "vital interests," would be prepared to initiate nuclear war at least on a limited scale.

But a war-fighting doctrine need not be coupled with a provocative threat to initiate nuclear strikes. As noted earlier, it is in the interests of both the United States and NATO that they should announce a policy of no use of nuclear weapons on Warsaw Pact territory as long as the other side reciprocates. Under these circumstances, the development of capabilities to respond to aggression in a flexible and credible manner, even to the point of having some war-fighting capability, should cause few objections.

CIVILIAN POPULATIONS AND NUCLEAR WAR

The central purpose of a nation's security policy is the defense of the lives and property of its citizens. This requires a policy of restraint in which every step is taken to reduce the possibility of war. If, despite everything, deterrence fails, the objective should be to bring a quick end to the conflict with the lowest possible level of damage and casualties on all sides. In addition to a policy of deterrence by denial and defense coupled with a restrained no-first-offensive-use doctrine, steps should be taken to develop and strengthen inhibitions against attacks on noncombatants.

With the introduction of the airplane to warfare, there arose the possibility of total war. This possibility generated serious concern during the 1920s and 1930s, and the nations of the world generally renounced the terror bombing of civilian populations. Military sentiment in America was overwhelmingly opposed to attacks on innocent civilians, and military planning excluded such attacks.

With the coming of war in Europe in 1939, President Roosevelt called upon the belligerents to adhere to international law and to refrain from attacks on civilians. For some time, both sides acted with restraint.[27] But as the war progressed, restraints broke down, and civilian populations lay open to enemy bombers. Area (people-killing) attacks became common. However, for most of the war (until 1945), the Americans refused to join the British in these area attacks but instead concentrated on precision bombing attacks on German war industries.

In the Pacific, both sides were also initially restrained. When the Japanese attacked Pearl Harbor, they were careful to attack only military targets, and only one stray bomb fell on Honolulu. But in contrast to the war in Europe, American restraint broke down quickly in the war against Japan. From the incendiary attacks on Tokyo to the nuclear attacks made without warning on Hiroshima and Nagasaki, civilians as well as industries became targets.

In retrospect, World War II, although terrible in the destruction it caused, was perhaps even more damaging to Western civilization because the idea of total war—war against the guilty and innocent alike—regained a foothold. While total war was then only a theoretical possibility, the advent of nuclear weapons can make that possibility a reality.

The American policy of deterrence through threats of retaliation against Soviet cities evolved over a number of years. By the early 1960s, Secretary of Defense McNamara had formulated a policy of assured destruction in which he suggested that the capability to destroy 25 to 30 percent of the Soviet population and one-half to two-thirds of Soviet industry would serve as an effective deterrent.

With the Nixon administration came a shift in policy. Targeting to prevent rapid Soviet recovery after a nuclear war became the new goal. Although this policy set new criteria for measuring the success of retaliation (destruction of some high percentage of the economic, political, and military assets of a country), actual changes in the National War Plan (the Single Integrated Operational Plan or SIOP) were probably minimal. Military targets have long been a part of the SIOP, and the new policy only serves to acknowledge this fact openly. Although residential areas are no longer directly targeted, collateral civilian casualties would undoubtedly be comparable to previous expectations under the McNamara criterion. Thus, the threat to civilian populations still remains; the casualties are just no longer quantified.

The dilemmas—both moral and practical—that result from the continued reliance on a doctrine that threatens to destroy civilian populations in the event of war have often been discussed, if not resolved.[28] Retaliating against innocent civilians (and we must assume that the Soviet population has little or no control over the actions of the Communist party leadership) runs counter to Western traditions of justice and decency.[29] Furthermore, as a practical matter, if deterrence fails, this policy will almost inevitably lead to catastrophe for the United States. However, some observers, such as Wolfgang Panofsky, have argued that the massive nuclear arsenals of the Soviet Union and the United States preclude the alteration of the mutual hostage relationship between the two populations.[30] But it is precisely because the mutual hostage relationship is inherent in the system that everything possible must be done to break the "inevitability" of counterpopulation attacks.

An early attempt to set guidelines for a policy of restraint was provided by Secretary McNamara, who was probably the first major public official to advocate a policy of placing cities off limits in a nuclear war. In his Ann Arbor address in 1962, McNamara stated:

> The U.S. has come to the conclusion that to the extent feasible, basic military strategy in a possible general nuclear war should be approached in much the same way that the more conventional military operations have been regarded in the past. That is to say, principal military objectives, in the event of a nuclear war stemming from a major attack on the Alliance, should be the destruction of the enemy's military forces, not of his civilian population.
>
> The very strength and nature of the Alliance forces make it possible for us to retain, even in the face of a massive surprise attack, sufficient reserve striking power to destroy an enemy society if driven to it. In other words, we are giving a possible opponent the strongest imaginable incentive to refrain from striking our own cities.[31]

This new controlled response doctrine, which included both counterforce and no-cities policies, was designed primarily to restore the weakened credibility of America's promise to defend Europe with an all-out attack against the U.S.S.R. If attacks on cities could be precluded, it would be possible (without great risk) to launch a massive counterforce damage-limiting strike against the relatively small Soviet strategic force. It was hoped that this attack would leave the United States in a position to coerce the Soviet Union into submission. This policy had some credibility because at that time a disarming attack might have been possible, particularly in a war of attrition fought over a fairly lengthy period of time.

However, this policy faced significant opposition. The other members of NATO opposed the strategy because they saw it as increasing the chances for making Europe a nuclear battlefield while American and Soviet cities remained safe. Opposition also came from those who saw the counterforce strategy as indistinguishable from a first-strike posture, particularly when the Kennedy administration explicitly refused to rule out a first strike. Indeed, in order to be effective in insuring that the damage to the United States would be limited, it would be essential for the United States to attack Soviet weapons before they were launched. Presumably, this attack would only have been in response to Soviet aggression in Europe.

In addition to the American and NATO criticisms, the Soviets refused to cooperate. Because the object was to disarm the then much weaker Soviet Union, they perceived the strategy as an attempt by the United States to retain a unilateral coercive advantage and publicly rejected the idea that nuclear war could be limited.

As the Soviets built more ICBMs and more strategic missile submarines, McNamara gradually de-emphasized the damage-limiting strategy (holding it to be infeasible) and relied more heavily on the threat of assured destruction to deter Soviet attacks on the United States and NATO. Because an effective counterforce capability was lacking, the no-cities policy gradually disappeared as an official doctrine.

The two aspects of controlled response, damage-limiting counterforce and no-cities, should be separated. In principle, either or both strategies could be followed in an attempt to prevent an enemy from using his weapons against American cities. One strategy works through forcible disarmament; the other, by providing the enemy with an incentive not to attack even if he has the weapons to do so. Although the two strategies can be complementary, they are not necessarily linked; in some cases, they may even be incompatible. For example, a massive counterforce campaign is not only likely to confuse the enemy regarding the other side's intentions (by disrupting communications and distorting his understanding of what is actually taking place), but it could also blur the distinction between strictly military targets and civilian targets. In an attempted disarming attack, many millions of civilians might be killed (if they were unprepared), and this could significantly lower incentives to be restrained or to bring the war to an early conclusion.

Since there is little prospect of the United States obtaining a significant damage-limiting capability (even in a first strike), counterforce strikes for this purpose offer little hope of American civilians being spared. If damage is to be limited, it will have to result from Soviet restraint. Thus, it is not just a moral concern over attacking Soviet noncombatants that suggests a policy of restraint, but also a concern for American self-interest.

Thus, the United States should reaffirm that a policy of deliberate attacks on noncombatants is inconsistent with international law, human rights, and common decency. It should develop a targeting doctrine that precludes such attacks and call upon all nations to renounce civilian attacks. If deterrence fails and war ensues, any U.S. threat to attack Soviet cities makes little military sense, particularly in the early stages of a war. Economic factors are likely to become important only if the war becomes protracted, as was the case in World War II. In the nuclear age, the potential for destruction is so great that the military issue is likely to be resolved fairly quickly—perhaps not in hours, but very likely in a matter of days or weeks. The kind of policy that the United States should adopt, a war-fighting strategy geared to defeating Soviet military actions, has already been discussed. Traditional military objectives are likely to seem far more important than cities if war actually breaks out.[32]

A policy that precludes attacks on civilians is not only more consistent with American ideals, it also offers the possibility of actually containing and stopping the war at a low level. But, it is argued, the restraint shown by the United States may not be reciprocated by the Soviet Union. The critics are correct in pointing out that present technology does not allow an escape from this threat (even though it could be mitigated to some degree by civil defense). Thus, the United States should offer every incentive to the Soviet Union to prevent it from attacking U.S. civilians. By initiating attacks on Soviet cities, the United States would remove both the coercive power it may have over the Soviets and the reason for their own restraint. Once their cities are attacked, there may be no hope of bringing about an early truce.

Of course, the Soviets might still attack U.S. cities if they thought that the self-restraint policy precluded an effective response. Thus the United States must maintain the capability to retaliate against Soviet cities. However, this does not mean retaliating against civilians. Retaliatory attacks on cities should only come after several days' warning, thus giving civilians time to evacuate. Because the Soviets already have plans to evacuate most of their urban population in a severe crisis, this act of restraint on the part of the United States may be superfluous—the United States may not have the option of attacking civilians. Nevertheless, the concept of restraint as a deliberate policy is important to the development of a general policy of limiting casualties if deterrence fails.

Declaratory policies are thought by many to be of little value because they cannot be enforced. And yet, prohibitions can work when they are in the self-interest of both parties. One example is the prohibition against gas warfare that lasted throughout World War II, which was otherwise unrestrained. The destructive potential of nuclear warfare is so great that there are strong incentives to do everything possible to prevent the indiscriminate slaughter of civilians. Of course, reducing the possibility of and the incentive for war is perhaps the surest way to achieve this goal. But even if the probability of nuclear war is quite small, one can never be certain that it will never occur—perhaps not deliberately but through some accident or crisis that inadvertently gets out of hand. Under these circumstances, every attempt should be made to incorporate in international law the idea that civilian noncombatants are off limits to nuclear attack. If this is adopted as an explicit, declared policy, there may be some chance of resolving a conflict short of the ultimate catastrophe.

Although the Soviets have in the past rejected the idea that nuclear war can be limited, this rejection occurred at a time when the Soviet Union was weaker than the West. They always viewed such restraints as an attempt to give the West coercive freedom of action without having to pay the consequences. However, if this is combined with a no-first-strike pledge, the Soviets should have no objections and might find themselves at a political disadvantage if they refused to join in an agreement.

In any case, a policy of restraint that tries to limit the scope of nuclear war (if it should occur) and the deaths of innocent civilians is not only in America's self-interest, but is also more consistent with American ideals of human rights and justice.

DETERRENCE IN THE 1980s

This book has sought to bring into focus some of the critical issues affecting peace in the next decade. It is clear that during this period the West will continue to be faced by a militarily strong Soviet Union that is likely to try to extend its power and influence throughout Western Europe and the rest of the world. While seeking détente, the West must be prepared to continue its struggle with the Soviet Union on ideological, political, and economic fronts as well as countering their arms buildup. Whether this "peaceful" confrontation will spill over into a direct military struggle will depend to a large extent on steps taken by the United States in the near future to secure the survivability of its strategic forces and to strengthen its deterrence policies.

APPENDIX A

Strategic Forces

TABLE A-1

Estimated U.S. Strategic Nuclear Forces

1978

Launcher	Number	Warheads per Launcher	Total Warheads	Yield (Megatons)	Equivalent Megatons	Total Megatons	Total Equivalent Megatons	Circular Error Probable (nm)
Minuteman II	450	1	450	1.0	1.0	450	450	0.2–0.3
Minuteman III	550	3	1,650	0.17	0.31	280	511	0.1–0.15
Titan II	54	1	54	9.0	4.33	486	234	0.5
Subtotal, ICBMs	1,054		2,154			1,216	1,195	
Polaris	160	1*	160	0.6	1.03	96	165	0.5
Poseidon	496	10	4,960	0.04	0.12	198	595	0.25
Subtotal, SLBMs	656		5,120			294	760	
B-52 G/H	255	4 SRAM	1,020	0.2	0.34	204	347	
		4 Bombs	1,020	1.0	1.0	1,020	1,020	
B-52D	75	4 Bombs	300	1.0	1.0	300	300	
Subtotal, Bombers	330		2,340			1,524	1,667	
Total	2,040		9,614			3,034	3,622	

1985

Launcher	Number	Warheads per Launcher	Total Warheads	Yield (Megatons)	Equivalent Megatons	Total Megatons	Total Equivalent Megatons	Circular Error Probable (nm)
Minuteman II	450	1	450	1.0	1.0	450	450	0.2
Minuteman III	250	3	750	0.17	0.31	127	232	0.1
Minuteman III (with MK–12A)	300	3	900	0.34	0.49	306	441	0.1
Titan II	54	1	54	9.0	4.33	486	234	0.5
Subtotal, ICBMs	1,054		2,154			1,369	1,357	
Polaris	80	1*	80	0.6	1.03	48	82	0.5
Poseidon	320	10	3,200	0.04	0.12	128	384	0.25
Poseidon C-4	160	8	1,280	0.10	0.22	128	282	0.25
Trident I	168	8	1,344	0.10	0.22	134	296	0.25
Subtotal, SLBMs	728		5,904			438	1,044	
B-52 G/H	135	6 SRAM	810	0.2	0.34	162	275	
		4 Bombs	540	1.0	1.0	540	540	
B-52D	75	4 Bombs	300	1.0	1.0	300	300	
B-52CM	120	20 Cruise Missiles	2,400	0.2	0.34	480	816	0.05
Subtotal, Bombers	330		4,050			1,482	1,931	
Total	2,112		12,108			3,289	4,332	

SOURCES: *Counterforce Issues for U.S. Strategic Nuclear Forces* (Washington, D.C.: Congressional Budget Office, 1978), pp. 18–19. Congressman Les Aspin, "SALT II or No SALT" (Press Release, Jan., 1978).
*The Polaris A3 missile carries three un-MIRVed 200 kT warheads.

TABLE A-2

Estimated Soviet Strategic Nuclear Forces

1978

Launcher	Number	Warheads per Launcher	Total Warheads	Yield (Megatons)	Equivalent Megatons	Total Megatons	Total Equivalent Megatons	Circular Error Probable (nm)
SS-9	158	1	158	20.0	7.37	3,160	1,164	0.5
SS-11	705	1	705	1.5	1.31	1,058	923	0.5
SS-13	60	1	60	1.0	1.0	60	60	0.7
SS-17	75	4	300	1.0	1.0	300	300	0.15–0.2
SS-18	150	10	1,500	1.0	1.0	1,500	1,500	0.15–0.2
SS-19	250	6	1,500	1.0	1.0	1,500	1,500	0.15–0.2
Subtotal, ICBMs	1,398		4,223			7,578	5,447	
SS-N-5	21	1	21	1.5	1.31	31	28	1.5
SS-N-6	528	1	528	1.0	1.0	528	528	0.5
SS-N-8	312	1	312	1.5	1.31	468	409	0.5
SS-N-17	16	3	48	0.5	0.63	24	30	0.2–0.3
SS-N-18	80	3	240	0.5	0.63	120	151	0.2–0.3
Subtotal, SLBMs	957		1,149			1,171	1,146	
Bear	100	2	200	5.0	2.92	1,000	584	
Bison	40	2	80	5.0	2.92	400	234	
Subtotal, Bombers	140		280			1,400	818	
Total	2,495		5,652			10,149	7,411	

1985

Launcher*	Number	Warheads per Launcher	Total Warheads	Yield (Megatons)	Equivalent Megatons	Total Megatons	Total Equivalent Megatons	Circular Error Probable (nm)
SS-11	300	1	300	1.5	1.31	450	393	0.5
SS-17	100	4	400	1.0	1.0	400	400	0.1 or less
SS-18	308	10	3,080	1.0	1.0	3,080	3,080	0.1 or less
SS-19	400	6	2,400	1.0	1.0	2,400	2,400	0.1 or less
Subtotal, ICBMs	1,108		6,180			6,330	6,273	
SS-N-6	320	1	320	1.0	1.0	320	320	0.5
SS-N-8	312	1	312	1.5	1.31	468	409	0.5
SS-N-18	408	3	1,224	0.5	0.63	612	771	0.2–0.3
Subtotal, SLBMs	1,040		1,856			1,400	1,500	
New Cruise Missile Carrier/Bomber	100	10	1,000	0.2	0.34	200	340	
Total	2,248		9,036			7,930	8,113	

SOURCES: *Counterforce Issues for U.S. Strategic Nuclear Forces* (Washington, D.C.: Congressional Budget Office, 1978), pp. 16–17; Congressman Les Aspin, "SALT II or No SALT" (Press release, Jan., 1978); Colin S. Gray, *The Future of Land-Based Missile Forces* (Hudson Institution, 1977), pp. 107–117; "The Military Balance 1977/78," *Air Force Magazine* Dec., 1977, pp. 62–70; "Current U.S. and Soviet Strategic Offensive Forces," *Aviation Week & Space Technology* Apr. 18, 1977, p. 18.

*All MIRVed ICBMs and SLBMs could be replaced by newer follow-on MIRVed missiles by 1985. The SS-11 may also be replaced by a new missile with a single, large warhead. Some of the SS-N-6 and SS-11 missiles carry 3 non-MIRVed warheads, each with a yield of about 0.5 MT (giving an EMT of 1.9 per missile).

†The Soviets could have about 400 Backfire bombers in 1985.

TABLE A-3

Comparison of Forces

Equivalent Megatons

System	1978 U.S.	1978 U.S.S.R.	1985 U.S.	1985 U.S.S.R.
ICBMs	1,200	5,450	1,400	6,300
SLBMs	750	1,150	1,000	1,500
Subtotal, Missiles	1,950	6,600	2,400	7,800
Bombers*	1,650	800	1,900	300
Total	3,650	7,400	4,300	8,100

*Excludes Backfire.

Warheads

System	1978 U.S.	1978 U.S.S.R.	1985 U.S.	1985 U.S.S.R.
ICBMs	2,150	4,200	2,150	6,200
SLBMs	5,100	1,150	5,900	1,850
Subtotal, Missiles	7,250	5,350	8,050	8,050
Bombers*	2,350	300	4,050	1,000
Total	9,600	5,650	12,100	9,050

*Excludes Backfire.

APPENDIX B

ICBM and Bomber Survivability

The following sections briefly describe the mathematical models used to calculate U.S. ICBM and bomber survivability and present a discussion of U.S. counterforce capability.

ICBM SURVIVABILITY

The important parameters affecting the survivability of an ICBM in its hardened silo are discussed in chapter 3. This section describes in more detail the calculation of ICBM survivability.[1]

The distance at which a nuclear weapon can generate an overpressure equal to the silo hardness is called the kill (or lethal) radius. An approximation[2] of the kill radius r_k is given by

$$r_k = (16\ Y/H)^{1/3}$$

where r_k is in nautical miles (nm), the yield Y is in megatons (i.e., the energy equivalent to that released by a million tons of TNT), and the silo hardness H is in pounds per square inch (psi). For example, the kill radius of a one-megaton (MT) weapon against a silo strengthened to 1,500 psi is 0.22 nm. Thus, if a 1-MT weapon is exploded within 0.22 nm of a 1,500 psi silo, it is assumed to "kill" it.

This approximation for the weapon kill radius holds for hard silos (greater than 300 psi) when weapons are exploded on the ground ("groundburst"). Weapons exploded in the air ("airburst") at the appropriate optimum altitude will generate the same pressure at a larger range than a groundburst weapon. This approximation thus underestimates somewhat the kill radius if a weapon is airburst at the optimum altitude.

The accuracy of a missile is usually measured in terms of its CEP (circular error probable or circle of equal probability) given in nautical miles. CEP is the median miss distance; that is, it is the radius of a circle centered on the target within which half the reentry vehicles would fall if the missile test were repeated many times.

If the distribution of the impact points (due to repeated firings) around a target is Gaussian or circular normal (which is usually the case), then the probability of survival P_s of a target is given by

$$P_s = 0.5^{(r_k/CEP)^2}$$

The probability of kill P_k is then

$$P_k = 1 - P_s = 1 - 0.5^{(r_k/CEP)^2}$$

Appendix B

or using the approximation for r_k

$$P_k = 1 - 0.5^{(Y^{2/3}/CEP^2)(16/H)^{2/3}}$$

The formula for kill probability assumes that the warhead will always arrive at the target and explode. Of course, missiles and warheads are not completely reliable, and some will fail. If the overall reliability of the system, ρ, is taken into account, then the probability of kill will be diminished by a factor ρ. Thus the probability of kill becomes

$$\tilde{P}_k = \rho(1 - P_s)$$

and the probability of survival becomes

$$\tilde{P}_s = 1 - \tilde{P}_k = 1 - \rho(1 - P_s) = 1 - \rho + \rho P_s$$

If a missile silo is attacked by n warheads (all coming from different missiles), then the overall probability of survival is given by

$$(\tilde{P}_s)^n = (1 - \rho + \rho P_s)^n$$

assuming that each missile has the same P_k and ρ.

For the case of a two-on-one attack, the overall probability of survival is then given by

$$(\tilde{P}_s)^2 = (1 - \rho + \rho P_s)^2$$

where $P_s = 0.5^{(r_k/CEP)^2}$ The probability of kill is then

$$(\tilde{P}_k)^2 = 1 - (\tilde{P}_s)^2 = 1 - (1 - \rho + \rho P_s)^2$$

Under some circumstances, a two-on-one attack can have its effectiveness limited by "fratricide" effects. That is, if precautions are not taken to properly time an attack, the second RV can be destroyed (or deflected) by the explosion of the first RV. The probability of survival $\tilde{P}_s$ of a missile silo that is attacked by two RVs (having the same reliability) in the case where the second RV is always killed by the first (when the first RV actually arrives on target) is given by

$$\tilde{P}_s = \rho P_{s1} + (1 - \rho)(1 - \rho + \rho P_{s2})$$

where P_{s1} and P_{s2} are the probabilities of survival when attacked by the individual RVs. If $P_{s1} = P_{s2} = P_s$, then

$$\tilde{P}_s = (2 - \rho)\rho P_s + (1 - \rho)^2$$

As an example, consider the case of a warhead with a yield of 1-MT and a silo with a hardness of 1,500 psi. The kill radius of this weapon is, as noted earlier, 0.22 nm. If the missile has a CEP of 0.15 nm, then the probability of survival is

$$P_s = 0.5^{(.22/.15)^2} = 0.225$$

and the probability of kill is

$$P_k = 1 - 0.225 = 0.775$$

Thus, if the 1,000 Minuteman silos were attacked by 1,000 reliable 1-MT warheads, each with a CEP of 0.15 nm, 775 silos would be expected to be destroyed. However, if the reliability of the attacking missiles is only 85 percent, only 850 silos will actually be attacked, and thus only $(0.775)(850) = 659$ silos will be killed. Or, alternatively, the probability of survival (with 85 percent reliability) is

$$\bar{P}_s = 1 - \rho(1 - P_s) = 1 - 0.659 = 0.341$$

and 341 Minuteman would be expected to survive.

If two warheads were assigned to each silo (from separate missiles, each with a reliability of 0.85), then the probability of survival would become

$$\bar{P}_s^2 = (0.341)^2 = .116$$

and only 116 Minutemen would be expected to survive.

If the timing of the attack were poor and fratricide resulted in every case, then the probability of survival would increase to

$$\tilde{P}_s = \rho \bar{P}_s + \rho \bar{P}_s(1 - \rho) + (1 - \rho)^2$$
$$\tilde{P}_s = 0.85\ (0.225) + 0.85\ (0.225)\ (0.15) + (0.15)^2 = 0.242$$

and 242 Minutemen should survive. Thus, although a two-on-one attack with fratricide is an improvement over a one-on-one attack (with 341 survivors), it is considerably worse than a well executed two-on-one attack without fratricide.

Appendix B 141

As the accuracy of the attacking missiles improves, fratricide becomes less critical. At a CEP of 0.1 nm, the probability of kill of a 1-MT warhead is 0.965; but with only 85 percent reliability, this drops to 0.82 for a one RV attack. A two-on-one attack raises this back to 0.968. Thus, without fratricide, about 32 Minutemen would be expected to survive. Even with full fratricide, however, the number surviving would only increase to about 55. Therefore, at low CEP, targeting two RVs on each target is a convenient way to make up for reliability problems and is advantageous even if the timing constraints caused by fratricide cannot be overcome. (Fratricide is, in fact, not likely to be a problem—see chapter 3.)

U.S. COUNTERFORCE CAPABILITY

The Soviet capability against the U.S. ICBM force is discussed in some detail in chapter 3. The following section explores the other side of the counterforce equation: present and future U.S. capabilities against Soviet ICBMs.

Table B-1 lists the properties of the force structures assumed for both sides during the next decade. Figure 9 in chapter 4 shows that the present Minuteman system has only a limited capability against Soviet ICBMs and that even if its accuracy is improved to 0.1 nm and all Minuteman III warheads are given twice their present yield (the Mk 12A warhead), it is likely that 400 or more Soviet ICBMs will survive an attack. These Soviet missiles could carry around 1,000 warheads, each having a yield of about 1-MT. The limited capability of the Minuteman system (even with improvements) is due to the limited number of warheads available and to the massive effort the Soviets have made to harden their new silos.

Given the expected accuracy and low yield of Minuteman, it is important to target at least two RVs per silo to achieve a high expectation of success in destroying a silo. For example, the Mk 12A has a single-shot probability of kill of only 75 percent against even a 1,000 psi target (assuming an 85 percent missile reliability). Although there are 2,100 Minuteman RVs (only 1,650 being Minuteman IIIs), there will probably be 1,300–1,400 Soviet silos in the 1980s, of which at least 800 will be the "superhard" variety. Thus, 300 or so silos would have only one RV assigned to each of them.

The other problem is that when the Soviets began deploying the new generation of ICBMs, they completely removed the old silos and replaced them with much more massive ones. These silos are thought to be much harder to nuclear effects than either the older silos or U.S. silos. It is reported that the intelligence community estimates that these new Soviet

TABLE B-1

U.S. Counterforce Capability

U.S. ICBM Capability

Missile	Year	Number of Missiles	Number of Warheads	Yield (MT)	CEP (nm)
Minuteman II	1977	450	450	1	0.2
Minuteman III	1977	550	1,650	0.17	0.15
Minuteman II	1980	450	450	1	0.2
Minuteman III*	1980	550	1,650	0.17	0.1
Minuteman II	1985	450	450	1	0.2
Minuteman III	1985	550	1,650	0.34	0.1
Minuteman II	1988	450	450	1	0.2
Minuteman III	1988	400	1,200	0.34	0.1
MX	1988	150	1,200	0.3	0.07

*This assumes all Minuteman III warheads are replaced with the Mk 12A, although only a limited conversion is planned at present. See Harold Brown, *Department of Defense Annual Report, FY 1979*, p. 108.

Soviet ICBMs

Missiles	Year	Number of Missiles	Silo Hardness (psi)
SS-7, 8, 9	1977	347	500
SS-11, 13	1977	900	1,000
SS-17, 18, 19	1977	230	2,500–4,000*
SS-11, 13	1980–1988	560†	1,000
SS-17, 18, 19 & Follow-ons	1980–1988	800	2,500–4,000

*SOURCE: "Could U.S. Survive First Strike by Soviets?," *Human Events*, Sept. 24, 1977, p. 10.
†This number could be smaller, depending on the outcome of SALT II.

Appendix B

silos are at least 2,500–4,000 psi hard.[3] However, from the point of view of Minuteman, it makes little difference. If attacked by the full Minuteman III force with Mk 12As and a CEP of 0.1 nm, around 320 Soviet ICBMs would survive even if the new silos were only 1,500 psi hard. It is clear that a new system would be required to offer a more serious threat to the Soviet ICBMs.

The Missile-X or MX system has been proposed as a replacement for at least some of the Minuteman III missiles. The exact configuration of this missile and its actual capabilities are unknown since it has not been built. Theoretical accuracies of 0.05 to 0.1 are reported to be under consideration as design goals. If attacked by a nominal force of 150 MX missiles with an accuracy of 0.07 nm, the Soviets could be drawn down to 125-175 ICBMs. If the MX force were expanded[4] or its accuracy further improved, MX would obviously be even more effective as a hard-target counterforce weapon.

In summary, over the next decade the United States will have only a limited counterforce capability against Soviet ICBMs. Not until the introduction of the MX system (if the missile meets the proposed design goals) will the United States have the potential for an ICBM counterforce threat.

BOMBER PRELAUNCH SURVIVABILITY

The prelaunch survivability of the U.S. strategic bomber force is illustrated in figures 5, 6, and 7 in chapter 3. The basis for these figures is discussed below.

The probability of a bomber being destroyed by an SLBM barrage is calculated in the following manner. The time available for a bomber to escape an attack is found by subtracting bomber reaction time from missile flight time. This "escape time" when combined with the flyout characteristics of the bomber gives the radius of a circle within which the bomber must be located. If the attacker does not know the bomber flight pattern after takeoff, he must assume that the bomber flies off in a random direction and that it could be anywhere within this circle. The probability of a bomber being killed can be determined by how much of this area can be covered by lethal nuclear effects.

The area of uncertainty A_u in which the bomber must be located is given by

$$A_u = \pi R_u^2$$

where R_u is the maximum range of the bomber when the SLBMs arrive. Since the lethal area A_L of a warhead is simply

$$A_L = \pi R_L^2$$

where R_L is the lethal radius, the probability of kill of a reliable attacking missile is

$$P_k = (R_L/R_u)^2, \text{ for } R_L \leq R_u$$

and the probability of survival is

$$P_s = 1 - P_k = 1 - (R_L/R_u)^2$$

If more than one RV is used to barrage the area of uncertainty, the probability of survival is

$$P_s = 1 - n(R_L/R_u)^2$$

where n is the number of reliable RVs attacking each bomber base. However, for values of P_s less than about 50 percent, the geometry of overlapping nuclear explosives must be considered. This increases the value of P_s somewhat and is included in the calculations in chapter 3.

The value of the parameters used in calculating prelaunch survivability is discussed below. (Much of the data comes from Quanbeck and Wood's book *Modernizing the Strategic Bomber Force*.)[5]

Missile Time of Flight

The time required for a missile to fly a minimum-energy trajectory to a range of 1,100 nm is about fourteen minutes. Quanbeck and Wood assume that by depressing the trajectory, the Soviets could reduce the time to about seven minutes.[6] However, this flight time of seven minutes is a theoretical number that ignores the initial powered phase of flight and the slowing down of the reentry vehicle as it reenters the atmosphere. These two factors should add about two minutes to the total flight time. Thus, for this analysis, a nine-minute time-of-flight to a range of 1,100 nm is used for Soviet SLBMs flown in a depressed-trajectory mode. The time-of-flight to other ranges is assumed to change at a rate of 200 nm/min. That is, the time-of-flight to 900 nm is eight minutes; to 700 nm, seven minutes, etc.

Appendix B

Lethal Radius

Quanbeck and Wood estimated that the hardness of the B-52 is about one pound per square inch (psi). They further assumed that Soviet SLBMs carry 1-MT warheads, although sizes up to 2 MT or more seem likely based on U.S. technology. For a 1-MT warhead, they assumed a lethal radius of 55,000 feet against a 1-psi target, although a 1-MT weapon detonated at the optimum height of burst gives an overpressure of 1 psi at a range of over 75,000 feet. Nevertheless, the Air Force criticized the 55,000 feet range as too high.[7] In view of this criticism, a lethal radius of 45,000 feet (7.4 nm) is used for this analysis, but this figure is somewhat optimistic from the U.S. point of view, particularly considering the possibility that these missiles carry higher yield weapons.

Bomber Flyout Characteristics

The "distance versus time from takeoff" curve for the B-52 is unclassified and included in Quanbeck and Wood.[8] Table B-2 summarizes these flyout characteristics.

As an illustration of this method, consider the example of a submarine 200 nm off the coast attacking a bomber base 800 nm inland. If it takes 120 seconds after the SLBMs have been launched for the bomber to start down the runway (the bomber "reaction time"), there are about 390 seconds left for the bomber to escape before the missiles arrive (because the missile flight time is about 510 seconds). In 390 seconds, the bomber could be about 34 nm at maximum from the base. If four SLBMs are used to barrage the area around the base, the following calculation can be made:[9]

$$P_s = 1 - n(R_L/R_u)^2 = 1 - 4(7.4/34)^2 = 0.81$$

Thus, a bomber would have an 81 percent chance of survival under these conditions.

TABLE B-2

B–52 Flyout Characteristics

Time (sec)	100	200	300	400	500
Range (nm)	4.0	11.5	21.5	34.0	46.0

Notes

CHAPTER I

1. The exact definition of "assured destruction" has varied from administration to administration. In the event of an all-out war, present policy calls for the destruction of some high percentage of the economic, political, and military targets in the Soviet Union. See chap. 6.

2. Secretary of State John Foster Dulles announced this "massive retaliation" doctrine in a speech to the Council on Foreign Relations on January 12, 1954. At that time, the U.S. had about 1,500 B-47 medium bombers and over 200 B-36 heavy bombers and was beginning a program to build over 500 B-52s. The Soviets possessed only a small number of medium-range propeller-driven bombers.

3. Of course, the situation now is reversed, and there is great concern that the Soviets will soon be in a position to exercise (or threaten) these coercive counterforce tactics against the United States and its allies.

4. Critics argued that a damage-limiting strategy would fuel the arms race because the Soviets would naturally try to achieve survivability by building more weapons. The whole "action-reaction" process was seen as undermining strategic stability and increasing the chances of war. (See Jerome H. Kahan, *Security in the Nuclear Age* [Washington, D.C.: Brookings Institution, 1975], p. 134.) See also chap. 6 for a further discussion of the McNamara policy.

5. This is contradicted by the NATO doctrine of "flexible response" in which the United States holds out the possibility of initiating an attack against the Soviet Union. But because the United States has not really pursued the development of damage-limiting capabilities, this doctrine does not change the reality of the situation. Even Secretary of Defense Schlesinger's attempt to reintroduce counterforce strategies was on a very limited scale and for reasons other than damage limiting (see chap. 5).

6. Quoted in Leon Goure, "Soviet Military Doctrine," *Air Force Magazine*, March, 1977, p. 47.

7. For a detailed description of Soviet military doctrine, see V. D. Sokolovskiy, *Soviet Military Strategy*, trans. and ed. Harriet Fast Scott (New York: Crane, Russak & Co., 1975); and Leon Goure, Foy D. Kohler, and Mose L. Harvey, eds., *The Role of Nuclear Forces in Current Soviet Strategy* (Coral Gables, Fla.: Center for

Advanced International Studies, University of Miami, 1974). The latter book contains extensive quotations from original Soviet sources. See also Richard Pipes, "Why the Soviet Union Thinks It Can Fight and Win a Nuclear War," *Commentary*, July, 1977, pp. 21–34. Professor Pipes, a Russian historian at Harvard, chaired one panel of the "B Team," a group formed by President Ford to give an independent assessment of Soviet intentions and capabilities (see William R. Van Cleave and Seymour Weiss, "National Intelligence and the USSR," *National Review*, June 23, 1978, pp. 777–780).

8. Quoted in Pipes, op. cit., p. 33.

9. Since the late 1950s preemption has been a key element in Soviet doctrine and strategy. See, for example, Goure, Kohler, and Harvey, op. cit., pp. 102–112.

10. See chap. 3.

11. For an analysis of the Soviet civil defense program and the high level of importance attributed to it by the Soviet leadership, see Leon Goure, *War Survival in Soviet Strategy* (Coral Gables, Fla.: Center for Advanced International Studies, University of Miami, 1976); John L. Frisbee, "The Imbalance of Civil Defense," *Air Force Magazine*, Feb., 1977, p. 53; and Major George Kolt, USAF, "The Soviet Civil Defense Program," *Strategic Review* 5, no. 2 (Spring, 1977): 52. See also *Soviet Civil Defense* (Washington, D.C.: Director of Central Intelligence, July, 1978).

12. Although the number of blast shelters for the general population is steadily increasing, at this point, evacuation of cities and construction of "hasty" fallout shelters are probably the primary methods that the Soviets plan to use to protect the general public.

13. See the section on "Overkill" in chap. 2.

14. Gen. George S. Brown, chairman, Joint Chiefs of Staff, quoted in Edgar Ulsamer, "'Cheap' Deterrence Could Be Fatal," *Air Force Magazine*, Aug., 1977, p. 33.

15. In any nuclear exchange, a large part of the strategic weapons of the Soviet Union (strategic submarines at sea, dispersed bombers, and ICBMs in hardened silos) and many of the shorter range delivery systems (the mobile SS-20 and the medium range bombers) should survive. Survival of much of the army and navy can be assured by prewar dispersal of these forces.

16. The Soviets would have a large number of nuclear weapon systems to use for blackmail and coercion and a large nuclear-equipped land army for defense (China), suppression (Eastern Europe), and possibly invasion and conquest (Western Europe, Middle East) if necessary.

17. The United States is also committed to the defense of Japan; but here, there is no confrontation with a massed Soviet army, and the defense problems and strategies required are quite different from those for Europe. Even in Korea, the prospect of a nuclear war with the Soviet Union or China is quite remote.

18. The consensus of the intelligence community in 1976 was that the Soviets were in fact seeking superiority. (See David Binder, "New CIA Estimate Finds Soviet Seeks Superiority in Arms," *New York Times*, Dec. 26, 1976, p. 1.)

19. Henry A. Kissinger, ed., *Problems of National Security* (New York: Praeger, 1965), p. 5.

20. Perhaps a more fundamental limit on a policy of deterrence is that the problems confronting the West in its struggle with communism are not only, or perhaps

even primarily, military but also ideological and political. Although the West has done a fairly good job of containing the expansion of the Soviet empire after its initial successes in Eastern Europe, in the ideological sphere, the West continues to falter. Of course, if the Soviets achieve a first-strike capability, their willingness to intervene abroad might increase greatly. But at that point, the central concern is likely to be the fate of Western Europe and the United States rather than that of the Third World.

21. James R. Schlesinger, *Department of Defense Annual Report, FY 1976 and FY 197T*, p. I–13.

22. E.g., Paul Nitze, "Nuclear Strategy: Detente and American Survival," in *Defending America*, James R. Schlesinger, et al. (New York: Basic Books, 1977), p. 97. A counterforce attack might also include attacks on the bombers and strategic submarines.

23. See Walter Slocombe, *The Political Implications of Strategic Parity*, Adelphi Paper no. 77 (London: International Institute for Strategic Studies, 1971), for an interesting discussion of this concept.

24. Because there is little else the Soviets could do at this point to bring political pressure on the United States to acquiesce to their demands, they might well fail in their objectives. As long as the United States retains an assured-destruction capability, the Soviets are themselves deterred from extending an attack to cities. (At any rate, the American hostages may only be completely in jeopardy for a short time because a spontaneous exodus from American cities once nuclear bombs start going off anywhere is likely.) In fact, the Soviet attack might act to redouble the resolve of the American government because persevering in the crisis would be all the more important for future credibility, and it might also be the only immediately available way to retaliate against the Soviet Union effectively.

25. A large Soviet ICBM throw-weight advantage can, of course, make it more difficult to maintain the survivability of America's ICBMs.

26. Albert Wohlstetter, "The Delicate Balance of Terror," *Foreign Affairs* 37, no. 2 (Jan., 1958): 211–234.

27. This is why, regardless of whether one believes that it is necessary to be concerned about orchestrated counterforce wars designed to change the Soviet ICBM throw-weight advantage from four-to-one to seven-to-one, there should be extreme concern about the central core of that scenario—the vulnerability of U.S. ICBMs. Given the uncertainties regarding the survival of other U.S. systems, this vulnerability could have serious consequences for deterrence.

CHAPTER II

1. Alain C. Enthoven and K. Wayne Smith, *How Much Is Enough? Shaping the Defense Program, 1961–1969* (New York: Harper & Row, 1971), p. 175.

2. One particular problem is that there is often a large bias in the United States towards high-technology solutions to technical problems. This approach is not always shared by the Soviets, and they often seek solutions through approaches that U.S. engineers might reject out of hand.

3. After combining available surveillance data with technological evaluations, the intelligence community offers its assessment of the most likely value (the so-

called "best estimate") for a particular characteristic of a weapon system. An uncertainty band is also usually given, and it is assumed that the value of the quantity being discussed is unlikely to fall outside the upper and lower limits of this band.

4. See David Binder, "New CIA Estimate Finds Soviet Seeks Superiority in Arms," *New York Times*, Dec. 26, 1976, p. 1, and chap. 3 for details.

5. See chap. 3 for the magnitude of the difference.

6. John S. Foster, Jr., "The Impact of Intelligence on National Security," *Journal of International Relations* 2, no. 3 (Fall, 1977): 210.

7. See the last section of this chapter.

8. If the Soviets simultaneously launch an attack on the ICBMs and bombers, the SLBMs used to attack the bomber bases will begin arriving some fifteen to twenty minutes before the Soviet ICBM attack on U.S. ICBMs. Some suggest that the United States could launch its ICBMs during this period. This is a variation of the "launch-on-warning" or "launch-on-attack assessment" doctrine. There are a number of political and technical reasons that make this doctrine ineffective and unacceptable (see chap. 4).

9. The ICBMs rely mainly on hiding in "chaff" clouds and on decoys, while the SLBMs rely on saturating a defense with a large number of reentry vehicles.

10. The other forces could, of course, be expanded. However, attempts to expand and modernize the bomber forces (by procuring the B-1) have already been cancelled and are unlikely to be revived. Furthermore, the proposed new Trident submarine is so large and so expensive that few are likely to be built. Even with expansion, a strategic diad would remain a much more concentrated force than the triad.

11. For a discussion of sabotage and covert attacks on submarines, see chap. 3.

12. As an example of this attitude, consider the following statement by former Secretary of Defense James R. Schlesinger in 1967: "All too many Americans deceived themselves into regarding a Soviet 'bolt from the blue' as a relatively probable event. This tendency may have been strengthened by some underlying 'Pearl Harbor complex' reflecting that traumatic event in recent American history." (Quoted in William H. Kincade, "A Strategy for All Seasons," *Bulletin of the Atomic Scientists* 34, no. 5 (May, 1978): 15.

13. "Surprise Attack by Russia Still 'Unthinkable'?," *U.S. News and World Report*, Sept. 5, 1977, p. 18.

14. The article cited above continued: "But the planners expect a period of warning even longer than a few days. A surprise attack with any chance of success, they say, would have to come after a period of growing tension and intense preparation, much as the Japanese attack on Pearl Harbor culminated months of diplomatic conflict in which there was a clear danger of war ahead." Considering the Japanese success at Pearl Harbor, this is hardly comforting. (Ibid., p. 18.)

15. This point is discussed in detail in chap. 3.

16. Roberta Wohlstetter, *Pearl Harbor: Warning and Decision* (Stanford: Stanford University Press, 1962), pp. 3, 387.

17. Barton Whaley, *Codeword Barbaroosa* (Cambridge, Mass.: M.I.T. Press, 1973), p. 242.

18. Avi Shlaim, "Failures in National Intelligence Estimates: The Case of the Yom Kippur War," *World Politics* 28, no. 3 (Apr., 1976): 355.

19. Ibid., p. 369.

20. Abraham Ben-Zvi, "Hindsight and Foresight: A Conceptual Framework for the Analysis of Surprise Attacks," *World Politics* 28, no. 3 (Apr., 1976): 381–395.

21. Ibid., p. 388.

22. It is not unlikely that if both sides are on alert at the time and the Soviets decide that war is inevitable, no action will be taken until relative calm has returned to the international scene and U.S. forces have returned to their normal, day-to-day alert status.

23. E.g., "Declaration on the Nuclear Arms Race," *Bulletin of the Atomic Scientists* 34, no. 3 (Mar., 1978): 8–10; and Michael D. Mann, "Curbing Weapons on the Drawing Board," *Los Angeles Times*, Dec. 13, 1977, part 2, p. 9.

24. See the section on arms control in chap. 4.

25. Ruth Leger Sivard, "Let Them Eat Bullets," *Bulletin of the Atomic Scientists* 31, no. 4 (Apr., 1975): 6.

26. The explosive yield of a nuclear weapon is given in terms of its TNT energy equivalent—usually in kilotons (thousands of tons of TNT) or in megatons (millions of tons).

27. For an even more extreme estimate, see Richard J. Barnet, *Roots of War* (Baltimore: Penguin Books, 1973), p. 4, where he stated that "the American nuclear arsenal holds the equivalent of ten thousand tons of TNT for every man, woman, and child on earth." The actual number is about five to ten tons of TNT per person. (See Thomas A. Brown, "Number Mysticism, Rationality and the Strategic Balance," *Orbis* 21, no. 3 (Fall, 1977): 483.)

28. Jack Kemp and Les Aspin, *How Much Defense Spending Is Enough?* (Washington, D.C.: American Enterprise Institute, 1976), p. 6.

29. The United States can try to compensate for this problem by cross-targeting; that is, each leg of the triad can be assigned some targets in each category of targets.

30. EMT or equivalent megatons is a measure of the area "killed" by a nuclear weapon and is defined as $Y^{2/3}$ where Y is yield of the weapon in megatons.

31. This figure is very optimistic for the United States in the 1980s and is used for purposes of illustration only. It could be much lower; see chap. 3.

32. In principle, several hundred more EMT could be available if the bombers were kept on a higher alert status. However, most of their inventory megatonnage is accounted for by the four 1-MT bombs each bomber can carry. Not even the most optimistic observers assume that a bomber can penetrate defended targets to deliver these bombs. Instead, the bombers hope to rely on the lower yield (0.2 MT) SRAM missiles to attack defended targets. If the bombs are used at all, they will most likely be used against less important, undefended targets (see chap. 3).

33. A recent study by the National Academy of Sciences shows that even massive use of nuclear weapons on both sides would not pose the threat of a worldwide disaster (ecological or otherwise) to parties not directly involved in the war. The report states: "Proceeding in a highly disciplined manner, the study addressed the *long-term, worldwide* consequences of the hypothetical nuclear exchange by examining, *independently*, possible effects upon, respectively, the atmosphere and climate, natural terrestrial ecosystems, agriculture and animal husbandry, the aquatic environment, and both somatic and genetic effects upon humans. Reasoning from

available information and understanding, it is concluded that, a decade or so after the event, in areas distant from the detonations, surviving humans and ecosystems would be subject to relatively minimal stress attributable to the exchange. If the detonations were limited to locales in the northern hemisphere, this conclusion can be stated with high confidence with respect to the fate of the southern hemisphere." (*The Long-Term Worldwide Effects of Multiple Nuclear-Weapons Detonations* [Washington, D.C.: National Academy of Sciences, 1975], pp. 2–3.)

34. Fallout is directly proportional to the yield (rather than EMT) of a weapon. The total nuclear yield of the U.S. strategic arsenal reached a peak in 1960 and has steadily declined ever since. (See Albert Wohlstetter, "Racing Forward or Ambling Back?" in *Defending America*, James R. Schlesinger, et al. [New York: Basic Books, 1977] p. 137.) This reduction is due to the decline in the number of bombers and to the MIRVing of the strategic missiles. Although MIRVing increases the number of warheads, it reduces the total yield. For example, the single warhead on Minuteman II has a yield of one to two megatons. The MIRVed Minuteman III carries three warheads, but each has a yield of only 0.17 megatons.

35. T. K. Jones, *Effects of Evacuations and Sheltering on Potential Fatalities from a Nuclear Exchange* (Seattle: Boeing Aerospace Company, 1977). This analysis assumed that a full force of B-1s would be available in 1985 and thus considerably overestimated the size of the U.S. retaliatory force.

36. In an earlier study, Boeing concluded that "If the U.S. were to program all its surviving weapons to detonate at ground level . . . with favorable weather conditions, a lethal level of fallout could be spread over up to 15 percent of Soviet territory. However, simple shelters can be constructed in a few hours to protect people against fallout until the radiation intensity decays to a nonlethal level. . . . Within a week after a worst-case U.S. retaliatory attack, the Russians could be out of their shelters for at least an 8-hour work day in 97 percent of Soviet territory." (*Industrial Survival and Recovery after Nuclear Attack: A Report to the Joint Committee on Defense Production, U.S. Congress* [Seattle: Boeing Aerospace Company, 1976], p. 7.)

37. Of course, if a war should come, 10 million casualties would be preferable to 110 million.

38. This is not to suggest that a belief in "overkill" is the only or even the primary reason for opposition to strategic force procurement. Reactions to the Viet Nam war, distrust of the "military-industrial complex," fear of an "arms race," hopes for détente, and other factors are also undoubtedly important.

39. In fact, the Soviets did produce large numbers of bombers and missiles during the projected period, but they were medium-range forces oriented towards Europe rather than the U.S. directly.

40. Albert Wohlstetter, op. cit., pp. 116–135.

41. W. T. Lee, "Intelligence: Some Issues of Performance," in *Arms, Men and Military Budgets, Issues for Fiscal Year 1978*, ed. Francis Hoeber and William Schneider, Jr. (New York: Crane, Russak & Company, 1977), pp. 286–321.

42. McNamara used the idea of a "greater-than-expected" threat (or as it has come to be called, the worst-case threat) in order to guide research and development as a hedge against possible Soviet technological breakthroughs. Critics have seized on the phrase to suggest that the Defense Department uses an exaggerated threat to argue for the *procurement* of forces.

43. General George S. Brown, former chairman, Joint Chiefs of Staff, at the conclusion of his tenure as chairman made the following comment regarding his testimony before Congress: "I have come before this Committee on three previous occasions and my message generally was: Well, *there is no reason for concern*, we are moving along, but the Soviets are improving rather markedly, if not dramatically, in some areas." (Emphasis added.) (U.S., Congress, House, Committee on Appropriations, Subcommittee, *Department of Defense Appropriations for 1979*, 95th Cong., 2nd sess., 1978, part 2, p. 712.)

44. U.S., Congress, House, Committee on Appropriations, Subcommittee, *Department of Defense Appropriations for 1975*, 93rd Cong., 2nd sess., 1974, part 1, pp. 345, 347.

45. Of course, this new policy was not just an attempt to rationalize the procurement of new weapons systems; it played an integral part in trying to reconcile the growing Soviet military force with America's continued determination to extend its nuclear umbrella over its allies.

46. Edgar Ulsamer, "A Blueprint for Safeguarding the Strategic Balance," *Air Force Magazine*, Aug., 1976, p. 69. With 200-300 MXs deployed, this would mean that 30-45 of these missiles would survive along with about 105-120 Minutemen.

47. U.S., Congress, House, Committee on Appropriations, Subcommittee, *Department of Defense Appropriations for 1978: Hearings on S. 1210,* 95th Cong., 1st sess., 1977, part 2, p. 221.

48. Ibid., p. 326.

49. Although this point is now conceded by the Defense Department, as late as April, 1977, Air Force Intelligence was still arguing that the fratricide problem could not be overcome by the Soviets. (See U.S., Congress, Senate, Committee on Armed Services, *Fiscal Year 1978 Authorization for Military Procurement, Research and Development, and Active Duty, Selected Reserve, and Civilian Personnel Strengths*, 95th Cong., 1st sess., 1977, part 10, p. 6862). See chap. 3 for a discussion of the fratricide issue. Many defense critics continue to argue that no changes in the Minuteman system are necessary on the basis of this issue.

50. Quoted in "Could Russia Blunder into Nuclear War? An Interview with Harold Brown," *U.S. News and World Report*, Sept. 5, 1977, p. 21. Also see Harold Brown, *Department of Defense Annual Report, FY 79*, p. 63.

51. Department of Defense, press release, July 1, 1977.

52. See chap. 3. The fact that the Navy plans to replace the Poseidon C-3 with the C-4 on only 12 of the 31 Poseidon SSBNs is an indication of this lack of concern.

53. U.S., Congress, House, Committee on Armed Services, *Hearings on Military Posture and HR 5068: Department of Defense Authorization for Appropriations for FY 1978*, 95th Cong., 1st sess., 1977, part 1, p. 309.

54. There are, of course, individuals within both communities who are not reluctant to voice their concerns. However, they have had little impact on the "official" positions.

CHAPTER III

1. According to Secretary of Defense Harold Brown, these missiles are being deployed at a rate of 100–150 per year. "In addition, the Soviets have a fifth generation of ICBMs in development, estimated to consist of four missiles. Flight testing

of one or two of these missiles could begin at anytime, with the others following by the early 1980s." (H. Brown, *Department of Defense Annual Report, Fiscal Year 1979*, pp. 49–50.)

2. Lethality is considered a measure of the hard-target capability of a warhead and is often used to compare U.S. and U.S.S.R. capabilities. But, taken by itself, lethality is meaningless as a measure of comparison unless one assumes the target hardness is the same for the two weapons (or group of weapons) being compared.

3. See Colin S. Gray, *The Future of Land Based Missile Forces*, HI-2599-P (Croton-on-Hudson, N.Y.: Hudson Institute, 1977), p. 108; and "MX Deployment Urged for Parity," *Aviation Week & Space Technology*, Dec. 5, 1977, p. 14. This last article suggests that the CEP of MX will be 0.067 nm.

4. D. F. Hoag, "Ballistic Missile Guidance," in *Impact of New Technologies on the Arms Race*, ed. Feld et al. (Cambridge, Mass.: M.I.T. Press, 1971), p. 100.

5. This data is taken from Gray, op. cit., p. 107, and other unclassified sources. See fig. 3 on p. 17 of Gray's work for a similar depiction of ICBM accuracies.

6. See also U.S., Congress, Senate, Committee on Armed Services, *Fiscal Year 1978 Authorization for Military Research and Development, and Active Duty, Selected Reserve, and Civilian Personnel Strengths: Hearings on S. 1210*, 95th Cong., 1st sess., 1977, part 10, pp. 6868–6869.

7. The numbers reported in these estimates are usually the so-called "best estimate," and some band of uncertainty (higher and lower) about these numbers exists. One should, therefore, not interpret the B Team estimate as the lower bound on the uncertainty band regarding Soviet missile CEPs. The reported B Team value is their "best estimate" of the CEP, and in fact, the Soviet missile CEP could have been (in 1976) substantially lower than 0.15 nm. See ibid.

8. E. Kozichaw, "Across the Board Gains in Soviet Forces Detailed," *Aviation Week & Space Technology*, Aug. 29, 1977, p. 17.

9. See Gray, op. cit., p. 108; Brown, op cit., p. 108; and *Counterforce Issues for the US Strategic Nuclear Forces* (Washington, D.C.: Congressional Budget Office, 1978), p. 18.

10. Clarence A. Robinson, Jr., "Soviets Boost ICBM Accuracy," *Aviation Week & Space Technology*, Apr. 3, 1978, p. 14. The article stated that "it is clear to a number of US strategic weapons experts that the demonstrated potential for accuracy [resulting from a new series of ICBM tests] puts the Soviet Union three to five years ahead of Carter Administration estimates."

11. Ibid.

12. Ibid. However, the data had not been fully analyzed at that point, and the number of tests was probably too small (four SS-18 tests and two SS-19 tests) to allow complete confidence in the assessment.

13. In the analysis that follows, only attacks on the 1,000 Minuteman missiles are considered because the 54 Titan IIs are relatively soft in comparison and thus could be easily eliminated by a small number of Soviet missiles.

14. See Edgar Ulsamer, "The Equal Sign in the SALT II Equation," *Air Force Magazine*, Jan., 1978, p. 29. See also Gray, op. cit., p. 49.

15. Testimony of John B. Walsh, deputy director, Strategic and Space Systems, Defense Research and Engineering, Department of Defense in U.S., Congress, House, Committee on Appropriations, Subcommittee, *Department of Defense Appropriations for 1978*, 95th Cong., 1st sess., 1977, part 2, p. 200.

16. Gray, op. cit., p. 109; *Counterforce Issues for the US Strategic Nuclear Forces*, op. cit., p. 16; C. A. Robinson, Jr., "Current US and Soviet Strategic Offensive Forces," *Aviation Week & Space Technology*, Apr. 18, 1977, p. 18.

17. Congressman Les Aspin, a noted defense critic, maintains that the yield of the Soviet warheads is 2 MT. See "SALT II or No SALT" (Press release, January, 1978), p. 19.

18. The second wave of RVs would arrive only a few seconds after the first wave.

19. Lt. Col. Joseph J. McFlichley, USAF, and Dr. Jakob W. Seeling, "Why ICBMs Can Survive a Nuclear Attack," *Air Force Magazine*, Sept., 1974, pp. 82–85; and John D. Steinbruner and Thomas M. Garwin, "Strategic Vulnerability: The Balance Between Prudence and Paranoia," *International Security* 1:1 (Summer, 1976): 138–181.

20. Because the fireball is opaque to radar for only a brief time, attacks with three or more airburst weapons are probably feasible, although this may considerably complicate the attack due to interactions from weapons attacking other nearby silos.

21. Testimony of Gen. Alton D. Slay, USAF, deputy chief of staff, Research and Development in U.S., Congress, *Department of Defense Appropriations for 1978*, op. cit., part 2, p. 208.

22. See Steinbruner and Garwin, op. cit., p. 160.

23. In this case, complete (or full) fratricide means that the second RV is destroyed by the explosion of the first RV. Obviously, if the first RV does not arrive on target or fails to explode, the second RV will not be affected.

24. See below for a description of U.S. early-warning detection systems.

25. Alton H. Quanbeck and Archie L. Wood, *Modernizing the Strategic Bomber Force: Why and How* (Washington, D.C.: Brookings Institution, 1976), p. 47.

26. U.S., Congress, Senate, *Congressional Record*, 94th Cong., 2nd sess., 1976, 122, p. 6621.

27. Francis P. Hoeber, *Slow to Take Offense: Bombers, Cruise Missiles, and Prudent Deterrence* (Washington, D.C.: Center for Strategic and International Studies, Georgetown University, 1977), p. 84. This assumes a 90-second delay from SLBM launch until the warning at the base is sounded.

28. See "The Military Balance 1977/78," *Air Force Magazine*, Dec., 1977, p. 62; and Gen. George S. Brown, *The United States Military Posture for FY 1979*, pp. 27–30. The Soviets may begin replacing the SS-N-6 with the solid propellant, MIRVed SS-N-17, which has a somewhat greater range. The Soviets are also now deploying the SS-N-18 in the Delta III class SSBNs. This is a MIRVed SLBM with a range at least as great as that of the SS-N-8.

29. See Quanbeck and Wood, op. cit., p. 59.

30. Ibid., p. 48. See also appendix B.

31. If, in fact, the bombers do not fly a random pattern and the Soviets are aware of this and target appropriately, this could have a devastating effect on bomber survivability because it greatly simplifies the attacker's problems and considerably lowers the number of weapons required.

32. George Brown, op. cit., p. 35. In contrast, the United States has essentially dismantled its air defense system. It now has 331 interceptors (more than half in the Air National Guard), 57 surveillance radars, and no strategic SAMs. ("The Military Balance 1977/78," op. cit., p. 64.)

33. For example, see Quanbeck and Wood, op. cit., chap. 5; and U.S. Congress, House, *Department of Defense Appropriations for 1978*, op. cit., part 2, pp. 160, 178, 179.

34. See Barry Miller, "USAF Simulates Soviet Defense Systems," *Aviation Week & Space Technology*, May 30, 1977, pp. 43–49 for descriptions and photographs of U.S. models of some of these systems.

35. Ibid., p. 48.

36. "Perry Gives Cruise Missiles Edge Over B-1 in Penetration," *Aerospace Daily*, July 28, 1977, p. 144.

37. John F. McCarthy, Jr., "The Case for the B-1," *International Security* 1, no. 2 (Fall, 1976): 96.

38. "Perry Gives Cruise Missiles Edge Over B-1 in Penetration," *Aerospace Daily*, July 28, 1977, p. 144.

39. Miller, op. cit., p. 44.

40. The Soviets may now be deploying a new, high performance missile, the SA-10. (See Rowland Evans and Robert Novak, "Does Russia's SA-10 Eclipse the Cruise Missile?," *Washington Post*, Feb. 17, 1978, p. 17.)

41. Although the B-1 bomber would have been an improvement over the B-52 in penetrating air defenses, even it could not have been confidently relied on. The B-1 would, however, have eased the prelaunch survival problem because it could have escaped its base faster and was somewhat "harder" to nuclear effects.

42. Many would consider the firepower in the alert SSBNs to be marginal at best as a deterrent, and some consider it to be inadequate. (See Paul Nitze, "Nuclear Strategy: Detente and American Survival," in *Defending America*, James R. Schlesinger et al. [New York: Basic Books, 1977], p. 105.)

43. Quoted in Harry S. Bradsher, "Vulnerability Growing for US Sub-based Missiles?" *Washington Star*, Dec. 12, 1977, Focus section, p. 1.

44. There are two acoustic techniques used for detecting the presence of submarines: passive and active. Passive techniques use acoustic equipment (sonar) and listen for the noise generated by a submarine, either from the propeller and water flowing around the hull or, at low speeds, from machinery aboard the submarine. Active sonar generates a pulse of sound and then detects the echo reflected from a submarine. For a discussion of acoustic ASW techniques and problems, see Richard L. Garwin, "Antisubmarine Warfare and National Security," *Scientific American* 227, no. 1 (July, 1972): 14–25.

45. Larry L. Booda, "Undersea Warfare Improved Effectiveness Awaits Major Top Level Decisions," *Sea Technology*, Nov., 1976, p. 13.

46. Ibid., p. 12. Of course, the detection range depends on the noise level of Soviet submarines. It is not clear what the detection range is against the newer and presumably quieter Soviet submarines.

47. It should be noted that the Soviets maintain a fleet of 128 diesel-powered attack submarines in addition to their 39 nuclear-powered attack submarines (see "The Military Balance 1977/78," op. cit., p. 69). Diesel submarines running on batteries are even quieter than U.S. nuclear submarines. Thus, a threat of a *covert* trial may exist, particularly for those SSBNs operating out of European ports.

48. Booda, op. cit., pp. 13, 40. For a description of the current U.S. program, see Harold Brown, op. cit., pp. 181–182.

49. With a detection range of 50 nm (on either side of the boat), twenty ves-

sels towing these arrays at a speed of ten knots (nm/hr) could search an area of one million square nautical miles in about two days.

50. The Soviets could use larger sources. By 1970, high-energy transducers that could generate acoustic power in the millions of watts were available. (Even a noisy submarine radiates less than one watt of acoustic power.) Dr. Victor Anderson of the Scripps Institution of Oceanography predicted that this technology, when combined with the advances in signal processing that enable the returning signal from a submarine to be distinguished from background noise, could in effect make the oceans transparent, and submarines would no longer be safe from detection. The Soviets could deploy such transducers from large, stable, surface platforms in the open ocean. However, the effectiveness of this approach is unclear. Because these large platforms could be easily detected, the United States could employ countermeasures. The outcome is uncertain because attempts to jam the receiver with noise might be overcome by adaptive processing techniques (which, in effect, filter out the noise from the jammer). (See V. C. Anderson, "Ocean Technology," in *Impact of New Technologies on the Arms Race*, ed. Feld et al. [Cambridge, Mass.: M.I.T. Press, 1971], pp. 201–216.)

51. The effectiveness of this approach depends to a great extent on the false-alarm rate. If only the seventeen SSBNs are detected, it may take 150 1-MT warheads to barrage the area in which the submarines are thought to be located. (This assumes that the SSBNs patrol at five knots, that their initial positions are known within a radius of 15 nm, and the warheads arrive one hour after detection.) If there are 100 total targets (only seventeen actually being submarines), the Soviets will have to use about 800 warheads to cover the area of uncertainty. They could, in theory, do this with 100 SS-18 ICBMs and still have around 1,300 ICBMs left. However, warheads exploded at or near the ocean surface are not as effective against undersea targets as those burst at some depth under the ocean surface. Thus, this approach might require the development of a warhead that could withstand the impact of hitting the ocean surface or the use of more warheads if a surface burst were used.

52. Booda, op. cit., p. 40.

53. Testimony of Adm. Donald P. Harvey, in U.S., Congress, Senate, Committee on Armed Services, *Fiscal Year 1978 Authorization for Military Procurement, Research and Development, and Active Duty, Selected Reserve, and Civilian Personnel Strengths: Hearings on S. 1210*, 95th Cong., 1st sess., 1977, part 10, p. 6655.

54. Testimony of Adm. James Holloway, chief of Naval Operations, in ibid., part 2, p. 1043.

55. Until about 1965, the Soviets wrote quite openly about most of these nonacoustic techniques. For a review of the Soviet literature, see K. J. Moore, "Antisubmarine Warfare," in *Soviet Naval Influence: Domestic and Foreign Dimensions*, ed. M. MccGwine and J. McDonnell (New York: Praeger, 1977), pp. 185–200.

56. Ibid., p. 192.

57. Testimony of Rear Adm. J. Metzel, in U.S., Congress, *Fiscal Year 1978 Authorization*, op. cit., part 10, p. 6655.

58. Moore, op.cit., p. 191. Infrared detectors deployed on aircraft can reportedly detect temperature variations on the sea surface of 0.2°C. (See *Strategy Survey, 1970* (London: International Institute for Strategic Studies, 1970), p. 14.

59. Moore, op. cit., p. 192.

60. "Focus On . . . ," *Air Force Magazine*, May 1978, p. 20. See also Henry S. Bradsher, "Vulnerability Growing for US Sub-Based Missiles?" *Washington Star*, Dec. 12, 1977, Focus section, p. 1.

61. Moore, op. cit., p. 191; and Bradsher, op. cit.

62. Hydrogen in concentrations of one part per million can be detected at 300-400 yards by laser resonance Raman spectrography. Whether the concentration of a hydrogen wake left by a submarine is greater or lesser than this is unknown.

63. Moore, op. cit., p. 190. See also Giordio Tacconi, "Fundamentals of ELF Communication and Detection," in *Applications of Remote Sensing to Ocean Surveillance*, AGARD Lecture Series no. 88 (Neuilly Sur Seine, France: NATO Advisory Group for Aerospace Research & Development, 1977) pp. 9–17, 9–18.

64. See Frank Chilton, Lowell Wood, and Rod Buntzen, *Electric and Magnetic Sensing Sensors: Applications*, UCID-17597 (Livermore, Calif.: Lawrence Livermore Laboratory, 1977). Also contained in *Applications of Remote Sensing to Ocean Surveillance*, op. cit., p. 10–1.

65. With a detection range of 10 nm (and a "sweep width" of 14 nm), 30 aircraft flying at 300 knots could search an area of one million square nautical miles in about eight hours. Of course, even smaller detection ranges could be quite useful.

66. As described by Fessenden and Cheng: "Since the early nineteen sixties, U.S. submarines have utilized trailing-wire antennas in order to remain submerged while maintaining RF reception with an antenna at or near the ocean surface. The trailing wire is simply an RF transmission line and/or single conductor encased in a buoyant, polyethylene foam jacket and is usually referred to as a buoyant cable. It is normally about 2000 ft (610 m) in length and may be divided, functionally, into three parts: transmission line section, antenna section, and drogue section (if any)." A typical configuration would have a 105 ft section at the end of the cable to receive very-low-frequency (VLF) up to high-frequency (HF) messages. (Charles T. Fessenden and David H. S. Cheng, "Development of a Trailing-Wire E-Field Submarine Antenna for Extremely Low Frequency (ELF) Reception," *IEEE Transactions on Communications* 22 [April, 1974]: 428.)

67. See U.S., Congress, *Fiscal Year 1978 Authorization*, op. cit., part 10, pp. 6690–6695.

68. Ibid.

69. For a photograph of the trailing wire floating on the surface, see ibid., p. 6694.

70. This approach has the possible drawback that it would take about two months before all the boats had been cycled through port and returned to sea with the sabotage devices aboard. This conflicts considerably with the general notion that a nuclear war would occur by accident or in the heat of a worldwide crisis. Of course, the crisis could come and appear to subside in the eyes of the West. The Soviet perception might be quite different. In the height of the crisis, the Kremlin might decide that war is inevitable and proceed with war preparations while giving all appearances of cooling the crisis and pushing for a return to the precrisis political atmosphere.

71. Testimony of Adm. Donald P. Harvey, in U.S., Congress, *Fiscal Year 1978 Authorization*, op. cit., part 10, p. 6620.

72. Bradsher, op. cit.

73. Testimony of Vice Adm. Robert Kaufman, director, Command, Control and Communications, in U.S., Congress, *Fiscal Year 1978 Authorization*, op. cit., part 10, p. 6756.

74. Ibid.

75. For a description of SOSUS and other U.S. ASW systems, see the November issues of *Sea Technology* for 1974, 1975, and 1976.

76. John M. Collins and John S. Chwat, *United States and Soviet City Defense, Considerations for Congress* (Washington, D.C.: Government Printing Office, 1976), p. 73.

77. Ibid., pp. 75–76.

78. Ibid., p. 75.

79. Ibid., p. 76. These are the PAVE PAWS radars.

80. For a more detailed description of these aircraft and wartime procedures, see the special issue of *Aviation Week & Space Technology*, May 10, 1976.

81. Ibid., p. 57.

82. Ibid., p. 49.

83. SAC could adopt a policy of launching the bombers whenever contact is lost between the satellites or ground stations. However, the launching of the entire alert bomber force is a serious matter, both from a diplomatic and from a technical viewpoint. For example, when the bombers return to base following a false alarm, there is a period of time during which the fleet is at a lower readiness state. This solution would depend a great deal on how often false alarms occur. If they are fairly common, it is doubtful that this would be adopted.

84. U.S., Congress, House, Committee on Appropriations, Subcommittee, *Department of Defense Appropriations for 1979*, 95th Cong., 2nd sess., 1978, part 3, p. 622.

85. Ibid.

86. See Henry S. Bradsher, "Soviet ABM Efforts Have Pentagon Worried," *Washington Star*, Feb. 16, 1978, p. 11.

87. Ibid.

88. Ibid. These mobile missiles have mobile, phased array radars associated with them. The Soviets also appear to be developing other ABM radars that can be quickly deployed. (See *Aviation Week & Space Technology*, Oct. 21, 1974, p. 14.)

89. Bradsher, "Soviet ABM Efforts," suggests the high altitude SA-5 would be used as the middle system of a tri-level, layered ABM. He also states that the Soviets have tested the SA-5 against ballistic missiles RVs, although there is some debate over the accuracy of this contention.

CHAPTER IV

1. See chap. 2.

2. To pindown the Minuteman missiles until the Soviet ICBMs arrive might take 200–300 warheads depending on the hardness of Minuteman and the yield of the Soviet warheads. The Soviets now have over 900 SLBMs.

3. E. g., U.S., Congress, House, Committee on Appropriations, Subcommittee, *Department of Defense Appropriations for 1979*, 95th Cong., 2nd sess., 1978, part

3, p. 611; Richard L. Garwin, "Effective Military Technology for the 1980s," *International Security* 1, no. 2 (Fall, 1976): 50–77; and C. A. Robinson, Jr., "Quickened Pace Sought in Missile Defense," *Aviation Week & Space Technology*, May 22, 1978, p. 16.

4. U.S., Congress, *Department of Defense Appropriations for 1979*, op. cit., part 3, pp. 618, 630.

5. The 400 or more Soviet ICBMs that will survive a U.S. attack in 1985 could carry about 1,000 warheads, each having a yield of about 1 MT. See appendix B for the methodology of countersilo calculations, the data used, and a discussion of U.S. counterforce capability.

6. For this calculation (which assumes a nominal force of 150 MX missiles with an accuracy of 0.07 nm), the Soviets could be drawn down to 125–175 ICBMs. If the MX force is expanded (with either more missiles or more RVs per missile) or its accuracy further improved, MX can obviously be even more effective as a hard-target counterforce weapon.

7. See Leon Goure, Foy D. Kohler, and Mose L. Harvey, eds. *The Role of Nuclear Forces in Current Soviet Strategy* (Coral Gables, Fla.: Center for Advanced International Studies, University of Miami, 1974), pp. 102–112.

8. If a Soviet attack occurs, it may be far more advisable for the United States to retain its remaining ICBMs (as a deterrent against city attacks) rather than using them to attack Soviet ICBMs.

9. Donald Rumsfeld, *Department of Defense Annual Report, Fiscal Year 1978* p. 71.

10. In any event, if a Soviet counterforce strike occurs (presumably directed at the more vulnerable bomber and submarine bases), any requirement to retaliate against remaining Soviet silos can be met by using the highly accurate cruise missiles. Of course, because the cruise missiles are slow, the Soviets may launch their ICBMs before they can be destroyed; but this is also true of an attack by MX.

11. Originally expected to be available in 1983, the MX system may not be available until 1987 or later and then only partially. The full system could not be completed until the early 1990s.

12. The conceptual approach described here was originated by Albert Latter. This approach is also being considered for basing MX. (See C. A. Robinson, Jr., "Salt Stance Allows New Missiles," *Aviation Week & Space Technology*, Apr. 24, 1978, pp. 16–19; and U.S., Congress, *Department of Defense Appropriations for 1979*, op. cit., part 3, p. 618.)

13. J. F. W. Parry, *Austere Silo Concept* (Marina del Rey, Calif.: R & D Associates, 1978).

14. These missiles are guarded by electronic sensors that warn of any intrusion into the fenced area, and troops from a central location are sent to investigate any irregularity.

15. Although, for the most part, environmental concerns are unwarranted for suitably selected sites, these concerns would no doubt generate many law suits and much public opposition, which could delay the system indefinitely.

16. The inspections could of course take place at random times also. A variation on this procedure would be to allow the Soviets to inspect the eight dummy cannisters but not the real one.

17. It may be possible to develop a system in which no one knows the location of missiles if the cannisters are loaded by one person who then gives them to an-

other person who in turn places them randomly about the complex. Because all cannisters would look alike, the driver would not know which cannister contained the missile, and the "dispenser" would not know in which hole the actual missile was placed.

18. Parry, op. cit.

19. This particular point should not be exaggerated, however, because most of this explosive power is due to the four one-megaton bombs that can be carried by each bomber. A bomber's chances for overcoming the defenses around important targets (because the bomber must overfly the target to deliver the bomb) do not appear great. Thus, a bomber must use the much lower yield, Short-Range Attack Missiles (SRAM) or cruise missiles to attack important targets.

20. Based on present freeway construction costs of $3 to $5 million per mile and austere facilities for the crews.

21. At present, crews can be involved in recreational or educational activities in other parts of the base. Although vehicles are available to take them to their aircraft if an alarm sounds, the time delay could be fatal.

22. The first B-52 fitted with twenty cruise missiles is scheduled to become operational in September, 1981. However, a full squadron of B-52s equipped with cruise missiles will not be operational until December, 1982. ("Cruise Missiles Called Costly to Counter," *Aviation Week & Space Technology*, June 12, 1978, p. 20.)

23. U.S., Congress, *Department of Defense Appropriations for 1979*, op. cit., part 2, p. 742.

24. A total of 400 Poseidon warheads are now assigned to support a theater nuclear war. This represents an increase of 250. (Ibid., part 2, p. 849.)

25. By converting twelve boats, the Navy expects to deploy a maximum of ten SSBNs; i.e., there will be times when less than ten boats are deployed due to overhauls. According to the Navy, it has increased the number of backfitted boats from ten to twelve, but "this does not require an increase in missile production because our missile procurement plans are based on deployed levels, not total levels. When a boat goes off-line for regular overhaul, its missiles are made available to the deployed force." (Ibid., part 2, p. 653). Thus, only C-4 missiles will be deployed in the ten Poseidon SSBNs under present plans.

26. It would also be possible to increase the range of present missiles by removing some of the MIRVed warheads. However, considering the small size of the force, this is not an attractive approach to the problem. If required, one or two boats could be kept in the present patrol area to handle time-urgent targets.

27. See H. F. Cooper, Jr., *An ICBM Basing Concept: Underground Missiles in Mesas (UMMS)* (Marina del Rey, Calif.: R & D Associates, 1978).

28. The Boeing 707s and 747s and the McDonnell Douglas DC-8s and DC-10s have ranges of 7000–9000 nm.

29. For one approach to overcoming these problems, see H. F. Cooper et al., *Description and Possible Capability of a Superhard Underground Command System (SHUCS) and Associated Technology Needs*, DNA-3755T (Marina del Rey, Calif.: R & D Associates, 1975).

30. These missiles might be encapsulated and dropped off some time before launch to maintain the submarine's safety.

31. Albert Wohlstetter, "Racing Forward or Ambling Back?" in *Defending America*, James R. Schlesinger et al. (New York: Basic Books, 1977), pp. 110–168.

32. See Bernard Brodie, "On the Objectives of Arms Control," *International Security* 1, no. 1, (Fall, 1976): 17–36, particularly pp. 29–33.

33. Consider, for example, the conflicts in the Middle East.

34. Agreements that save money without affecting security obviously can also be useful.

35. This is a policy aimed at developing a "first-strike" capability. Whether the intent is defensive or aggressive is a separate question (see chap. 1).

36. There are also likely to be unilateral restrictions on the throw-weight of U.S. ICBMs.

37. Cruise missiles are far more important to the United States than to the Soviet Union. Even if long-range cruise missiles are completely banned, it will not affect the Soviet Union (presuming they adhere to the ban) because their bombers have essentially a "free ride" when penetrating U.S. airspace because the American air defense system has been effectively dismantled. Furthermore, the Soviets already have (and have had for many years) hundreds of cruise missiles deployed on ships and submarines as well as on aircraft. Although these missiles are short-range, they can reach the 50 percent of the American population and industries concentrated along the U.S. coasts.

38. Congressman Robin L. Beard has suggested the following amendment to a SALT II treaty: "The development and testing of ICBMs for the purpose of allowing their deployment and launching from multiple aimpoints is allowed. The concept of deployment of multiple aimpoints includes ICBMs that are mobile and also ICBMs that are deployed at several redundant sites. Also the development and testing of associated cannisters, transporters, and launchers is allowed. If ICBMs are deployed in a multiple aimpoint mode, they will be counted under SALT limits in terms of the number of missiles and not in the context of launchers. The side undertaking such a deployment must provide for the adequate verification of the number of missiles deployed." (Edgar Ulsmer, "Focus on . . . ," *Air Force Magazine*, June, 1978, p. 17.)

39. Jack F. Kemp, "SALT Recess Urged," *Aviation Week & Space Technology*, June 5, 1978, p. 9.

40. See Congressman Les Aspin, "SALT II or No SALT" (Press release, Jan., 1978); and idem, *Bulletin of the Atomic Scientists* 34, no. 6 (June, 1978): 34. Henry Kissinger made similar arguments for accepting SALT I, but that agreement neither stopped Soviet momentum nor lessened the threat to Minuteman.

41. "New US Plan for Cruise Missile," *The Trib* (New York), Mar. 30, 1978, p. 14.

42. As noted previously, Secretary Brown has stated that these aircraft could not be available until 1988 or 1990.

43. If the Soviets continued to deploy missiles, the apparent throw-weight differential would increase (because the U.S. would only be deploying silos not missiles), but the usable Soviet throw-weight would not increase because each new Soviet missile would be "absorbed" by new U.S. silos. This illustrates another important feature of the multiple-aim-point (MAP) Minuteman system—it is a way of rectifying the throw-weight imbalance without increasing U.S. throw-weight. In the early 1980s, the Soviets would require only 300 (or less) of their 1,400 ICBMs to threaten the entire U.S. ICBM force, leaving considerable throw-weight for tasks beyond the counterforce role. However, a fully deployed MAP system could absorb

the entire Soviet ICBM force and reduce the usable Soviet ICBM throw-weight to zero but still leave half of the Minuteman missiles surviving. This would seem to preclude the Soviets from considering a deliberate, calculated attack on the United States.

44. See R. F. Herbst and A. L. Latter, *The Role of Strategic Forces* (Marina del Rey, Calif.: R & D Associates, 1972) for a discussion of many of the following points.

45. Other aspects of that proposal, such as severe limits on the number of cruise missile carriers, were less conducive to stability.

46. Paul C. Warnke, the chief U.S. arms control negotiator, has written: "I can hardly believe that there can be any continuing détente or any chance of a useful relationship unless arms control succeeds." ("Arms Control: A Global Imperative," *Bulletin of the Atomic Scientists* 34, no. 6 (June, 1978): 32.)

CHAPTER V

1. Actually, even during the 1950s and early 1960s, the United States did not have a unilateral deterrent in the sense that it could have coerced the Soviet Union. Although the Soviet Union had only limited long-range forces during this period, they did build a massive force of medium-range bombers and ballistic missiles in order to hold Europe hostage.

2. P. Gallois, "United States Strategy and the Defense of Europe," in *Problems of National Strategy*, ed. Henry A. Kissinger (New York: Praeger, 1965), p. 295.

3. Although these are considered to be "theater" forces by the United States, to the Soviet Union and Western Europe they obviously are of "strategic" importance.

4. Harold Brown, *Department of Defense Annual Report, FY-79*, p. 34.

5. Manfred Worner, "NATO Defenses and Tactical Nuclear Weapons," *Strategic Review* 5, no. 4 (Fall, 1977): 11–18. If the West has 24 to 36 hours of warning, 18 combat-ready NATO divisions would be facing 39 divisions of the Warsaw Pact. With three days of warning, it would be 25 NATO divisions versus 77 Pact divisions, and with a comprehensive mobilization (with ten to twelve days of warning) 32 NATO divisions would confront about 110 Warsaw Pact divisions at the beginning of the conflict. It should be noted that Soviet divisions are smaller than NATO divisions—about 11,000 troops compared to 16,000. As for active duty personnel along the Northern and Central European fronts, the Warsaw Pact has 945,000 troops compared with 630,000 for NATO. In main battle tanks, the Warsaw Pact leads 20,500 to 7,000. (See *Military Balance, 1977–1978* (London: International Institute for Strategic Studies, 1977) pp. 104, 106.)

6. Senators Sam Nunn and Dewey F. Bartlett, "NATO and the New Soviet Threat," in U.S., Congress, Senate, *Congressional Record*, 95th Cong., 1st sess., 1977, 123, part 13, p. 3.

7. Ibid., p. 4.

8. C. A. Robinson, Jr., "Increasing Soviet Offensive Threat Spurs Stronger Europe Air Arm," *Aviation Week & Space Technology*, Aug. 1, 1977, p. 46.

9. General Robert Close, *Europe Without Defense* (Brussels: Editions Arts and Voyages, 1976). See also "Surprize Attack Could Make Nuclear Weapons Useless," *London Times*, Mar. 15, 1976, p. 1.

10. U.S., Congress, Senate, *Congressional Record*, 95th Cong., 1st sess., 1977, 123, p. 14104.

11. Worner, op. cit., p. 15.

12. Secretary of Defense James R. Schlesinger, *The Theatre Nuclear Force Posture in Europe, A Report to the United States Congress* (1975), p. 13. The Carter administration expresses this in somewhat more muted tones: "But, for the most part, their military doctrine continues to stress the likelihood of escalation to nuclear conflict and the need for the combined nuclear and conventional operations. They continue to equip and train their forces to fight in both chemical and nuclear environments." (Brown, op. cit., p. 69.)

13. The SS-11 ICBM is also often tested in a shorter than full-range mode.

14. *Planning US General Purpose Forces: The Theater Nuclear Forces* (Washington, D.C.: Congressional Budget Office, 1977), p. viii.

15. Jeffery Record, "Theater Nuclear Weapons: Begging the Soviet Union to Preempt," *Survival* 19, no. 5 (Sept./Oct., 1977): 211.

16. The Soviets have about 600 SS-4 and SS-5 launchers in the western Soviet Union. With reloads, they may have from 1,000–3,000 of these missiles. Of course, the deployment of only 400 of the new SS-20s would provide an additional 1,200 accurate warheads for this task. The missile time-of-flight to NATO airbases is very short, and few if any aircraft would likely escape. The American aircraft carriers are under almost constant surveillance by Soviet submarines, ships, or aircraft—all of which carry missiles with nuclear warheads.

17. Brown, op. cit., pp. 67–68.

18. T. C. Schelling, *The Strategy of Conflict* (Cambridge, Mass.: Harvard University Press, 1960), chap. 3.

19. Richard Rosecrance, *Strategic Deterrence Reconsidered*, Adelphi Paper no. 116 (London: International Institute for Strategic Studies, 1975), p. 11.

20. Speech by General Alexander Haig, Oct. 13, 1976, reprinted in *Survival* 19, no. 1 (Jan./Feb., 1977): 34. More recently General Haig reiterated this position: "The core of our deterrent (in Western Europe) remains uncertainty on the part of a potential aggressor with respect to what our response would be." (*U.S. News and World Report*, June 5, 1978, p. 21.)

21. *White Paper 1975/1976: The Security of the Federal Republic of Germany and the Development of the Federal Armed Forces* (Bonn: Federal Minister of Defense, FRG, 1976), pp. 20–21.

22. There are a number of other contingencies besides a deliberate Soviet attack (such as the escalation of an Eastern European uprising or a crisis in Yugoslavia after the death of Tito) that are of concern to some analysts. However, there is no indication that NATO could effectively deal with these problems should they arise. A primarily defensive NATO posture (as will be suggested in the next chapter) would probably lower the likelihood of NATO involvement in these affairs and thus lower the likelihood of war.

23. The logic of this argument would seem to suggest that if the Europeans someday voted themselves into the Soviet orbit, an attack on the Soviet Union would then be appropriate.

24. As for the economic impact, although Europe is a valuable trading partner, it has no resources critical to the economic survival of the United States. The loss of the European trade would require some adjustments in U.S. industry (and perhaps some lowering of the American standard of living), but it would certainly not deliver a death blow to the economy. As for the rest of the world, it is unclear how effec-

tively the Soviets would be able to extend their empire beyond those areas close to their borders in an attempt to cut off all American trade. (The so-called vital resources may not even be all that important. Today, it is cheaper to import than to seek alternatives, but this does not mean that alternatives could not be developed.) At any rate, this threat would lie in the future, and thus U.S. counteractions might prevent the threat from materializing. On the other hand, U.S. attacks on the Soviet Union could result in an immediate full-scale nuclear war.

25. *Annual Defense Department Report FY 1975*, p. 38.

26. *Annual Defense Department Report FY 1976 and FY 197T*, p. II-3.

27. See Ted Greenwood and Michael L. Nacht, "The New Debate: Sense or Nonsense?" *Foreign Affairs* 52, no. 4 (July, 1974): 761–780.

28. B. H. Liddell Hart, *Deterrent or Defense?* (New York: Praeger, 1960), p. 254.

CHAPTER VI

1. See James Schlesinger, *The Theater Nuclear Force Posture in Europe, A Report to the United States Congress* (1975); Joseph D. Douglass, Jr., *The Soviet Theater Nuclear Offensive*, Studies in Communist Affairs, vol. 1 (Washington, D.C.: Government Printing Office, 1976); V. D. Sokolovskiy, *Soviet Military Strategy*, trans. and ed. Harriet Fast Scott (New York: Crane Russak & Company, 1975); A. A. Sidorenko, *The Offensive (A Soviet View)*, trans. U.S. Air Force (Washington, D.C.: Government Printing Office, 1974); L. Goure, F. D. Kohler, and M. L. Harvey, *The Role of Nuclear Force in Current Soviet Strategy*, Monographs in International Affairs, Center for Advanced International Studies (Coral Gables, Fla.: Center for Advanced International Studies, University of Miami, 1974). See also the "Posture Statements" submitted by the secretaries of defense to Congress since 1975.

2. Bernard Brodie, "Introduction," in *Toward a New Defense for NATO, The Case for Tactical Nuclear Weapons* (New York: National Strategy Information Center, 1976), p. 7.

3. See Harold M. Agnew, "A Primer on Enhanced Radiation Weapons," *Bulletin of the Atomic Scientists* 33, no. 10 (Dec., 1977): 6–8.

4. As part of the Soviets' campaign against NATO's deployment of the neutron bomb, they have "threatened" to deploy similar weapons. Of course, from NATO's point of view, far from being a threat, nothing could be more welcome. Since NATO plans to fight a defensive war, most Soviet nuclear weapons would be used on Western European soil. Anything that would lessen civilian casualties in the unhappy event of a war should be encouraged.

5. This policy could be called a "no first-strike" policy but should not be confused with the concept of an effective first-strike counterforce capability. The United States has eschewed (of late) the development of a first-strike damage-limiting capability but has nevertheless held that under some circumstances it might initiate nuclear strikes against the Soviet Union ("flexible response").

6. The Soviet Union and the other Warsaw Pact nations have over the years advocated a joint NATO–Warsaw Pact pledge of "no first use" of nuclear weapons. This has been correctly rejected by NATO because it would tie NATO's hands in dealing with a Warsaw Pact invasion. The proposal offered here would be politically

difficult for the Soviets to reject, however, since it is the equivalent to their proposal except in the event they are planning an attack on NATO. For a similar proposal distinguishing between defensive and offensive use of nuclear weapons, see Edward Teller, *In Search of Solutions for Defense and Energy* (Stanford: Hoover Institution, 1977), p. 9.

7. See below for a discussion of the relationship between a "no first strike" policy and a new strategy for deterrence and for limiting civilian casualties.

8. A "no first-strike" policy would also have an important impact on the question of U.S. civil defense. Rational discussion of civil defense has been greatly limited by the fear that if civil defense could be successfully achieved, it might tempt the United States to initiate a nuclear war under some circumstances. With this fear removed, a more realistic evaluation of civil defense as a prudent hedge against a nuclear war could be made.

9. Some might argue that the following approach could be implemented without any change in the official flexible response doctrine. However, because it would involve the possible early and extensive battlefield use of nuclear weapons, it is difficult to imagine that this proposal could get a hearing as long as the present doctrine remains in force. For a contrary view, which recommends both an early use of tactical nuclear weapons *and* the flexible response policy, see Jacquelyn K. Davis and Robert L. Pfaltzgraff, Jr., *Soviet Theater Strategy: Implications for NATO* (Washington, D.C.: United States Strategic Institute, 1978).

10. The concept was developed by Roland Herbst, S. T. Cohen, George Taylor, and others at R & D Associates. A similar approach (with a nuclear "kill zone" but without the physical barrier) was suggested by Col. Marc Geneste, French Army (Ret.); see "The Nuclear Land Battle," *Strategic Review* 4, no. 1 (Winter, 1976): 79.

11. Of course, breaking through with only conventional weapons would require the massing of a large Pact force, which could then be attacked by NATO forces before the barrier was breached. Because the fortifications would be hardened, they could withstand NATO's own nuclear explosions in the obstacle barrier or in front of it.

12. Aircraft based at easily targeted European airfields may have difficulty surviving a Soviet attack. The further development of vertical takeoff or short-takeoff aircraft that can operate out of open fields and from highways could provide some hope for maintaining a survivable tactical air arm.

13. These newly arriving aircraft might also orbit behind the lines and launch cruise missiles in close air support of the barrier or of units fighting those Pact forces that might have succeeded in penetrating the barrier.

14. Although the Soviets plan to use airborne raids behind the lines, the major threat comes from their surface-based forces. Slow transport aircraft are quite vulnerable to air defenses; the drop zones can be targeted with nuclear weapons; and, finally, the effectiveness of airborne bridgeheads is quite limited unless they are quickly linked with ground troops.

15. (In billions of dollars) Bunkers: $1.1; tunnels: $1.1; armored vehicle barriers: $0.84; weapons and equipment: $1.1; land: $0.5.

16. Charles Schultz et al., *Setting National Priorities: The 1972 Budget* (Washington, D.C.: Brookings Institution, 1971), p. 58.

17. One of the problems with a barrier concept is pyschological. A barrier immediately brings to mind the Maginot Line of fortifications that was supposed to

defend France from the Germans during the 1930s. Although this system has received much criticism since the war, it in fact was never attacked by the Germans. The Germans struck beyond the western end (along the Belgian border) of the incomplete Maginot Line. But even with the Line incomplete, the French could probably have successfully fought off an invasion by maintaining strong forces along the Belgian border. However, in the words of Liddell Hart: "What proved fatal to the French was not, as is commonly imagined, their defensive attitude or 'Maginot Line complex,' but the more offensive side of their plan. By pushing into Belgium with their left shoulder forward they played into the hands of their enemy, and wedged themselves into a trap. . . . With every step forward that these armies took in their rush into Belgium, their rear became more exposed to (the German's) flanking drive through the Ardennes. Worse still, the hinge of the Allied advance was guarded by a few low-grade French divisions, composed of older men and scantily equipped in anti-tank and anti-aircraft guns, the two vital needs. To leave the hinge so poorly covered was the crowning blunder of the French High Command." (B. H. Liddell Hart, *History of the Second World War* (New York: Putnam's, 1971, p. 70.)

18. Geneste, op. cit., p. 85.

19. Joseph D. Douglass, Jr., "Soviet Nuclear Strategy in Europe: A Selective Targeting Doctrine," *Strategic Review* 5, no. 4 (Fall, 1977): 19–32.

20. If the Soviets wish to destroy Western European cities, they have more than enough nuclear armed rockets to accomplish this feat. An invasion by its army would be superfluous for this objective.

21. A purely conventional war as presently envisioned by NATO could last months and result in destruction comparable to or worse than World War II. And the chances of an ultimate NATO victory would not be high.

22. A deterrence policy based on retaliation against Soviet cities may be credible against a Soviet invasion even though European cities were not struck. Although the threat might be suicidal, the Western Europeans might credibly argue that actual conquest and occupation (something that America would not be in danger of) would be to them worse than suicide. However, against anything other than an attack on European cities, this threat may not be politically viable. Considering the range of popular support in Western Europe for communist and socialist ideology, it may not be possible to embrace a pure retaliation doctrine based on a "better dead than red" policy. This might be particularly true of French and British responses to a Soviet attack on Germany.

23. A similar system now exists in NATO. German troops have nuclear weapons available to them, but the weapons are controlled jointly with the Americans and will be released to them by the Americans only in the event of war.

24. Michel Tatu, "The Devolution of Power: A Dream?" *Foreign Affairs* 53, no. 4 (July, 1975): 669.

25. In order to meet this problem, the United States could conceivably launch reconnaissance satellites during the war. (The prewar satellites in orbit are not likely to survive.) But the significant time delays involved in finding an appropriate target, relaying the data, assigning a weapon to a target, and then delivering that weapon are likely to make transcontinental targeting ineffective. In theory, bombers flying armed reconnaissance missions could attack important targets, but their chances of success against the Soviet air defense system are not great.

26. Attacks on Soviet strategic submarine bases and bomber bases could of course be profitable if the Soviets left these forces in place.

27. The German attacks on Warsaw in September, 1939, and on Rotterdam in May, 1940, while described in Allied countries as indiscriminate attacks on civilians seem to have been attacks against legitimate tactical military objectives and were apparently designed to defeat the military forces that were using those cities as defensive positions. The attack on Rotterdam was reported in London to have killed 30,000 civilians. Although the nature and extent of the German attack were exaggerated (the actual number killed was 980), the British cabinet, in response, approved the first air strike on industrial targets in the Ruhr. Later, on the night of August 24, 1940, about a dozen German aircraft accidentally dropped their bombs on London. The next day the British retaliated by attacking Berlin. Two more raids were carried out on August 30 and 31. On September 7, Hitler responded by beginning the London Blitz. Although designed to attack military and industrial targets, any night raid was bound to result in attacks on residential areas. By October 30, 1940, British directives indicated the clear acceptance of a policy of indiscriminate, area bombings. A new directive to British Bomber Command on February 14, 1942, emphasized that the primary objective was to be the terror bombing of civilians in order to destroy civilian morale. (See F. M. Sallager, *The Road to Total War: Escalation in World War II*, R-465-PR [Santa Monica, Calif.: RAND Corp., 1969], pp. 36–39, 59–61, 90–93; and B. H. Liddell Hart, *History of the Second World War* [New York: Putnam's, 1971] p. 594–597.)

28. See Michael M. May, "Some Advantages of a Counterforce Deterrence," *Orbis* 14, no. 2 (Summer, 1970): 271–283; Fred Charles Ikle, "Can Deterrence Last Out the Century," *Foreign Affairs* 51, no. 2 (Jan., 1973): 267–285; Wolfgang K. H. Panofsky, "The Mutual-Hostage Relationship Between America and Russia," *Foreign Affairs* 52, no. 1 (Oct., 1973): 109–118; Bruce Russet, "Assured Destruction of What? A Counter-Combatant Alternative to Nuclear Madness," *Public Policy* 22, no. 2 (Spring, 1974): 121–138.

29. One can reasonably argue that if the Soviets start a war, the moral responsibility for the death of Soviet citizens that results from any defensive actions by the United States lies with the leadership that started the war. This is true for those incidentally killed in defensive actions but hardly applies to those deliberately killed (or where no precautions at all are taken to avoid casualties) by massive attacks on cities.

30. This point of view, of course, denies the efficacy of the Soviet civil defense program, which many suggest could hold Soviet casualties to a few percent of the population.

31. Quoted in William W. Kaufmann, *The McNamara Strategy* (New York: Harper & Row, 1964), pp. 114–210.

32. As an alternative to both civilian attacks and war-fighting, some authors (see Bruce Rusett, op. cit.; and Bernard S. Albert, "Construction Counterpower," *Orbis* 20, no. 2 (Summer, 1976): 343–366) have suggested that targeting should be against the sources of the Soviet leadership's power, primarily tactical military forces and internal security forces. In particular, Soviet troops in Eastern Europe and along the Chinese border and KGB units are suggested as prime targets. However, these tactics are of doubtful merit. In Eastern Europe, the governments in power are not anti-Soviet. Although the people may resent Soviet control, it is not likely that there would be an immediate uprising, since strong communist governments would still be in power. In the Far East, it is not clear that the Chinese would move to take advantage of Soviet weaknesses. Although it would be a matter of strong con-

cern (particularly if a protracted war in Europe were expected), the Soviet Union would still have a strong nuclear deterrent against Chinese actions. In the throes of a nuclear war with the United States, the credibility of Soviet use of nuclear weapons against China in the event of a Chinese invasion would be quite high. Finally, the evidence for an internal breakup of the Soviet state if the KGB is attacked is nonexistent. Although most Soviet citizens would undoubtedly be glad to be rid of the KGB, internal revolt is likely to be the last thing on their minds in the midst of a nuclear war that could threaten their existence. But beyond the question of the usefulness of these attacks is the question of whether these targets can be attacked effectively. As has been pointed out, both the military and the KGB can move and are very likely to do so if war seems imminent. Thus, attempts to define and target the Soviet leadership's elusive power base are unlikely to prevent the Soviets from achieving their military objectives and thus will be of little deterrence value.

APPENDIX B

1. For a more detailed discussion of ICBM survivability calculations, see Lynn Davis and Warner Schilling, "All You Ever Wanted To Know About MIRV and ICBM Calculations But Were Not Cleared To Ask," *Journal of Conflict Resolution* 17, no. 2 (June, 1973): 207–242.

2. Derived from experimental data. See H. J. Carpenter, *On Nuclear Height-of-Burst Airblast at High Overpressures* (Marina del Rey, Calif.: R & D Associates, 1975), p. 6.

3. "Could US Survive First Strike by Soviets?," *Human Events*, September 24, 1977, p. 10.

4. There could be more RVs per missile or more missiles.

5. Alton H. Quanbeck and Archie L. Wood, *Modernizing the Strategic Bomber Force: Why and How* (Washington, D.C.: Brookings Institution, 1976). Appendix B of their book contains a somewhat more detailed discussion of the model used here.

6. Ibid., pp. 44, 51.

7. U.S., Congress, Senate, *Congressional Record*, 94th Cong., 2nd sess., 1976, 122, p. 6622. The Air Force states that this figure fails to take into account the capability of the "aircraft to climb-out above the triple point (Mach stem) effects generated by the nuclear weapon shock waves reflected off the earth."

8. Quanbeck and Wood, op. cit., p. 48.

9. This assumes that all the SLBMs are reliable. If the missiles are only 80 percent reliable, five SLBMs must be used to assure that four SLBMs arrived. More generally,

$$P_s = 1 - \rho n(R_L/R_u)^2$$

where ρ is the reliability.

Index

ABM systems, 10, 69; covert, 70; defense of Minuteman, 74; forward based, 62; R&D, 70
ABM Treaty, 63, 69, 74
Accuracy, missile: assessment of, 37; definition of, 35; history of improvements in, 36–38; intelligence estimates of, 37–39
Airborne command post, 67, 69, 84
Airborne launch control system, 67
Airburst, nuclear weapons: fuzing, 26, 44; and prevention of fallout, 26; and prevention of fratricide, 43
Air defense, Soviet, 9, 29, 51–56
Alert rate, strategic forces, 32, 46, 57, 64, 85
Alpha net, 68
Antiballistic missiles. See ABM
Antisubmarine warfare. See ASW
Arctic deployment of SSBNs, 87
Arms control, 22, 92–99
Arms race, 22, 93
Army. See Conventional forces
Assured destruction, 8, 72, 103, 113, 128; McNamara criteria for, 24, 126; Mutual assured destruction, 103
ASW: acoustic, 57–59; arms control limitations on, 99; intelligence uncertainties regarding, 63; nonacoustic, 59–64

B-1 bomber, 29, 84
Backfire bomber, 106; and SALT, 95–96
Balance of terror, 15

Ballistic Missile Early Warning System (BMEWS), 66
Barrier defense of Europe, 117–23
Ben-Zvi, Abraham, 21
Bluffing, as a deterrent, 109, 112, 113
BMEWS. See Ballistic Missile Early Warning System
Boeing Aerospace Company, 26
Bomber gap, 27
Bombers, U.S.: alert rate of, 21, 46, 85; basing of, 46–47, 50, 84; description of, 24, 45, 132–33; flyout characteristics of, 145; penetration tactics of, 52–53, 85; reaction time of, 46, 85, 143; survivability of, 29, 45–56, 84–85, 143–45
Booda, Larry L., 58
Brezhnev, Leonid, 9
Brodie, Bernard, 114
Brown, Harold, 29–30, 77, 104, 107
B Team, 18, 37–39, 44

C^3. See Command, control, and communications
Carter administration, NATO policy of, 106
CEP, 35. See also Accuracy
Circle of equal probability. See CEP
Circular error probable. See CEP
Civil defense, 8, 10, 26, 30
Civilians: bombing of in World War II, 126; and nuclear war, 125–30; renunciation of attacks on, 126, 128
Close, Major General Robert, 106

Coercion. *See* Nuclear coercion
Collateral damage, 78, 115, 120
Command, control, and communications (C³). *See* Strategic C³
Complacency, Defense Department, 27–31
Controlled response doctrine, 127–28
Conventional forces: European balance, 105–7; vulnerability to surprise attack, 21, 107
Counterforce capability: Schlesinger's views on, 27; of Soviets, 33–69; of U.S., 76–77, 141–43
Counterforce targeting, 8–10, 76–80, 124
Crisis stability, 16, 73
Cruise missile, 19; carriers, 85, 91, 97; for penetration, 85; and SALT limitations, 93–98; Soviet, 106, 161; for a strategic reserve, 91
Cuban missile crisis, 12–13

Damage limiting, 8–10, 15, 77, 103, 128; and Soviet doctrine, 9
Defense Support Program (DSP), 66, 69. *See also* Tactical warning
Depressed trajectories, 48–50, 83–84, 144
de Gaulle, Charles, 104
Détente, 58, 92, 99, 130
Deterrence, 7; assuring, 17; by denial and defense, 113; extended, 8, 16, 103–12; by retaliation, 8–9; Soviet views on, 9–11; U.S. views on, 8–9
Diad, 19–20, 72
Diversity, strategic forces, 19, 32
DSP. *See* Defense Support Program

EAM. *See* Emergency Action Message
Early warning systems. *See* Tactical warning
ECM. *See* Electronic countermeasures
Eisenhower administration, NATO policy of, 103
Electronic countermeasures (ECM), 55
Electronic surveillance systems, 18, 21, 65, 94
ELF communications, 62, 88
Emergency Action Message (EAM), 67, 69

Emergency Rocket Communications System (ERCS), 67, 69
EMT, 24, 132–35
Enhanced radiation weapon, 114, 121
Enthoven, Alain C., 17
Equivalent megatons. *See* EMT
Essential equivalence, 13, 28
European deterrent, 121–23
Extended deterrence. *See* Deterrence

Fallout, nuclear, 26, 115
First-strike, 8–9, 13, 15, 27, 127. *See also* Counterforce and Damage limiting
First use of nuclear weapons: defensive, 116; offensive, 103, 116. *See also* First-strike; Flexible response; and LNOs
Flexible response doctrine, 104, 107; credibility of, 109; morality of, 115; need for change of, 114
Forward defense, NATO policy of, 105–6, 109
Foster, John S., Jr., 18
Fratricide, 28, 36, 43; calculation of, 139

Gallois, Pierre, 103
Geneste, Colonel Marc, 120
Gorshkov, Admiral Sergi G., 56
Grechko, Marshal Andrei A., 9
Green pine system, 68
Ground control intercept (GCI), 52, 54

Haig, General Alexander, 108
Hard-target kill capability, 76
Harvey, Admiral Donald P., 59, 63
Hiroshima, 23, 126
Hitler, Adolph, 112
Hoag, D. C., 36

ICBMs, Soviet: accuracy of, 37–39; description of, 34, 134–36; role of, 9
ICBMs, U.S.: basing of, 34, 75, 80, 94; counterforce capability of, 76–77, 141–43; description of, 19, 24, 33–34, 39, 132–33; MX, 74–82; and SALT, 94–98; survivability of, 28, 33–44, 72, 80, 138–41
Intelligence: assessments, 18, 37; estimates, 27, 37–39; uncertainties, 18, 63

Index

Intercontinental ballistic missiles. See ICBMs
International law, 126, 128, 130
Interservice rivalry, 30

Joint Chiefs of Staff (JCS), 67

Kennedy administration, 13, 104, 127
Kill radius, nuclear explosion: against bombers, 145; against ICBMs, 35, 138
Kissinger, Henry, 12

Launch-on-warning, 72–74, 97
Liddell Hart, B. H., 112
Limited Nuclear Options. See LNOs
Limits of nuclear deterrence, 11–13
Linkage, strategic weapons and European defense, 107, 109, 111; decoupling of, 104, 115–16. See also Flexible response doctrine
LNOs, 78–110
Look-down/shoot-down system, 54
Looking Glass, 67, 69, 84

MAP system. See Multiple-aim-point system
Marxism, 12
Massive retaliation policy, 8, 103, 104
McNamara, Robert, 9, 20, 24, 104, 126–28
Minimum Essential Emergency Communications Network (MEECN), 67–68
Minuteman missile. See ICBMs, U.S.
Mirror Imaging, 22, 65
MIRVs, 32–33; SALT limitations of, 94
Missile gap, 27
Missiles. See Cruise missiles; ICBMs; SAMs; and SLBMs
Multiple-aim-point (MAP) system, 75, 80–83; and SALT, 82, 94
Multiple independently targetable reentry vehicles. See MIRVs
Multiple RV attack, 35, 42–43. See also Fratricide
Mutual assured destruction, 103
Mutual deterrence, 9, 13, 113
MX. See ICBMs, U.S.

National Command Authority (NCA), 64, 66, 73

National Intelligence Estimate (NIE), 27, 38
NATO defense: present capability, 105–7; a new policy for. See Barrier defense of Europe
NATO military doctrine, 103, 104; and incalculable response, 107, 108. See also Flexible response
Navy, role of Soviet, 9, 56
Neutron bomb. See Enhanced radiation weapon
Nixon administration, targeting policy of, 126
No-cities policy, 127–28
"No-first-offensive-use" policy, 114–16, 125
North American Air Defense Command (NORAD), 66
Nuclear coercion, 8, 10, 14–15, 79, 127
Nuclear escalation, 73, 108, 113–15
Nuclear Test Ban Treaty, 41, 75
Nuclear threshold ("firebreak"), 114, 115
Nuclear umbrella, 103, 122

On-site inspection, 82
Overkill, 23–27, 99

Panofsky, Wolfgang K. H., 127
Payload, missile. See Throw-weight
Pindown attack, 73
Polaris missile. See SLBMs, U.S.
Population fatalities, nuclear war, 10, 25–26
Poseidon missile. See SLBMs, U.S.
Positive control, strategic forces, 33, 64, 66
Post-attack C^3, 92
Pre-emptive nuclear strike, 9, 16, 76, 114
Probability of survival, strategic forces, 35, 138–44

Quanbeck, Alton H., 46, 144

Reed, Thomas C., 28
Reliability, missile, 35, 42
Research and Development (R&D), 22, 70
Restraint, policy of, 128–29
Rosecrance, Richard, 108
Rumsfeld, Donald H., 79

Sabotage, submarines, 62, 89
SALT, 95–98
SAMs, Soviet, 52–56, 70, 85, 105
Sanguine. See ELF communications
Satellites, 65–66, 69, 84, 89, 92
Schelling, Thomas C., 108
Schlesinger, James R., 13, 27, 110–11
Seafarer. See ELF communications
Silo hardness, 34; of Minuteman, 39; Soviet assessment of, 40; of Soviet ICBMs, 142–43
Shaped trajectories, 49, 56, 83
Shlaim, Avi, 21
Short Range Attack Missile. See SRAM
Single Integrated Operational Plan. See SIOP
SIOP, 67, 126
Slay, General Alton D., 28
SLBMs, Soviet, 46, 48–49, 83, 134–35
SLBMs, U.S., 19, 24, 30, 57, 87, 89, 132–33. See also SSBNs, U.S.
Sonobuoy surveillance, 59
Sound Surveillance System. See SOSUS
SOSUS, 57, 65
SRAM, 19, 52, 55, 85
SS-20, 106
SSBNs, Soviet. See SLBM, Soviet
SSBNs, U.S.: alert rate of, 32, 57; bases, 57; description of, 30, 57; deployment of, 57–58, 87, 98; survivability of, 30, 56–64, 86–90; Trident, 30, 56, 89
Strategic Arms Limitation Talks. See SALT
Strategic balance, 11–15, 136
Strategic C³: description of, 61, 67–68; improvements required in, 62, 88, 92; vulnerability of, 21, 69
Strategic forces. See Bombers; Cruise missiles; ICBMs; SSBNs
Strategic policy. See Assured destruction; Barrier defense of Europe; Controlled response; Damage limiting; Deterrence; Flexible response; Linkage; LNOs; Massive retaliation; "No-first-offensive-use"; Restraint; and Warfighting
Strategic reserve, 90–92
Strategic submarines. See SSBNs
Strategic warning, 21, 64–65
Submarine Launched Ballistic Missiles. See SLBMs

Submarines, restrictions on deployment areas, 98–99
Superiority: importance of, 11–12; numerical, 11; military meaning of, 14
Surface effects due to submarines, 60
Surface to air missiles. See SAMs
Surprise attack, 20–22, 24, 117
Survivability, 15, 17, 33, 71. See also Bombers; ICBMs; SSBNs

TACAMO, 69
Tactical nuclear weapons, 107
Tactical warning, 46, 66, 69, 84
Targeting doctrine, U.S., 24, 26, 126
Tatu, Michel, 122
Teller, Edward, 165
Theater nuclear forces, 106, 107
Theater nuclear war, Soviet doctrine, 104, 106, 114
Third world, Soviet influence in, 11, 12
Throw-weight, 14, 79
Time of flight: ICBM, 72; SLBM, 48, 72, 98, 144
Towed arrays, 58, 65
Training communications wire or buoy, 61, 88
Trailing of submarines, 58, 88, 99
Triad, 19, 20, 30, 32, 72
Trident. See SSBNs, U.S.
Trident I missile, 30, 87, 133

Uncertainties, 18, 20, 63, 72
United Europe, 121–23

Wakes, submarine, 60
Warfighting, 8–9, 15; and new strategic doctrine, 123; objections to, 125, 127
Warning systems. See Strategic warning and Tactical warning
Warsaw Pact, 104–10, 115–20, 123
Wilson, General Samuel V., 38
Wohlstetter, Albert, 15, 27
Wood, Archie L., 46, 114
Worner, Manfred, 106
Worst case planning, 27, 29, 99

Yield, warhead, 35, 41, 132–35, 145